Enjoy Your Own Funeral

Enjoy Your Own Funeral

and Live a Happy Forever

George W. Meek

1999
Galde Press, Inc.
Lakeville, Minnesota, U.S.A.

First Edition
First Printing, 1999

Library of Congress Cataloging-in-Publication Data
Meek, George W.
    Enjoy your own funeral : and live a happy forever / George W.
Meek.
        p.   cm.
    Includes bibliographical references.
    ISBN 1–880090–85–6
    1. Spiritualism.   2. Future life.   I. Title.
BF1261.M44   1999
133.9—dc21
                                                                99–27092
                                                                CIP

Galde Press, Inc.
PO Box 460
Lakeville, Minnesota 55044–0460

Contents

Introduction

During all of recorded history, people have wondered whether there is any life beyond the death of the physical body. Speculations through the passing centuries have been supplemented by thoughts and pronouncements of the occasional persons called sages, seers, mystics, prophets, and holy men.

The majority of religious thought systems have taught that there is perhaps some continuity of life, but where and how such life is possible is not for Man to know. The New Testament of the Christian religion speaks about eternal life some sixty times—without giving clues as to how such eternal life is possible. And even though Jesus spoke of His "Father's Many Mansions," there are few clues as to where they might be located, how they are constructed, and who lives in which mansions.

Well, the veil has at last been pulled aside. In just the last thirty years Man has:

1. Constructed electronic devices permitting the living to have two-way communication with the dead;

2. Operated simple and inexpensive black-and-white television sets to obtain pictures of persons known to have been cremated and buried; and

3. Perfected mental telepathy and deep-trance channeling to a degree that surpasses the previously rare, misunderstood, and very imperfect mind-to-mind communications achieved by the relatively few mystics, sages, prophets, and holy men in past ages.

Yes, the veil between Heaven and Earth has indeed been torn asunder. This book will provide you with an easily understood step-by-step report as to how science and METAscience have accomplished these three stunning breakthroughs in your lifetime.

It is a sobering thought to realize that billions of persons have lived and died on this planet without benefit of the body-mind-soul understanding that it has now been possible to assemble in this one book.

Part I

Back to School

How Is Continuing Life Possible?
(Things They Do Not Teach in Any
University Graduate School in the World)

All that follows in this book relates to the basic questions:
Am I both caterpillar and butterfly?
and if so, what happens to me when I live
in my butterfly body?

L et's start with this sobering thought: You are traveling a road that has a funeral at the end! It is natural to shy away from the very thought of what must then happen unless we have satisfying answers to such questions as:

Is death really the end?

After doing my best to struggle through this life, am I blotted out forever, as our materialistic scientists say?

Do I lose my personal identity and become some formless nonentity, absorbed in the great unconscious?

Can I believe the Biblical promises and accumulated lore about life after death…about eternal life?

Is there any truth about purgatory—about hell with fire and brimstone?

Why hasn't my minister, priest, or rabbi answered such questions for me?

And what about the scientists? Why can't they answer my questions?

Well, let's face the sad truth: At no time in recorded history have the ministers, priests, rabbis—or today's scientists—been able to answer such questions for you.

3

But cheer up. Our dozens of sources (listed in Appendix A) created exciting and useful information on the basic nature of man. This knowledge at last provides the soul-satisfying answers mankind has long sought.

We want to answer questions which are unanswered—and probably not even considered—by books you read in school or the reading you have done in the Bible, the Talmud, the Koran, or other holy books.

We want to answer the dozens of questions you have about what happens after you leave your physical body—about what can be a glorious or a most distressing experience.

In fact, we want to answer questions for which you would not find answers today in the best scientific libraries.

We want to share knowledge with you that will be given more exhaustive treatment in books not yet written, books available five to ten years from now.

Obviously this material could not be obtained, as present matters stand, by further study of the so-called hard sciences. In the pages which follow, we are going far beyond the current restrictions of chemistry, physics, microbiology, neurophysiology, brain research, psychiatry, and the findings of our best medical internists.

Skilled surgeons have been dissecting the body and brain for the last 150 years. Not one has located the "spirit" or "soul." No surgeon has been able to isolate the mind from the brain, to throw light on the question of survival of the individual mind, personality, and soul.

There is a vast contribution to be made by science, but it is still so new, so poorly understood, and so narrowly recognized by scientists themselves that they cannot tell you what will be happening after you leave the caterpillar-like body. This does not mean that they won't get the answers eventually. Dr. Fred Hoyle, the eminent British cosmologist, has said, "When science begins the study of nonphysical phenomena, it will make more progress in one decade than in all the centuries of its experience."

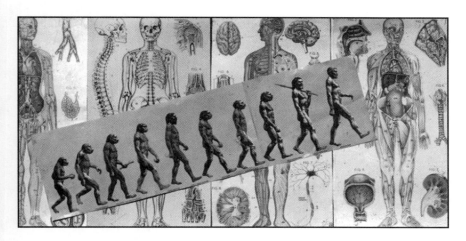

Fig. 1–1.—Evolutionary Development of Physical Systems

Science, however, may not make quite as rapid progress as Dr. Hoyle predicts. Dr. Hiroshi Motoyama, one of our advisory panel members, made an interesting observation. Dr. Motoyama, a scientist with an international reputation, is also a Shinto priest and psychic deeply schooled in spiritual matters. He is founder and president of the International Association for Religion and Parapsychology in Tokyo, Japan. Dr. Motoyama remarked, "In one sense the research will be more difficult than Dr. Hoyle anticipates. Science has limited means for its contact with and search for spiritual things."

But we need not wait five, ten, twenty, or thirty more years! The material assembled in this book will help give you many of the answers right now.

First, it is necessary to recognize the physical body for what it is: an electro-opto-biochemical mechanism of truly magnificent conception and design. The physical body has evolved (fig. 1–1) over the many millions of years since life first came ashore from the primordial seas. Think of its many systems: skeleton, blood circulation, nerves, etc. Think also of its many important organs, such as the brain, heart, lungs, pancreas, kidneys, liver, genitals, large and small intestines, and so on; the two to three square yards of skin which make up the body's all-enclosing envelope; and the organs that provide our five senses. Individually, each of these components is fantastically complex and perfected to an awesome degree. And, unlike any man-made mechanism or machine that must go into the repair shop for even a minor malfunction, the electro-opto-biochemical mechanism that is the physical body is endowed by its Creator with a built-in capability to automatically maintain and even repair itself.

Most of what we know about our surroundings is a result of the working of our five senses: touch, taste, smell, sight, and hearing. In fact, almost everything we think we know about our world and the universe has come to us through one or more of these sense organs. We feel quite content in our belief that we can rely on them to give us a completely factual, dependable, and highly accurate picture of the universe in which we are each immersed. But this is a false belief!

Consider the sense of sight. Our eyes can see the merest fraction of what is going on all around us. They can detect only matter that reflects light in the very narrow band of wavelengths we call the visible spectrum. Laboratory research has shown that there is much going on all around us in wavelengths that our limited sense organs cannot detect.

Supersensible Sight

In our laboratory in 1978, we could filter out all visible light so that as far as the eyes could tell, it was dark. But standard photographic color films can record wavelengths of light from objects that the eyes cannot detect (Fuji 400). Such color films record pictures of very strange living forms that baffle our scientific friends. Figure 1–2 is an example.

When figure 1–2 was taken, the room was dark except for certain wavelengths of light beyond the range of normal human vision. No flash was used. But when the film was developed, the unique object at the left was photographed in lovely shades of blue, pink, peach, red, and violet. (This small black-and-white reproduction does not show the delicate inner

Fig. 1–2.—Photo of Meek's Astral Body and Transparent Physical Body

workings or organs of this strange and normally invisible life form. They are much more apparent in the color enlargements.)

What was mind-bending was that such objects occupied space in our windowless laboratory and seemingly passed instantaneously through the solid brick walls. Such objects also passed through my body as if it were transparent—which, as a matter of fact, it is!

When the color negative of figure 1–2 was used to make color enlargements, we were astonished to see that the film had recorded in good detail the back, seat, and front legs of the chair on which I was sitting. It was even possible to see and count the upholstery tacks hidden behind my trouser-covered leg, as well as the chair back, which was concealed behind eight inches of flesh, blood, and bone!

Well, naturally I was shocked. Such a thing cannot happen in the world of our five senses. I showed this photo to scientists and photo specialists throughout the United States and abroad. They were at a loss to explain it. But there is a saying to the effect that "if you find even one white crow, that proves forever that not all crows are black." (If you are scientifically or photographically oriented, it is almost a mathematical certainty that you already have not one but several ideas for explaining the strange effects in figure 1–2. But consider these two points: First, I am not a photographic novice. I acquired my first thirty-five-millimeter camera sixty-six years ago, and in the following half-century I have used practically every type of camera and am familiar with all stages of the photographic process. Second, all qualified critics who have examined the color photographic blowups have found no error or faking upon the closest of examination.)

Science, quite rightly, insists on replication. By this, scientists mean that it is necessary to be able to repeat a phenomenon under controlled laboratory conditions. Hence we persevered in our search for "white crow number two." Many months and more than five hundred color photos later, we again succeeded in photographing the transparency of the human body. Those who are unfamiliar with the trials and tribulations of research may naturally wonder why it took more than five hundred photos before the next white crow was captured. I will explain.

Thomas Alva Edison was one of the world's greatest inventive geniuses. For forty-four winter seasons he operated a research laboratory in Ft. Myers, Florida, where our laboratory was formerly located. When Edison was trying to perfect the filament for the electric light bulb, his assistants became

very discouraged. One of them said, "Mr. Edison, in trying to find a filament which will be satisfactory, you have tried more than nine thousand
different materials which will not work." Edison replied, "Let's get busy
and find the one which will work."

Pioneering on the edge of the unknown, whether it be to encapsulate
light in a little glass bulb or capture spirit entities on film, is a slow and
sometimes discouraging job. Nature does not give up her secrets easily.

Supersensible Hearing

A similar situation exists with respect to what our ears are able to tell us
about what we call reality. The most acute hearing in an adult covers only
the range of twenty to sixteen thousand cycles per second. A dog has a
wider range of auditory perception. We are familiar with silent whistles for
calling dogs, that emit sound waves at vibratory frequencies beyond the
range of the human ear.

In the past few years, scientific research in our laboratory and that of
a colleague has been aimed at exploring phenomena beyond what our auditory system can detect. Just as we are pioneering beyond the capability of
our sense of sight, we are also exploring beyond our sense of hearing.

We were initially motivated to do this because of our research with
healers. We became intrigued by the many healers encountered in our worldwide studies who said they heard voices of departed spirits who guided
them in their healing work. As I explained in *Healers and the Healing
Process* (published in 1977 by the Theosophical Publishing House, Wheaton,
Illinois, and translated into Dutch, German, Portuguese, and Spanish), this
subject has been referred to for thousands of years in literature, both religious and secular.

We felt that the time had come to take a serious scientific look at the
subject. After all, at least some souls have been locked behind bars in mental hospitals all over the world because they committed the sin of hearing

voices that no sane person could hear. Ipso facto, there are no such voices and the person is obviously quite crazy.

Well, there *are* such voices, although few persons can hear them. Your auditory system can pick up the sound of your mother's voice as she asks you to help on some household chore. But that auditory system, marvel of perfection that it is, does not tell you that the room in which you are standing is filled with hundreds of voices being carried on the air waves of radio and television stations. Nor does it tell you that the room is also filled with the voices of spirit entities who once lived in physical bodies just like yours. Their voices are at wavelengths or frequencies much higher than even the radio and television signals you cannot hear.

Everything in our world, this universe, and the Cosmos results from energy, and energy manifests as vibration at some specific frequency.

The sound energy imparted to the molecules of air from a spoken word is at very low frequency—from a few hundred to a few thousand per second. Our radios receive waves of energy which vibrate at hundreds of thousands of cycles per second. Our telephone conversations are carried across the country, across the oceans, or to an astronaut in a spacecraft by energy with a vibrational frequency of millions of cycles per second. Light waves, with which we are able to see, have a frequency of roughly twelve trillion cycles per second! Soft x-rays, hard x-rays, gamma rays, etc., vibrate at progressively higher frequencies.

Just as it was necessary to supplement our hearing capability by inventing the radio to send and receive energy at higher frequencies than airborne audio sounds, man must invent new devices that will allow him to tune into the still higher frequencies of the voices of, say, the discarnate spirit doctors who are working with healers. Thus, this is a parallel to our work in developing photographic "seeing" capability to go beyond the energy wavelengths our visual system can detect. This means using magnetic tape to capture sounds (voices) we never knew existed and photographic film to see things that we never knew existed.

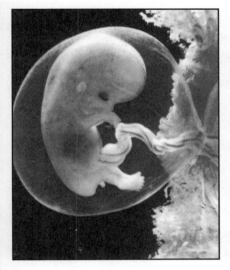 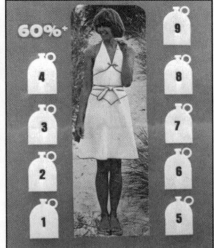

Fig. 1–3.—Human Embryo Suspended in Sea of Water

Fig. 1–4.—Water Content of Human Body

All of this knowledge is teaching us that we know very little about important aspects of our body, mind, and spirit. Our ignorance of what we know about the solid, everyday, material world can be described in one word: colossal. As will be shown later, these normally invisible sights and unheard sounds have a most important bearing on the question of life after death.

A Wet, Squishy Body

Just as the caterpillar has a soft squishy body, so do you and I. Each of us is born in a sea of water (fig. 1–3) and, when we step on the scales, most of what we are weighing is water. As we see in figure 1–4, more than sixty percent of the young woman's weight is water. It would take at least nine gallon jugs to hold an equivalent amount, and her brain is at least eighty percent water by weight.

Since we are trying to see what part of us survives the death of our physical bodies, it would seem we can narrow our search. Obviously the water will dry out after the person dies; it will evaporate. So whatever survives must be in the part which makes up less than forty percent of the physical body.

A Body Filled with "Empty" Space

Furthermore, the soft, wet, plastic mass which we are talking about is found to be "empty"! By this, I refer to the fact that our present-day insights into the nature of matter show us that most of the space taken up by the human body is more than ninety-nine percent void (leaving aside the possibility of the so-called ether or equivalent), Andrew Glazewski, the late scientist-priest of Britain, explains it thusly:

> To illustrate this, imagine borrowing an atom from, for example, a hand. For the sake of convenience let us accept the Bohr model of the atom, magnified so that the nucleus is the size of an apple—where would the next atom be? Between 1,000 and 2,000 miles away! Looking upon our bodies in this scale we would see a vast universe containing many millions of trillions of atoms forming billions of galaxies. If the nuclei of those atoms were shining, as they are centers of energy, we would confront a vast, celestial starry sky of unimaginable spaces. So you see, our body, of which we have only a statistical perception when using our senses, is actually a great "void" with little centres of energy in forms of atoms dispersed at enormous distances. One biological cell contains many millions of galaxies of atoms.

Now we can begin to understand why it was possible, as I reported a few pages earlier, for a camera to look right through the flesh, blood, organs and bones in my chest and record a picture of the chair's back. Like you, I am a wet, squishy mass largely filled with "empty" space.

How Much Does a Soul Weigh?

Since we would like to identify that portion of the individual person which survives the death of the physical body, it would seem we can now narrow our search even further. Obviously, the water portion will evaporate during the days, weeks, and months after death. Yet, as we will see later, there is rather solid proof that the essence—that is, the mind, personality, and soul—departs the physical body within a period of *minutes* to a maximum of three days. Thus, although Biblical writings are replete with references to "the water and the spirit," it does not seem that water as such is the carrier for mind, personality, and soul.

There have been a few serious attempts to measure the loss of weight that takes place at the instant of death. One piece of research stands out. While this work was done a long time ago, there has never been any serious question of the methodology, the integrity of the scientist who did the research, or the quality of the findings. (Carrington, H., *Dr. McDougall's Experiments*, Archives of the American Society for Psychic Research, Vol. 1, 1907. The later work of Crookall [see bibliography] provided good correlation with the McDougall data.) McDougall found the instantaneous weight loss at death varied between one-half and three-quarters ounce.

The research of McDougall seems to have been replicated in the work of five physicians at a Massachusetts hospital (John Langone, *Vital Signs— The Way We Die in America,* New York: Little Brown, 1974). These men built a large and very delicate balance. On one platform they would lay a person who was at the very point of death, while on the other platform they would place counterweights so as to bring the large pointer into a balanced condition. At the moment the heart stopped beating, the doctors said, "With startling suddenness the pointer moved, indicating a weight loss from the now dead patient's body. The amount of the weight loss that we encountered over such tests in a six-year period varied between one-half and one ounce."

Over the years, most of us familiar with these findings have found it difficult to believe that it could be possible to put the mind, personality, and soul into such a small package. Recently, however, with the advances in solid state physics, we have had dramatic indication of how Man himself is able to put a vast amount of information into a very small package. A small, crystalline chip weighing less than five percent of the above-mentioned weight loss can store one hundred million "bits" of information. So it no longer seems so preposterous that our Creator has devised an infinitely more compact and efficient method of "packaging" the individual human mind, personality, and soul.

These considerations have tremendous importance for us in trying to track down just what part of the caterpillar-like body it is that might have a chance to survive through eternity. But at this point it is only sensible for you to ask: How can anyone answer my questions about life after death in a scientific way when medical science has not even proven that Man has a mind or spirit? Since medical science has not proven that the brain is anything more than a collection of perishable cells (which are eighty percent water), how can my mind possibly survive the death of my physical body?

Your Brain Is NOT Your Mind

Certainly one of the greatest blocks we have in understanding life after death stems from having been told that the brain and mind are synonymous. However, a different picture emerges for those serious researchers into the nature of Man who can look beyond conventional notions. For such scientists it has become increasingly obvious that the brain and mind are *not* the same thing.

One of the most conclusive pieces of evidence was provided by the research of the eminent Canadian neurosurgeon, Dr. Wilder Penfield. He was considerably surprised at how large a piece of the brain he could surgically remove with little or no effect on the ability of the patient to carry on living as usual. To use a now out-of-date analogy comparing the brain with a telephone switchboard, it was almost as though several of the "operators" went

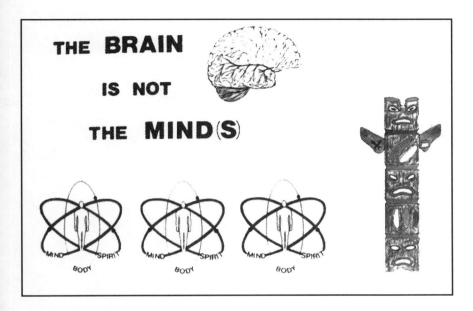

Fig. 1–5.—The Brain Is Not the Mind(s)

out for lunch, but as long as even one was still on duty, the calls could come in and go out much as usual.

In the same connection, it must be noted that neither Penfield nor any other brain surgeon has been able to identify any specific brain cells or regions of the brain as being what psychoanalysts refer to as the id, ego, or super-ego; neither could the psychologist identify the brain's site for conscious, subconscious, or superconscious states of mind. Yet concepts attributing three levels or aspects to the human mind existed hundreds of years before psychiatry and psychology came into existence.

For example, the native peoples of both the Pacific and American Plain recognized three levels of mind and represented them in their tribal totem poles. The totem pole shown at the right of figure 1–5 and in figure 1–6 was carved by a Cherokee Indian. It shows wings adjacent to the topmost level of the Indian's self. Centuries ago, the Indian knew that the highest level of

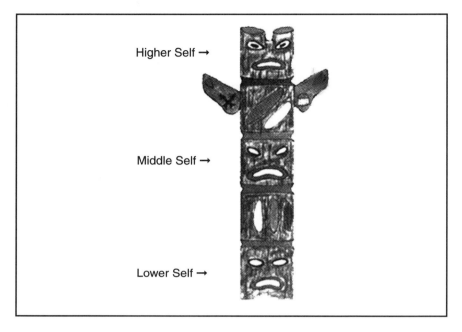

Higher Self →

Middle Self →

Lower Self →

Fig. 1–6.—American Indian and Polynesian
Concepts of the Three Levels of Being

his mind and spirit would leave the physical body at death, and like a butterfly, fly on to a higher level of existence. Only today is the white man discerning a scientific basis for much of the knowledge of the "primitive."

In this age of the computer, we find another analogy for helping to understand how the mind functions and can even operate as an entity distinct from the body and its brain. Like the computer programmer, the mind works *through* the brain but is *not* the brain.

We know that the brain controls all aspects of the body it serves. We can say that the body, the "bioelectrical mechanism," is controlled by its computer, the brain. We can go further and say that the brain is infinitely more sophisticated than the most advanced computer yet built by Man. But we also must say that the brain, like even the fanciest computer, is totally useless unless there is a programmer—some intelligence separate and distinct from the computer itself. It is only in the last three decades—a mere instant in humanity's long evolutionary climb—that science has given us a valuable tool that enables us to understand that the mind is the programmer, that it interpenetrates the "empty space" in our wet, squishy, physical body, and that it can control every single action of the more than sixty trillion cells that make up the physical body.

What is this mysterious and magical tool?

The Mind and the Jelly Mold

The wise old fellow who wrote about death in the Bible, perhaps thirty centuries ago, used a beautifully poetic description for which only the most recent scientific research gives basis for understanding. The writer of the twelfth chapter of the book of Ecclesiastes said, "...or ever the silver cord be loosed [severed] or the golden bowl be broken...." He was referring to the departure of the mind and soul from the bowl (skull). The separation involves the severing or cutting of the tenuous connection by which the mind and soul have been attached to the brain while cradled in the bowl or skull. To understand more fully the role the silver cord plays in life after death, let us consider the following analogy.

Jelly Molds and Energy Fields

If a cook wants to mold gelatin into an attractive shape for a salad or dessert, he or she must use a mold made of plastic, metal, or paper. The cook looks at the mold and knows what shape the watery, jelly-like material will assume when it cools and hardens. If the mold is battered and bent, the molded product will be shaped accordingly. *Energy fields behave like jelly molds.*

In beginning physics courses there is an experiment in which a magnet is placed beneath a piece of paper on which iron filings are randomly sprinkled. The invisible energy field of the magnet becomes visible as the filings are molded into the pattern of the lines of magnetic force. Thus the iron filings are *molded into a shape* by an invisible field of magnetic energy.

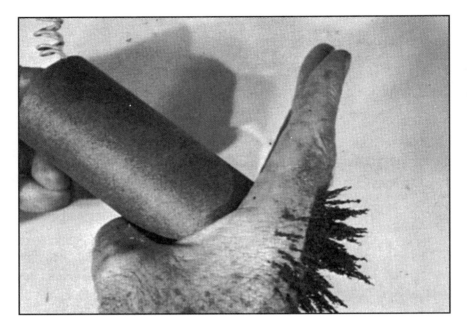

Fig. 1–7.—Magnetic Lines of Force Passing
Through Blood, Flesh, and Bones

You can see a jelly mold, but your limited eyesight cannot see an energy field. Yet the *invisible* energy field of the magnet is just as real as the metal or plastic jelly mold.

In figure 1–7, I show how a powerful magnet will send its energy field through the cells and bones of a hand and still organize iron filings. Even after passing through the hand, the energy field is so strong that it can overcome gravity and hold thousands of small pieces of steel in a precise pattern.

In figure 1–8, I performed a more modern experiment and placed a bar magnet in front of a color television screen. In brilliant colors, a fascinatingly complex picture of energy fields around the magnet became visible to the eye and was captured on color film.

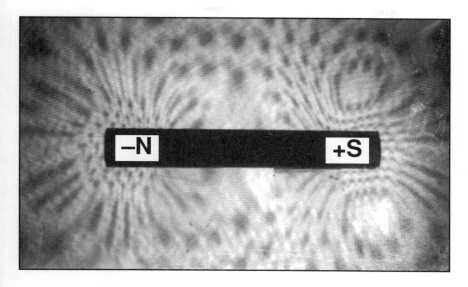

Fig. 1–8.—Energy Fields Around a Bar Magnet

The reader may be inclined to think, "Yes, these fields may surround and penetrate magnets and other material objects, but what about living objects such as plants and people? Do these have energy fields?"

Historically, the credit for answering this question goes to Dr. Harold Saxton Burr and F. S. C. Northrop, both of Yale University School of Medicine. In 1935, they published a paper, "The Electro-Dynamic Theory of Life." This pioneering work fully documented the existence of invisible but dynamic fields of energy interpenetrating and surrounding all living matter. This work went largely unnoticed for forty years because it just did not fit with accepted scientific attitudes about the nature of matter.

In the period between 1940 and 1960, the Kirlians, a husband and wife team of Russian scientists, refined an old technique of electro-photography pioneered by Bardouc of France at the beginning of the twentieth century. They were able to record on photographic film the otherwise invisible energy fields extending beyond the skin of men and animals. And in the late 1970s, a young British scientist, Rupert Sheldrake, had the temerity to hypothesize the existence of what he called anthropomorphic fields as a formative force in living bodies and tissues. His book, *A New Science of Life*, was held up to ridicule by the most prestigious British science magazine, *Nature*. The reviewer, probably frightened by the far-reaching implications for many fields of science, labeled it "a book fit for burning."

Also in the late 1970s, following the path pioneered by Barr, Northrup, and the Kirlians (but with no knowledge of the work of Rupert Sheldrake), I may have been the first to capture on photographic film the beautifully-colored energy fields of my own etheric body, momentarily projected into the space at the right of my physical body, as was shown in figure 1–2.

Simultaneously with the work of Sheldrake and Meek, two British scientists, Dennis Milnar and Edward Smart, were doing pioneering work with electro-photography. The illustration in figure 1–9 shows the energy fields around a freshly plucked leaf and the magnetized needle from a compass. Notice that the energy field surrounding the leaf is attracted or drawn to the field which exists around the magnetic pole of the compass needle.

Thus, for the first time in the history of Man, these various research projects have begun to provide insights suggesting that in some way Man's energy fields might provide a clue for the understanding of the nature of consciousness. To a "dreamer" such as I, there comes a "hunch" that Man's invisible energy fields might ultimately provide the key to solve the mystery of the survival of the human mind, memory banks, personality, and soul. The later chapters of this book will report on the extent to which this hunch has been verified.

When I talk about "energy fields," you naturally ask, "What kind of energy?" I will try to answer this question as nontechnically as possible. First, you should know that the physical body utilizes electricity. The cells have the ability to generate electricity, using as fuel the food we eat. Some of this electricity flows through a network of nerves just as the electricity in your house or apartment flows through its electrical wiring system.

Fig. 1–9.—Interaction Between Energy Field of Magnetized
Compass Needle and Freshly Plucked Leaf

Second, there is a very subtle type of energy that the Chinese discovered more than three thousand years ago. It seems to flow primarily on and near the surfaces of the body along what are called acupuncture meridians (fig. 1–10). The Chinese made such drawings of these energies centuries before the time of Christ.

Shortly after writing the above paragraphs, I was traveling in the People's Republic of China. In the museum in Soochow, I stood before a large bronze figure of a man—taller than my six-foot-three frame—and learned how *two hundred years ago* the medical students were trained to insert acupuncture needles at the proper locations. A very small hole had been drilled through the hollow bronze casting at the precise location of each acupuncture point. The bronze figure was then covered with a thick wax and filled with water. Students instructed to insert a needle for a particular malady would know they had not hit the right place unless they were greeted by a spurt of water.

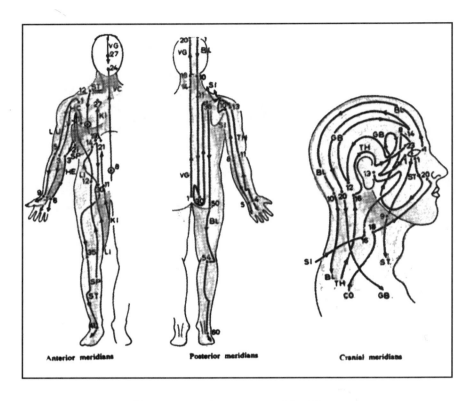

Fig. 1–10.—Acupuncture Meridians

Traveling on to Nanking, I got dramatic proof of the efficacy of acupuncture when used as an anesthetic. A small group, of which I was a member, visited the Nanking General Hospital. The general administrator, after giving us a talk on their use of acupuncture, took us on a tour of the outpatient and recovery wards and four operating rooms. Wearing surgical gowns and face masks, we proceeded to watch four operations, all major, in which acupuncture was the *only* anesthetic. I will describe one of these to give you a better understanding of the reality of these energies that I am discussing and about which our modern science knows very little.

One patient, a forty-year-old woman, was being operated on for an ulcerated stomach condition which had not responded to treatment. A few hours before the operation, she was given orally a very mild tranquilizer to ease the perfectly normal fear of the dangers which might lie ahead once she was wheeled out of her room and into the operating room.

Upon arrival in the operating room, a nurse inserted three small needles into the periphery of the patient's left ear. Each needle had a small wire extending to a nearby instrument about the size of a small tape recorder. This instrument supplied a six-volt direct current to each needle. *These three needles provided the only anesthetizing effect.*

Extending up from the patient's throat area was a cloth screen about one-foot square which prevented the patient from observing the actions of the surgeons. However, we could see the patient's face, as well as the actions of the surgeons. With the hospital administrator serving as translator, we were able to converse with the patient at all stages of the operation.

The two surgeons, standing on each side of the operating table, made the incision. Gradually they progressed to the point where they took the patient's stomach and lifted it up so that they could carefully inspect it. The condition they found apparently warranted their decision that it was necessary to remove fully sixty percent of the stomach. This they did. Then they completed the many details and closed the incision. At no time did the patient experience discomfort. She apparently had no knowledge of what was going on.

One of our group was an American surgeon in his sixties. Knowing nothing about the subtle and invisible energy systems and related energy fields of the human body, he was totally mystified. I observed him stand aside and through his face mask mutter, "Incredible. Absolutely incredible! There is just no anatomical basis for this nonsense." How right he was! (1978)

In the postoperative ward, we talked to patients who had had major operations in the preceding days. Most of them—provided their digestive tracts had not been operated on—were able to enjoy a full meal a few hours after the operation. Within twenty-four hours most were able to get out of bed and

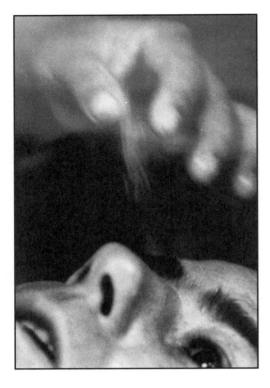

Fig. 1–11.—Stream of Healing Energy

walk. Few needed to stay more than two or three days.

Further evidence on the new vistas opened for medical treatment through a growing understanding of the invisible acupuncture meridians and the part they play in the functioning of our bodies was given when I stopped off in Tokyo to get up to date on the scientific research of Dr. Hiroshi Motoyama, the parapsychologist and Shinto priest I mentioned earlier. Dr. Motoyama has used his knowledge of acupuncture to devise an electronic system for making a medical diagnosis of a person in fifteen minutes that would otherwise take days of detailed and costly hospital tests. These diagnostic machines are now in daily use in many large hospitals in Japan.

While studying healers living in the rice fields of a northern part of the Philippines, we were fortunate enough to capture on film a red-orange stream of healing energy. Josefina Sisson was just starting to treat the eye of a patient who had come from the outback area of Australia. The momentary blast of healing energy was invisible to the members of the five-man team of specialists we had with us, but it was detected and recorded by the emulsions on the photographic film. (Unfortunately, the delicate colors do not show clearly in a black-and-white printed picture.)

Ancient writings speak of still another type of energy as being involved in human life and have called it by names such as *prana, od, odic force, ki, baraka,* etc. This subtle energy from the cosmos enters the body through whirling energy vortexes known as chakras, located roughly as indicated in figure 1–12. Only recently did an American scientist, Itzhak Bentov of Boston, Massachusetts, and the Japanese scientist, Dr. Motoyama, invent equipment which can prove that these normally invisible energy centers actually do exist.

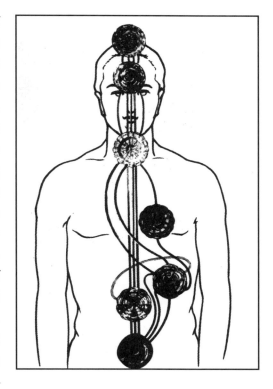

Fig. 1–12.—Diagram of Chakra Energy Centers

The foregoing comments on acupuncture have a very direct bearing on our search for evidence of life after death. Since no surgeon has ever opened a body and found a soul, we have to assume that the soul is not of the same material as the physical body, and, if it exists, it must be invisible. Since it is hard— almost impossible—for any of us to believe something unless we can see it, we can sympathize with my surgeon friend who could not even believe what he *saw* in the four operations, because in a lifetime of surgical practice no one had taught him about the reality of the energy fields of Man.

As of now, no dependable means exists for photographing or instrumentally detecting the subtle cosmic energies that activate and flow through the chakra system, a very important part of your own physical body. On rare occasions the energies present in a very gifted psychic person are so intense, so powerful, that they can effect the emulsion of a photographic film as they did in figure 1–13.

This photo is of an American scientist, who wishes to remain anonymous, and his small son. The father and son are highly psychic, as is his eight-year-old daughter, who snapped this extremely rare photo with a simple Instamatic-type camera with a built-in flash. It shows the energy stream bursting upward from the crown chakra of the boy and blending with the energy shooting upward from the father's crown chakra.

I have introduced you to these normally invisible and hard-to-detect-energy fields for a very important reason. Without such knowledge you could not understand how it is that the most significant parts of you—your mind, personality, and soul—*must* survive the death of your physical body.

I said in the opening pages that I would "keep it simple" and present concepts largely through photos and diagrams. I feel sure that enough has been presented to make it clear that the brain is not the mind, that the mind(s) are energy fields, and that these normally invisible energy fields shape, control, and animate all matter. (For the technically-inclined reader, one of the most interesting scientific pieces of brain-mind research is the development of the holographic model by K. Pribram and D. Bohm [see M. Ferguson, *Brain-Mind Bulletin*, July 4, 1977]. However, this new model does not recognize that the mind is something distinct from the brain and will survive and function normally long after the brain has returned to dust.)

Now we are ready to face up to a seemingly preposterous statement:

We Live on Seven Levels and in Two Worlds
We have examined the fantastically wonderful and complicated physical body. We have discovered that it is largely empty space. We have learned that energy fields can and do penetrate the physical body as though it were transparent and had little substance. We have learned that the brain is not

Fig. 1–13.—Head Chakra Energies

the mind. We have learned that the body is electrically powered and that it also utilizes two other anciently postulated energy systems of which twentieth-century science knows very little.

Hence it will not come as a great surprise that interpenetrating our physical body there is another body made up of a large number of energy fields, each of which collects and organizes cells into shapes or organs precisely the same way the magnet in figure 1–7 organizes the thousands of iron filings into a specific pattern.

In fact, *there is an energy field for every major organ and bone in the physical body,* and these control all of the individual cells. They provide what we might call the intelligence that builds the organ in the first place, provides it with the life force, keeps it running in harmony with the other parts of the body, and repairs and maintains the organ or bone.

For centuries, occult literature has called this vast collection of energy fields the "etheric body." Western scientists have been very slow to investigate this "body" because up to now it has been invisible and could not be weighed. (Science is largely dependent on the ability to observe and measure whatever it is that is being studied. Moreover, most scientists have been conditioned to pay attention only to those they measure and weigh and observe that fit within the framework of contemporary science.) Russian scientists have been readier than Western scientists to undertake research on the etheric body of Man. They have become convinced of its reality and have coined their own name for it—the "bioplasmic" body.

The physical body operates primarily on electricity. The bioplasmic body utilizes the energy systems that are involved in acupuncture meridians and the chakras.

But once we have started to take Man apart and have found that he is actually living on two levels of being, this is not the end of the matter. There are actually *five additional* levels of being!

How can we possibly picture in our minds seven levels of being? Well, we are certainly familiar with the physical body. Now that we have learned that it is largely empty space, we can even imagine that there is another energy occupying the same space as the physical body. So, since we can think of "bodies," let us just imagine there are five additional bodies. After all, when we look at an onion, we have no trouble discerning that there are many layers making up that onion.

Or let us recall an experience most of us have had when we were purchasing a new dress or a new suit of clothes. We put the garment on and then stood between mirrors arranged so we could see over our shoulder in order to check the fit of the back of the garment. At the same time, we could also see our image repeated several times, each image looking a bit smaller and farther away behind our back. Note the arrangement in figure 1–14— an extension of a common experience.

Our next step is to *identify* these levels of being.

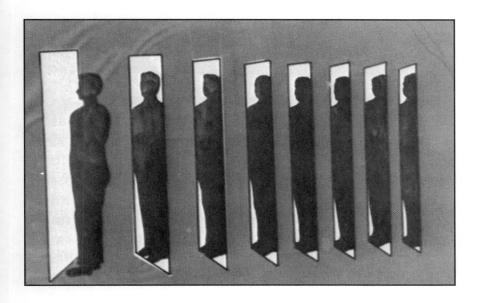

Fig. 1–14.—Multiple Image (Body) Concept

We have already identified the physical body and its interpenetrating bioplasmic body. Then we come to the mind. From our earlier discussion, you will recall that long before the writings of Dr. Sigmund Freud of Vienna, Austria, the American Plains Indians and the Polynesians utilized their knowledge of the three levels of mind.

Now it is quite appropriate for us to think of these three minds as being three separate bodies. This is not as fanciful as it might seem. Only in the last few years has it been discovered that most of the many millions of cells in the physical body have what the scientists call communication capability. This means that the cells can send and receive messages. We are also learning that the cells go beyond this function; it is almost as though each cell has a mind of its own. Now we can begin to understand that not only is the brain not the mind, but that the mind function extends throughout the entire body.

But—and this is extremely important, as we will see shortly—nature has put the soul and the levels of mind in a nice, neat package. For the last few centuries, occult and esoteric literature has called this package the "astral body." So now let us put it all together and arrive at figure 1–15.

As of now, our scientific instrumentation is such that we can detect and measure energy relating directly to only the physical and the bioplasmic bodies. The other so-called bodies or energy fields are "invisible," as indicated in figure 1–16. That is, we do not have instruments that will measure them. Actually, this is not the serious barrier it might appear to be. Modern physics includes many concepts that even today are not confirmed by anything more solid than informed speculation.

Please note that in some of the diagrams I use the word "spirit" and in others I use the word "soul." I do this because for most readers the terms are interchangeable. Properly speaking, however, the word "spirit" distinguishes the nonphysical portions of our being from the physical body, whereas "soul" relates to that *individualized portion* of the Creator that resides in each of us. Indeed, the soul might be defined as that individualized spark or portion of spirit energy which originated in and emanated from what Man has called the Creator, God, the Godhead, Cosmic Consciousness, Universal Mind, Higher Power, etc. This spark manifested downward into the denser realms of spirit, where it is involved in working, learning, loving, and growing back to the divine source from which it came. The soul already resides in and will always continue to reside in what I will later refer to as "the worlds of spirit"—where Jeannette D. Meek is enjoying her continuing life, as you will learn in later chapters.

This concept of multiple bodies gives us a method of visualizing how parts of the individual person—the real, the everlasting "I" of Jeannette—survives death. This is portrayed in figure 1–17.

If the minds and spirit or soul of the individual person are nonphysical, it is not such a strain on the imagination to conceive of this portion surviving the death of the physical body. Recalling the brain-computer

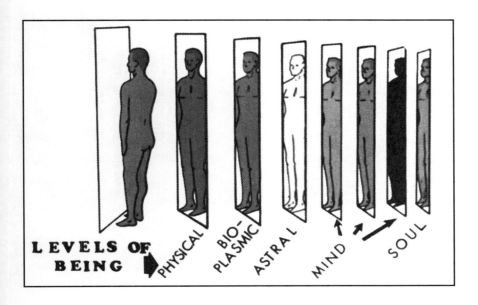

Fig. 1–15.—Man's Multiple Levels of Being

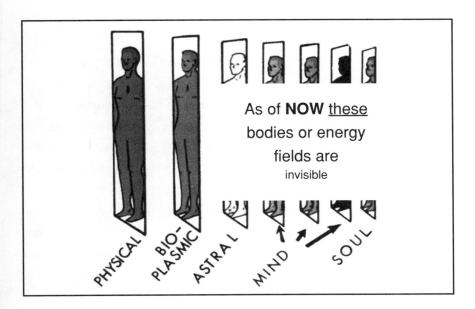

Fig. 1–16.—The Invisible Levels of Being

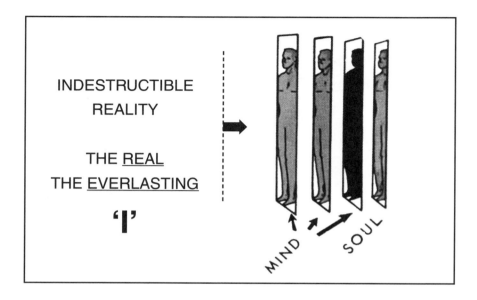

INDESTRUCTIBLE
REALITY

THE <u>REAL</u>
THE <u>EVERLASTING</u>

'I'

Fig. 1–17.—The Real, the Everlasting "I"

analogy, the computer may be damaged or even destroyed, but the intelligence that acted as programmer for the computer is still very much alive.

In figure 1–18, I have separated the two sets of bodies to help you further visualize this process. This begins to suggest the mechanism by which a good clairvoyant sees what, since Biblical times, has been called "the silver cord" (marked by the letter "c" in the diagram). Literature is full of accounts of how a good clairvoyant observes the gradual loosening and then the separating of the silver energy cord as a person is dying.

This multiple body analogy also begins to help parapsychologists visualize how it is that while the physical body of a sensitive is relaxing and lying peacefully in bed, his consciousness can travel far and describe scenes en route. In other words, this helps you to understand the mechanism of the out-of-body experience or OBE, to use parapsychological terminology. This is what has been known for thousands of years in occult literature as

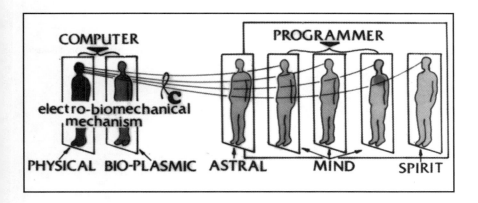

Fig. 1–18.—The Programmer of the Electro-biochemical
Mechanism We Call the Physical Body

astral travel. Notice particularly that term astral travel. It is a marvelous
clue to the reality of life after death.

Figure 1–19 sums up these ideas in a slightly different way. Just as the
skin covers all the internal organs and skeleton of our physical body, the
astral body functions as a skin or covering for the three levels of mind and
soul. It contains them and makes a unit of them. This package or bundle is
the real you. It contains the more enduring parts of your memory banks,
your emotional patterns, your personality, and your soul.

This is the programmer of which I wrote earlier. It is connected to and
works through your wet, squishy, physical brain—that quart or so of water
that is in your personal computer.

It is still material, but not in the sense of matter as you know it. It is of
such fine, rapidly vibrating energy that it is similar to what you think of as
light rays.

Normally, it stays well within the confines of the physical and bioplasmic bodies. But at night when you are in deep sleep, it can leave your
body and travel. During life in the physical body, it always remains

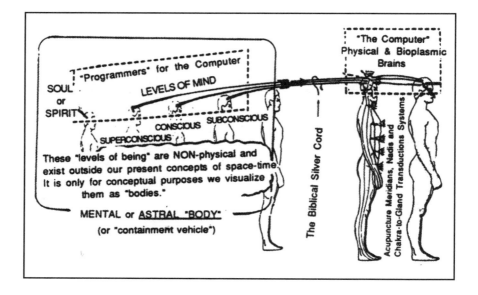

Fig. 1–19.—Figure 1–18 Presented in a Different Form

connected to your physical body by an invisible elastic web-like "wiring harness" that is attached to the brain—the so-called silver cord.

Now, just as we have bodies interpenetrating each other, some scientists tell us that we can have interpenetrating worlds. (The term they prefer is "space-time systems.") But for our purposes in discussing life after death, let's just say there is an astral world that occupies the same space as our physical world while our astral body lives and functions in the interpenetrating astral world.

Perhaps your mind is still reeling from all the theories about seven bodies and the statement that you live in two worlds at the same time. With so many problems and so much strife, all of us frequently feel like the person who called out, "Stop the world! I want to get off." But it really isn't so complicated as it might seem at first.

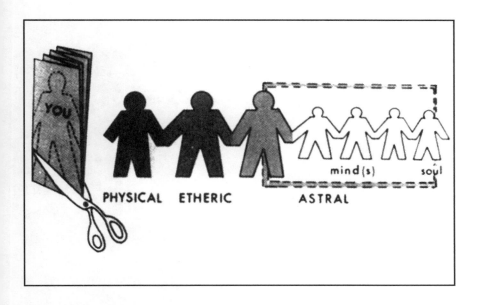

PHYSICAL   ETHERIC   ASTRAL

mind(s)   soul

YOU

Fig. 1–20.—Figure 1–19 Presented in a Different Form

It may also help to recall how as a child you took scissors, folded a sheet of paper back and forth on itself three times, and then cut out a paper doll. Now that you are older and a bit more creative, it is no problem for you to cut out dolls and label them as I've done in figure 1–20.

When we are born, we are all folded into one nice, neat package. As we progress through life, we continue to stay largely within the confines of the physical body, the package that also contains our bioplasmic and astral bodies. But every man, woman, and child on the planet shares the same fate. *At some time the package breaks open.* At some time, sooner or later, the physical body reaches the end of its usefulness. From illness, violent accident, suicide, homicide, death in war, or just plain old age, our physical body becomes inoperative. It dies.

What happens to the bioplasmic body when the physical body dies? Well, that body also dies. But usually it stays around for just a little while,

Fig. 1–21.- Interpenetrating Worlds

sometimes only for a few hours. In the majority of cases, it will have dis-integrated completely within three days. It is reabsorbed into the great cosmic supply of the energies, normally invisible to people, which activate the acupuncture and chakra systems. The etheric body has served its pur-pose of molding matter into the many organs used to form the physical body and has served to channel the cosmic energies required to keep the body operational.

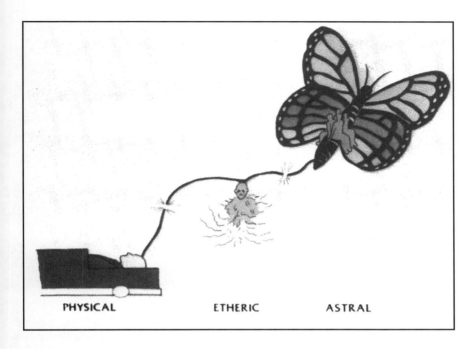

PHYSICAL   ETHERIC   ASTRAL

Fig. 1–22.—Symbolic Survival of Bodily Death

And what happens to the astral body? Aha! This is the crucial question. It is completely alive and functional after the death of both the physical body and the etheric body. It continues to live in the same second world in which it has always lived—the astral world that completely interpenetrates and occupies the same space that the physical world does. This is symbolically portrayed in figure 1–21.

This individual astral body contains all the memory banks, emotional patterns, personality, and soul that it had before it departed from the physical body. These are all neatly contained in one package. When you someday find yourself without your physical body, you will find that your personal baggage is all neatly packed and that you—like the butterfly—are ready to fly (fig. 1–22). (Jeannette will describe later how strange it was to leave behind her physical body.)

Unlike the caterpillar, you need not waste time spinning a cocoon. There is no need for you to spend a season or two before you can split your cocoon and emerge as a beautiful creature ready to enter on flights of exploration. In making Man, our Creator surpassed even His handiwork in making the caterpillar and butterfly.

You are all packed and ready to fly!

Summary of Chapter 1

- We are far more than our physical body.
- Our mind(s) and soul are nonphysical.
- These nonphysical portions contain our memory banks, our soul, and our own very individual personality.
- These memory banks, soul, and personality can and do survive death of the physical body.
- Even during the first instant after the death of the physical body, the mind, memory banks, personality, and soul are just as vibrantly alive (although they may initially be at rest or sleeping) as they were during the years when we temporarily wore that physical body given to us by our parents and ancestors.

Chapter Two
Where Are the Spirit Worlds and What Are They Like?
(A Road Map and Guide Book)

Millions of spiritual creatures walk the earth
Unseen, both when we wake, and when we sleep.

What if earth and heaven be to each other like
More than on earth is thought?

—John Milton

Putting It All Together

What actually happens when the day comes—as it does for each of us—to leave behind the physical body we are temporarily wearing? You ask, "What happens then? Where do I go?"

We need a blueprint, a diagram that can help to locate and identify the many mansions the Nazarene said are "in my Father's house."

The blueprint of immortality that I now present is based upon:

• The experiences of many saints, sages, seers, prophets, and mystics over the ages;

• The experiences and reports of certain enlightened persons who in the last two hundred years have reached levels of cosmic consciousness;

• Similar experiences of my close personal friends and fellow researchers around the world...and most importantly, my wife and co-author, Jeannette.

If you are as skeptical as I was, you probably are already questioning, "Just how accurate, how dependable, and how specific is this blueprint you propose to show me?" While the years ahead will doubtlessly provide additional details, most of the basic information presented has been authenticated by *present occupants* of the "mansions," brought through by mediums and telepathic channels of proven reliability—and in some areas by electronic systems!

Does one have to be an architect, engineer, or college graduate to read the blueprint? No. If you will follow carefully just three simple steps, you will have a good basis for comprehending what Jesus himself had in mind when He spoke poetically about the many mansions in His Father's house.

Packing for the Trip

Let us recall the essence of the concept we considered in figure 1–17, reproduced here for easy reference in figure 2–1. This simple diagram helps us to understand that the multiple levels of our minds and our souls constitute the indestructible portions of our being, which the Apostle Paul two thousand years ago termed the spiritual body. Now with the knowledge you gained in chapter 1, you know that the various levels of the mind and soul are nonphysical and, still more important, that they are composed of invisible energy fields that are indestructible.

But, you ask, "Where does this surviving body go? What happens to it? Where does it travel to?"

Using a Road Map

Our most careful research led us to believe that the best clues to answering these questions were given in the Nazarene's own statement of two thousand years ago—"In my Father's house are many mansions."

This may not seem very specific, but recall that His listeners were not scientifically informed to the degree that we are. His listeners never heard of energy fields (nor did anyone else for the next 1,900 years)! Jesus was

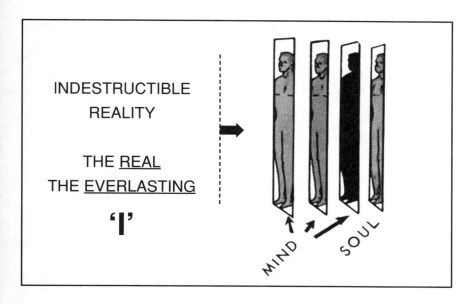

INDESTRUCTIBLE
REALITY

THE <u>REAL</u>
THE <u>EVERLASTING</u>

'I'

Fig. 2–1.—The Real, the Everlasting I

forced to use poetic language to create a picture in the minds of His listeners. Fortunately, now, at the close of the twentieth century, we can locate
the mansions—and we have learned enough in our twenty years of research
to provide a rather accurate road map. Figure 2–2 charts the general terri-
tory to a degree never before possible. And it can be presented now only
because of hundreds of hours of recorded conversations (via superb telepathic channels and electronic systems) with persons who are today actually dwelling in the various mansions!

Strange and unbelievable as it may seem, the Nazarene was telling the
literal truth when He said, "The kingdom of heaven is within you." He was
not speaking in parables. The only problem is that during almost all the
past two thousand years Man and his science have not known enough about
the nature of Man's own existence and the so-called material world to be
able to comprehend His teaching.

There is no need to picture these mansions, planes, levels, or resting places as being in some faraway heaven, on some planet or in a far-out space above the earth. Most of these levels are surrounding and interpenetrating us now. Recall the disclosure in chapter 1 that introduced you to the knowledge that (a) our bodies and all of the material world are more than ninety-nine percent empty space, and (b) we live in two worlds at the same time.

However, it does strain the imagination less if we simply picture these levels, planes, "mansions," or resting places stacked one above the other, with the lowest plane starting just above the earth's atmosphere. This simple sketch in figure 2–2 provides us with a good preliminary blueprint or road map.

Do not be concerned about the names of the planes or levels. There is not yet an agreed-upon terminology. Any serious student of the accumulated mystical, occult, esoteric, and religious lore will recognize that we have greatly oversimplified both our discussion and our diagrammatic representations of the planes (in both the lower and higher worlds of spirit). For instance, each of the three planes we have designated as astral will be found to contain within themselves many different vibratory levels. The same is true of the still higher planes. Recently, a "teacher" on one of these higher planes expressed it this way: "There are many, many planes of life. We may be on a plane beyond yours; but believe me, my friend, there are planes beyond ours, far, far beyond ours, of which we know very little."

Needless to say, we can only dimly comprehend the nature of the levels above the celestial level. We know they exist and we know a little about them—again from some of the current inhabitants of those higher levels. However, rather than trying to contemplate the possibility of additional reality systems, it is better to develop a solid comprehension of planes 1 through 5 so that they may become goals and promises for us when we leave earth's dwelling.

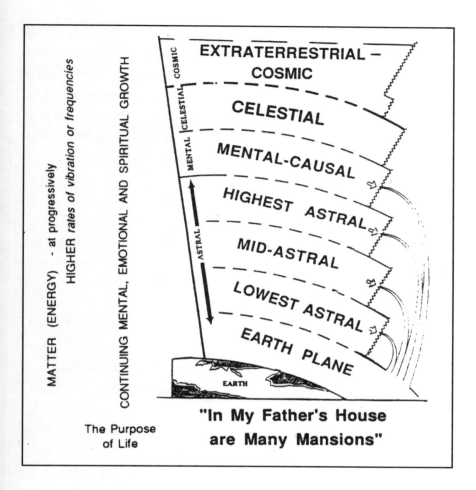

Fig. 2–2.—Interpenetrating Levels of Life and Consciousness

Finding Lodging

Now that we have the excellent road map provided in figure 2–2, let us see just who dwells on the various planes of consciousness and what type of daily activities are offered for the occupants on each. We will treat each level or mansion in a paragraph by itself, numbered to correspond to the titles in figure 2–2.

In a first reading of the six paragraphs that follow, it is best not to stop
and try to understand all of the words in detail, nor to be concerned if some
of the ideas are new, "far out," questionable, or even upsetting. In some cases
you may not have been exposed to these ideas by your minister, priest, or
rabbi simply because he himself has never been exposed to such information! Just read slowly and thoughtfully each of these paragraphs, holding
your questions in abeyance until you have finished reading them all.

1. The Earth or Physical Plane

Here, on the surface of the earth, you now live in your physical body and
also in your interpenetrating etheric and astral "bodies." The etheric and
astral bodies are nonphysical. (This explanation is offered to the technical
or scientific reader: we use the term "nonphysical" to refer to a finer and
higher type of "matter-energy" undetectable by our present instrumentation. According to Motoyama, the "bodies" and "minds" of the physical,
etheric, or bioplasmic and astral levels of being exist simultaneously and
independently, are closely related and are connected with one another—
making up one human being. See his article on "The Realization of Holistic Health and Its Science" in *Journal of Religion and Parapsychology* 20,
June 1979, Tokyo.) They are a finer form of matter involving vibrating
energy fields. The interpenetrate the physical body just as hundreds of radio
and television waves are doing at this instant.

Your soul, personality and emotions, memory banks, and mental or
causal body are all contained in your astral body (fig. 1–18). When your
physical and etheric bodies die (here called the first death), the "real you"
is still fully alive in your astral body. Usually within minutes to within a
few days you find yourself functioning on that particular astral plane to
which the quality of your life on earth has entitled you.

2. Lowest Astral Planes

This dark, dismal, dangerous, and often frightening world, which the Bible
describes as "outer darkness, weeping, wailing, and the gnashing of teeth,"

is the habitat of greedy, self-centered, unloving, resentful persons. Often they have fierce bodily desires and lusts. Here, too, may be drug addicts, sex perverts, unrecovered alcoholics, murderers, and suicides. It is also the abode of the less desirable creatures of nonhuman lines of evolution.

This vibratory or thought level is traditionally referred to as Hell, Hades, or Purgatory. It is the human astral bodies from this plane that attach themselves to the magnetic auras or astral bodies of persons living on the earth plane (an act of obsession). Such a possessed person may act abnormally, be judged insane, and be institutionalized or commit suicide.

3. Intermediate Astral Planes
On this vibratory or thought level, the person awakens minutes, days, or weeks after departing the physical body, or months, years, or centuries after arrival on the lowest astral plane.

This is primarily a rest and rehabilitation region, complete with hospitals and their staffs and institutions of learning and teachers. Help is given to diseased souls, persons who had traumatic experiences and/or sudden death, and persons with inflexible or erroneous mental, emotional, or religious beliefs. The body is still material, but of finer substance at a higher vibratory rate. Its appearance accommodates each individual's personal preference—usually the prime of earth life.

Here communication is by both thought and the spoken word. Each person is encouraged to continue mental and spiritual growth. By such growth one progresses to the higher astral and mental planes, or from this level decides to re-embody for further learning and personal growth on the earth plane.

4. Highest Astral Planes
This wonderful vibratory or thought realm of existence is what the Christian generally calls heaven. Another appropriate term is the summerland. There is no pain or suffering. There are happy meetings with those for

for whom a bond of love is felt, or groups formed of like-minded persons. There are unlimited opportunities and encouragement for each soul to grow in mental and spiritual consciousness. Interest in activities on planet earth decreases. There are encounters with angels—lovely and helpful beings of both human and nonhuman evolution. (This is where Jeannette arrived after departing her physical body.)

Wider perspectives, greater vistas, magnificent panoramas! But eventually the soul must decide whether to return to the earth plane for more experience or to accept the second death. In the latter case, the mind and soul may shed its astral body or containment vehicle and be reborn into the mental level for which it has become qualified. When reborn, the soul will function in its mental body. (This is what happened to Jeannette eight months after her transition.)

5. Mental and Causal Planes

These vibratory or thought levels offer unlimited scope for the further development of the individual mind and soul. There is access to all of the accumulated wisdom of the ages on the earth plane and throughout other parts of our solar system.

There is no jealously, judgement, or selfishness. There is complete brotherhood. Most human inventions, scientific advances, poetry, inspired prose, art, and music originate on the causal planes and are passed down, through the process called intuition, to receptive minds on the earth plane. For this reason, the intelligences on this level "cause" much of the good, beautiful, and inspiring activities of the lower planes.

This is the final opportunity to choose to return to the earth plane for more earth-life experience and growth; or, if all factors are favorable, then comes the final rebirth into the celestial planes.

6. Celestial Planes

The nature of these planes of consciousness (as well as those still higher galactic, universal, and cosmic levels 8, 9, 10, and 11) are largely beyond the comprehension of those now living on earth. The celestial planes are the location of Jesus the Christ, Buddha, and spiritual leaders of other great religious persuasions on the earth plane. In the Bible it is referred to as the third heaven.

On these planes there is preliminary understanding of the universal life and energy systems of our solar system. The tapping of such levels of consciousness enabled the Nazarene to perform miracles. This path is open to each of us. This is what He meant when He said, "These things I do, you will do also; and greater things than these will you do."

After your initial study of figure 2–2, I suggest you lay it aside until you come to the end of chapter 14. By then you will have increased your understanding through the study of forty-four questions about life after death—and their answers. These questions and answers will make it much easier to grasp the important concepts in figure 2–2.

Now you can comprehend how it is that we are functioning not only on the earth plane, but also in the very lowest and densest portion of the astral plane. When the physical body dies and the etheric body disintegrates, we do not really have to go on a far journey. We will be automatically on whatever vibrational level we deserve to be on, based on the quality of life we have lived while in the physical body.

As you ponder the answers to the questions and the implications of the blueprint, you will glimpse the sublime vistas and the grandeur of the overall scheme of life God has created for all of humanity—regardless of race, color, caste, sex, or religion. You will note that while the blueprint forever strips away most of the controversial dogmas and creeds that separate the world's religions, it does not discredit the central spiritual teachings of the major religious systems.

Gradually, the overall concepts will become familiar and more comfortable. There will be less reason to cringe or become frightened by the implication that you are each a spark of the Universal Godhead. You have the opportunity to start living a life right now in ways that will lay up for ourselves treasures in heaven"—another of the Nazarene's gentle admonitions.

No longer can we fail to realize that our every act is a "cause"—and that each cause must have an "effect" on our lives in the countless centuries of life which lie ahead for all of us!

No longer can the scramble to meet the monthly payments on a never-ending list of material wants—or the effort to climb a little higher in the economic or social rat-race—be quite so irresistible.

No matter how dull, dreary, and unrewarding this moment of life may be, the path beginning with the next moment can be the stepping stone into a glorious and ever-unfolding future of great promise.

No longer can a political system fail to recognize that its citizens are far more than one-lifetime, soulless cogs in a materially oriented world, facing personal extinction at death.

Even if you disagree with many details of figure 2–2, accept your immortality. You have come to realize that immortality is an alternative to your assumption of personal extinction at death.

And if the term "immortality" has any negative connotations for you, perhaps we should take a lesson from the men who edited the Bible. "Immortality" is not mentioned in the Bible. But "life eternal" is mentioned seventy-two times. On that authority and on the basis of twentieth-century research into the nature of Man, let us close part I with the assurance:

Life is Eternal
This is still just a glimpse, perhaps, but it is a clearer, more meaningful, exciting, stimulating, challenging, and easily understandable glimpse than anyone can picture without full perception of the grandeur of "the many mansions" of infinite progression that lie ahead for each of you.

Part II

Can the "Dead" Speak?

Chapter Three
Via Instrumental Systems
(Part 1)

Perspectives, Predictions, and Parallels

Throughout mankind's history, there have been men and women who have dared look beyond the present moment and dream of ways by which the quality of life might be improved. These "dreamers" often developed an idea that left its impact on the forward movement of society. This movement in every field of human endeavor has resulted from what has been called "constructive discontent" with things as they were.

Late-twentieth century Man looks out from his present perspective and is horrified by what he sees—a materialistic world seemingly running amok. He watches helplessly as some fellow passengers daily do their utmost to destroy each other—and even the planet on which all are moving through the cosmos. It is in such situations that prophecies are born.

For most of this century, there have been predictions that mankind would develop an instrumental system to permit the enlightened souls of heaven or the spirit worlds to converse with and bring enlightenment to persons in fleshly bodies. Of the several dozen predictions that have been made, these five illustrate the point:

1931. Sir Arthur Conan Doyle, medical doctor, creator of Sherlock Holmes, and an untiring exponent of spiritualism, returned after his death by way of a series of messages channeled through the mediumship of Grace Cooke. Some of Doyle's unpublished material referred to design details for electrically-activated devices to serve as an instrumental communication from the spirit world. I made a visit to the Cooke home in 1974 to investigate. I found that, indeed, serious effort had been made to build the equipment, but there was no success.

1935. *Open the Door*, a book telepathically channeled by Wilfred Brandon through Edith Ellis of New York City, was published. On page 23 he states:

> Yet science is on the verge of discovering the secret of life after "death"; it is all but able to connect with our plane. Marconi and those who study the marvels of the ether will in time find the connecting wave length and we shall then be united in a common understanding of the Law of Life. In the meantime all automatic writing and trance mediums are makeshifts which we must use until we can, through them work with your radio engineers, until we can perfect a mechanism that we can use automatically. This is possible and will doubtless be the next step after television.

1944. *Psychic Press,* London, published an article containing prophecies and predictions about a heaven-to-earth communication system. In trance sessions recorded in 1944, spirits of departed scientists talked about fluidal electronic rods covered with layers of ectoplasm to produce human voices. The main obstacle was how to overcome the problems of high frequencies in the spirit world.

1944. The book, *Esoteric Healing*, channeled through Alice A. Bailey, carried a "Letter to a Scientist" dictated by the Tibetan master Djwhal Khul. On pages 376 and 377, he prophesied: "Towards the close of this century, electric devices will be used to contact departed souls, together with photographing of thought forms, thus opening a new area of spirit photography." "...The first demonstration of existence after death in such a way that it can be registered upon the physical plane will be via the radio because sound waves always precede vision. No radio now exists which is sufficiently sensitive to carry sound waves from the astral plane."

1972. From the Stainton Moses recordings: "...ere long there will be an instrument that will make contact between the two worlds a fact, so that the most highly skeptical will be convinced of life after death. When that time comes, all the barriers that now stand will be broken down."

These predictions should be viewed in the context of the key events that led to the development of mankind's already existing communication systems.

In 1558, Giovanni Battista della Porta proposed a message-sending device that would utilize magnetism. Man had known about magnetism since ancient times, but it was almost three hundred years before the development of electromagnets made della Porta's dream a reality.

Fig. 3–1.—Della Porta

In 1838, Samuel F. B. Morse, a portrait painter with an inventive bent, built a crude contraption which demonstrated that clicks from an electromagnet could carry a message along a wire. After much experimentation and assistance from Joseph Henry, a message was sent over forty-five miles of wire stretched from Washington to Baltimore: "What hath God wrought?"

In 1867, Alexander Graham Bell, a teacher of speech, demonstrated with a very crude device that wires could carry not only

Fig. 3–2.—Morse

Fig. 3–3.—Bell

Fig. 3–4.—Edison

Morse's dots and dashes, but the tones of the human voice itself. The first words were transferred over a wire only seventeen feet long.

In 1877, Thomas Edison, with no formal education, used a sewing needle to capture the vibration of the telephone mouthpiece, first on paraffin paper, then on tinfoil, and then on wax. Crude as his device was, he had invented the forerunner of today's magnetic audio and videotape recording systems.

By 1896, Guglielmo Marconi was demonstrating that dots and dashes of telegraphy could be transmitted over long distances without a wire—even over the Atlantic Ocean. It did not take long for Lee DeForrest to show that Marconi's signal could be detected by a device that used the flame of a Bunsen burner and platinum electrodes with a coating of hydroxide. He followed this device with the invention of the first "audion" vacuum tube detector, and by 1907 the voices of singers could be heard on the airwaves. Following in the steps of these pioneers came dozens of inventors bringing regenerative circuits in 1912; superheterodyne radio in 1918; the first complete television system in 1926; and the first broadcast from a commercial station of color television in 1940. In 1969, when mankind made its first landing on the moon, millions of persons participated in that historic action via both radio and television. Today, we regularly see photographs sent back to earth from cameras traveling more than a thousand million miles out in space.

With this veritable flood of inventions and technical achievements of the last one hundred years, it is easy to see that the stage has been set for a whole series of breakthroughs that will fulfill the predictions and prophecies quoted earlier in this chapter.

Breakthrough Number One: The Electronic Voice Phenomenon

Following in the footsteps of Marconi and Edison are some pioneers whose names will not be as familiar to you. In 1956, two men from California, a photographer named Atilla von Szalay and a writer named Raymond Bayless, began an era of what has come to be known as EVP (electronic voice phenomenon). They recorded on magnetic tape some paranormal voices— voices that should not, logically, have been there. Bayless reported their experiments in the *Journal of the American Society for Psychical Research* in the winter of 1959. The announcement made hardly a ripple. Not a single person contacted the society or the researchers to inquire about their work.

But across the Atlantic, things were about to heat up in the field of EVP research. In the summer of 1959, a Swedish film producer named Friedrich Juergenson came up with some extra voices on his recordings as he was trying to capture bird songs on tape in the countryside. Amid the bird songs he heard a faint human voice, a male voice speaking Norwegian, saying something about "bird voices of the night." Like anybody would in that situation, Juergenson wondered whether the voices weren't just radio signals. But the more he listened carefully to his tapes, the more voices he detected that could not be explained as radio transmissions. The voices included some personal messages, such as, "Friedrich, you are being watched." A few weeks later, he recorded what he recognized to be the voice of his mother, who had died four years earlier, saying in German, "Friedel, my little Friedel, can you hear me?"

Juergenson continued his experiments and published a book about them in 1964. In addition to using the tape recorder with a microphone, he experimented with making recordings from the radio, then studying them to see if he could detect extra voices.

His book was read by Dr. Konstantin Raudive, a psychologist and author of books on philosophy, who lived in Germany. After visiting Juergenson and listening to his tapes, Raudive decided to experiment himself in order to answer the question of whether or not the voices were somehow connected with Juergenson's particular personality. For three months Raudive could detect nothing paranormal on his tapes. Then he heard a whispered, "That is correct," in his native Latvian language. This was in response to his remark that spirit-world inhabitants, like those on the earth, might face certain limitations.

Raudive was encouraged, and he went on to collect a huge number of voice recordings. By the time he published the first book on his work in 1968, he had recorded some seventy thousand phrases. Also, he had added some new techniques. He learned that if he turned his radio to the so-called "white noise" between stations, the tapes recorded at those wavelengths would contain voices. Word of Dr. Raudive's work spread, and scientists and engineers in Europe tried to duplicate his experiments. One of those was Alex Schneider, a Swiss physicist, who helped Raudive develop a new method of recording. The two discovered that voices not heard by the human ear at the time of the recording could be detected on the tape when it was played back.

Other pioneers who cooperated with Raudive included Theodore Rudolf, a high-frequency engineer who worked for Telefunken. Rudolf developed his own recording device called a goniometer. Another colleague of Raudive was Dr. Franz Seidl, an electronics engineer in Vienna who developed a device he called a Psychophon.

Engineers and scientists were not the only people to become interested in experimenting with the electronic voice phenomenon. Many lay people did also, after reading Raudive's book. So many began experimenting, in fact, that a German woman, Hanna Bushbeck, started a newsletter in 1969 to help the experimenters keep in touch and exchange ideas. Today, there are more than a thousand people in Germany alone recording, analyzing, and cataloging paranormal voices. One Catholic priest in Switzerland, Father Leo Schmid, has recoded thousands of phrases.

And that is only in Europe. Not until 1971 was Raudive's book brought out in English under the title of *Breakthrough: An Amazing Experiment in Electronic Communication with the Dead.* It was published by the British firm of Colin Smythe, which is a fascinating story in itself. Smythe was handed a copy of Raudive's book at a book fair in Germany with the suggestion that he might want to consider publishing it. He turned it over to an associate, Peter Bander, who was skeptical about the whole matter—until, that is, Smythe himself tried some experimenting with the voices and came up with the voice of Bander's mother, who was dead. The two publishers decided to have Raudive brought to England so that his tapes and his methods could be checked out by scientists and engineers under controlled conditions. Convinced that Raudive had, in fact, come up with unexplained voices on tape, they published the book, along with a recording of some of the voices. As a result, many more scientists and laymen throughout the world began experimenting with EVP.

As with so many aspects of serious research into the almost unexplored realms of the lower worlds of spirit, it is necessary to be constantly on guard and try to separate the wheat from the chaff. So far, I have said little about the content of the messages these researchers are receiving. Frankly, there have been serious problems with these recordings. Up to this time, the voices heard speaking the majority of such words or sentences that are purported to be coming from other planes is so weak that only a person who has spent many months trying to attune his hearing can distinguish the words from the background noise or sound that is a necessary part of the energies involved. This fact naturally results in much of the material being subject to misinterpretation.

There is another problem. Bits and pieces of the experimenter's own thoughts can be impressed on the recording tape. To date, only relatively few researchers have obtained sentences or groups of sentences that are distinct enough that ten people listening to them can agree on what it is they are hearing. Moreover, it is very rare to get a complete sentence. In 1981, Alexander MacRae, a Scottish researcher, made a statistical study of many hundreds of EVP voices and found the average length to be only 1.8 seconds.

In spite of such discouragements, the membership of the two German electronic voice associations and the American Electronic Voice Association are diligently pursuing this line of research to perfect a communication system for conversing with persons who are very much alive but no longer have physical bodies.

Breakthrough Number Two: The METAscience Research

My reading over many years in the fields of psychiatry, psychology, and psychic research opened up exciting vistas for research into the basic nature of the human being. In 1970, I terminated my professional career as an engineering and management consultant specializing in directing industrial research laboratories in the United States and Europe. In this role I had made forty-four transatlantic trips. With the prospect of royalty income from certain inventions I had made for Swedish clients, I then embarked, at age sixty, on what I hoped would be a fifteen-year self-directed and self-financed research program. (It actually took twenty years.)

The Ghost of 29 Megacycles by John G. Fuller gives an in-depth report on my work and that of others during this period. It was published in England in 1985 and in the United States in 1986 by the New American Library.

Since the answers I sought did not exist in any laboratory in the world, I developed my personal research program, using the same techniques and principles that had made millions of dollars in profit for my professional clients. Knowing that no one of the major sciences, nor any combination of them, could supply the answers I sought, I conceived a *meta-science* approach. In the sense that *meta* means over, above, transcending all fields of science and including the best of the world's accumulation of religious, psychic, and metaphysical lore.

Over the next decade, five trips around the world and many shorter foreign trips brought me into personal contact with a few dozen creative thinkers in the fields of medicine, psychology, parapsychology, psychic research, metaphysics, science, religion, psychiatry, and so on. My close collaboration with these persons, often leaders in their specialties, resulted in the eventual formation of an International Advisory Panel of more than two dozen members in twenty countries.

In 1971, two electronic specialists and I had opened a small private research laboratory in Philadelphia to work exclusively on the project that had foiled Marconi and Edison—a communication system capable of two-way conversation with the higher levels of consciousness. Through good fortune this laboratory activity had the benefit of two outstanding telepathic channels, an advertising executive in his sixties and a minister in her late fifties. Through the superb clairaudient abilities of these two persons, contact was established with Dr. William Francis Gray Swann (see appendix C). Dr. Swann, prior to his passing into the spirit world eight years earlier, had been a physics professor at several distinguished universities and had written the then-definitive book on cosmic rays.

Dr. Swann desired to help us in our research and assembled a large team of colleagues from the highest astral and the mental-causal planes. Many weekend sessions with Dr., Swann and his colleagues gave valuable insights as to the nature of our design problems, both numerous and of great complexity!

During this period, my twice-yearly trips for research in Europe delved deeply into the electronic voice phenomenon research just reported. By 1975, my engineering analysis indicated, at least to me, that the EVP approach held very little prospect of achieving meaningful and extended two-way conversation at higher levels of consciousness.

Several decades of organizing and directing research had taught me that at times it is prudent to carry on simultaneously two or more somewhat parallel lines of research. Hence, in 1975, I established a second research activity in the home of William J. O'Neil, a colleague who was a radio and television technician. Bill was also a most remarkable psychic who could clairvoyantly see and clairaudiently hear spirits dwelling in the lower and middle astral planes. One of these was a former medical doctor with whom Bill had once had single-sideband ham radio contact when he was still alive. Doc Nick suggested that instead of the white noise traditionally used by the EVP researchers, we should use certain audio frequencies. These would serve as an energy source against which the sounds produced by Doc Nick's vocal cords (in his rather dense astral body) could be projected. He said the result would be that our ears and the tape recorder would then be able to pick up his voice. This suggestion sounded plausible to us because we had observed that all of the EVP voices had to steal energy from radio frequencies, spoken or sung words, music, or artificially created white or pink noises or sounds.

After some experimentation, we had the great thrill on October 27, 1977, of hearing Doc Nick's first words, just barely, coming through the quite loud mixture of tones Bill had provided as a starting point.

Bill: Try it again.

Doc Nick: All right, Do you hear me now, Bill? Can you hear me, Bill?

Bill: Yeah, but you make it sound like—oh boy—a robot on television (chuckling).

Doc Nick: Yes, we always will, when we...we will. The one thing...you hear, Bill. You hear, Bill?

Bill: Yeah, okay (sounding as though he is shaken up by the happenings.) You have to forgive me, but— I know this is—you have to admit this is kind of scary.

Doc Nick: (Unintelligible.)

Bill: It's all garbled. I can't understand you.

Doc Nick: I said, why are you…leave it alone, leave it alone. Did you hear me, Bill? Do you hear what I say?

Bill: Yeah, I got it now, Doc. You asked what I was doing on the Vidicom, right?

Doc Nick: Yes.

Bill: Dr. Mueller wants me to get busy on this, you know.

Doc Nick: Oh yes, *that* man.

Bill: Yeah, that man (chuckling). You have to forgive me, but it is not that easy, it is not easy. [Tones shift slightly in pitch.] That frequency changed again.

Doc Nick: Yes, I know, Bill. It is much better now. I feel [echo effect], I feel, I feel more comfortable with this frequency. Don't change it anymore. As I told you before, you must be careful of these frequencies. Mark the frequency change.

Bill: Oh, yes—yes, sure. I am supposed to guess what these frequencies are. I don't have any way of monitoring these frequencies.

We really can't blame William for being a bit scared when he had his first communication with someone who had been among the so-called dead for seven years. But he showed his own good sense when he remarked to Doc Nick, "Who do you think will believe anything like this?'

Our position in releasing a tape recording of this communication was precisely that of Doc Nick when he replied, "Don't worry about that. It is not important, believe me!" Those who scoffed at this information, even after carefully evaluating the tape and the related printed materials, were in the embarrassing position of one member of the French Academy of Sciences years ago. He told his learned colleagues, "I personally have examined Mr. Edison's phonograph and I find it is nothing but the clever use of ventriloquism."

Noise-filled, broken, and disjointed, and disappointingly brief as it was, this was history-making at its best. It was the first meaningful two-way conversation of this quality of which we have any record. None of the tens of thousands of EVP phrases recorded have had such significance. And it certainly ranks in clarity with what is said to have been the first communication over Alexander Graham Bell's first crude telephone: "Come here, Watson!" or Edison's squeaky tinfoil recording of "Mary Had a Little Lamb" on his first phonograph.

In some respects, this historic voice exchange between Doc Nick and William O'Neil may be even more momentous. It could be called the start of a communication system between the living and the dead—between heaven and earth, between mankind on planet earth and higher levels of consciousness. But science demands replication, and in this case prolonged instrumental voice contact with Doc Nick was not accomplished. Thereby starts the trail to the third major breakthrough.

Breakthrough Number Three: Hours of Sustained Communication
Of course it was disturbing, even disheartening, when shortly after that historic conversation, Doc Nick seemed to go off in a disgruntled manner. What happened was however more interesting. You will recall that Bill mentioned that he was also doing some work with a Dr. Mueller. At that point, Doc Nick remarked, with seeming disapproval, "Oh yes, *that* man!" and Bill answered, chuckling, "Yeah, that man."

At this period in our research, in 1978, Bill was clairaudiently and clairvoyantly collaborating in his research with both Doc Nick and Dr. George Jeffries Mueller. These two dwellers in the interpenetrating worlds of spirit had totally different personalities and professional backgrounds. Doc Nick had been the first to collaborate with Bill and he definitely regarded Dr. Mueller as a "Johnny-come-lately." However, sad as we were to see our friend Doc Nick break off contact, he had made a historic appearance, had helped Bill to further develop his already great psychic abilities of clairaudience clairvoyance, had introduced the idea of using certain audio frequencies, and had generally set the stage for what was, within three years, destined to become the third major breakthrough.

Earlier we mentioned the apostle Paul's admonition two thousand years ago to test the spirits to make sure they were who they professed to be and were not mischievous impostors or pranksters. Bill had learned this lesson well and between us we proceeded to put Dr. Mueller on trial. The research over the next two years resulted in notebooks filled with data and reports.

It must be one of the best documented cases of survival in more than two hundred years of psychic research. Here are the highlights in abbreviated form:

Education: Dr. Mueller told us of his undergraduate work at the University of Wisconsin in Madison, of social and glee club activities, his earning a master's degree in physics, his doctoral work at Cornell University in Ithaca, New York, and his subsequent instructorship in physics at Cornell. Parapsychologist Dr. Walter Uphoff visited the registrar's office at the University of Wisconsin and was able to verify Dr. Mueller's statements. Dr. Norman Uphoff, Walter's son, was at this time on the staff at Cornell and was able to verify Dr. Mueller's statements regarding his work there.

Death: Dr. Mueller voluntarily gave the name of the small town in California where he had been living when he suffered a fatal coronary attack. We were able to obtain a copy of the death certificate, confirm the cause of his death, and get additional vital statistics.

Social security number: Dr. Mueller obliged us by providing his social security number! We were able to verify this.

Survivors: We verified the existence and name of four surviving members of his immediate family. They were as he had given them to us.

Personal appearance: Bill described Dr. Mueller the way he saw him clairvoyantly. We then wrote to his wife at the time of his death and asked her to describe her former husband. Then a comparison was made of the two descriptions. They agreed as to body build, weight, and mannerisms. They disagreed in one particular. Bill described him as having wavy brown hair, whereas in fact he was bald at the time of his demise. This discrepancy is easily explained. Even if you, the reader, make the transition at the age of ninety and are old and decrepit, you will have the privilege of "manifesting" a spirit-body that suits your fancy! As we said in the last chapter, most persons choose their appearance at what they consider the prime of life. Dr. Mueller had wavy brown hair as a younger man.

Intimate conversations: In the period from 1978 to 1981 (prior to the two-way instrumental conversation with Dr. Mueller), Bill recorded on tape dozens of extended clairaudient conversations on a great variety of subjects. Our investigations confirmed many of the intimate items Dr. Mueller shared.

Personality: Again in deference to Dr. Mueller's privacy, we will refrain from presenting a personality profile, but from his dozens of hours of one-to-one contact with Bill we got a very clear picture of his personality and mannerisms. We found our observations confirmed by a few contacts we made with persons who knew him. Basically, we can say he was a warm-hearted man with a wonderful sense of humor. Due to his great intellect and scientific expertise, he naturally had a communication gap with Bill, a high school dropout. For example, Dr. Mueller could never bend to the point of addressing William as "Bill."

Professional resume: Dr. Mueller dictated to Bill two pages of details, which he said were contained in the last printed copy of his professional resume. Apparently the details were quite accurate, because one family member was of the opinion that we "must have done some research and uncovered this material in the files of one of Dr. Mueller's consulting clients." While we certainly had not had any access to the files of Dr. Mueller or his clients, it was evidential to have such a statement from a family member.

His book: Dr. Mueller referred to a small booklet he wrote in 1949 for the U.S. Army. Several times he requested that Bill locate a copy and read pages 66 and 67. After a search of two years that involved contacts with several departments in the Pentagon, the Library of Congress, and the Army library at West Point, a copy was located in the Army section of the archives of the State Historical Society of Wisconsin, Dr. Mueller's home state. Comments regarding these two pages and their amazing relevancy are presented in appendix G.

Scientific knowledge: On several occasions, Dr. Mueller dictated a scientific discourse—at least as scientific as possible with Bill's limited knowledge of scientific terms. One of these, dealing with the origin of music in the earliest civilizations, is a most enlightening document.

A useful invention: Dr. Mueller, prior to the death of his physical body, had a deep interest in arthritis. He gave Bill the wiring diagram for a device to treat arthritis. He called it the Integrated Frequency Response Therapy Unit. We built samples and had them tested in several locations. We have received dozens of affidavits signed by patients who benefited. My wife Jeannette and I, as well as some of our friends, are among the many persons who have benefited from the use of this device.

Our main interest in contacting Dr. Mueller, of course, was not just to gather evidence, as impressive as it may be. We wanted his help in our research work. And one of the most dramatic examples of Mueller's help was the way he applied the knowledge he had acquired from a lifelong hobby—the study of the theory of music. From this background, he provided a suggestion that helped make his voice audible in Bill's laboratory. He instructed Bill to create a recording on a cassette tape of thirteen specific tones that spanned the adult male voice—from 121 to 701 cycles per second—for use as a source of audio energy in the instrumentation Bill was devising. Wonder of wonders—the third breakthrough! It occurred on September 23, 1980. Here it is:

MUELLER: William, I think that's much better, right there, William. Now, William, did you understand? W i l l i i a a m m?

BILL: Yes, sir, I understand, Doctor.

MUELLER: Very well. I will give you a count from one to ten. One. Two. Three, four, five, six, seven, eight, nine, ten. One moment, William.

BILL: Okay.

MUELLER: Very well, then. [Reciting] Mary had a little lamb, the lamb would go-ooo-goooooo [deliberately holding the last syllable]. Play that back for me, William. William?

BILL: Yes, sir.

MUELLER: Play that back for me.

BILL: All right, Doctor. I am sorry; I was lighting a cigarette.

MUELLER: Oh, those cigarettes again! [Bill played the tape back, then they resumed their conversation.] Did you change it, William?

BILL: Yes, I did, Doctor.

MUELLER: Very well. I am back about three feet now, I am back about three feet. I will give you another test. One, two, three, four, five, six, seven, eight, nine, ten. I'd change that frequency again, William.

BILL: Very well, Doctor.

MUELLER: One, one, one, one, two, three, four, five. This is somewhat better, William. Play that back, if you will.

Well, "Mary's Little Lamb" certainly added to its claim to immortality! But since one of the first rules of science is that of replication, nothing could be more gratifying than to have Dr. Mueller's conversation confirmed that we had at last established meaningful instrumental communication with a person who had shed his physical body.

The great value of the technical assistance given by Dr. Mueller is dramatically shown in the next excerpt, taken from a conversation in April 1981. Near the start, he gives his reactions to one of the audio frequencies and then proceeds to pinpoint an electronic circuit problem on the video apparatus on which he and William are working.

Spiricom is the name we gave to the electronic device we used to talk to the spirits. *Vidicom* is the name we coined for the video device which we had hoped would do the same thing, but with pictures as well as sound.

BILL: Just a minute, Doctor. Yes, I know you are here, but I got to—I am gonna cut down the volume of these other frequencies.

MUELLER: Very well, William.

BILL: I want to cut them down to a level that won't uh, ah...

MUELLER: I am not sure, William, but—I don't feel too comfortable with that one frequency.

BILL: Well, we will see. Maybe we can change it later on, Doctor.

MUELLER: Very well. Oh, yes, William?

BILL: Yes?

MUELLER: Ah, I think we have a problem with the Spiricom we are working on.

BILL: Spiricom? Oh, you mean Vidicom.

MUELLER: Oh, yes, William. I am sorry, Vidicom. I think the problem is...television receiver. William, I think the big problem is an impedance mismatch into that third transistor.

BILL: Third transistor?

MUELLER: Yes, the transistor that follows the input.

BILL: I don't understand.

MUELLER: The pre-amp, the pre-amp!

BILL: Oh, the pre-amp?

MUELLER: Yes, I think that I can easily correct that by introducing a, by introducing a 150 or 100—I am not sure, William—a 150-ohm one-half-watt resistor in parallel with a .0047 microfarad ceramic capacitor. I think we can overcome that impedance mismatch.

BILL: Oh, boy, I'll have to get the schematic back.

MUELLER: You'd rather have the schematic?

BILL: I'd rather mark it on the schematic, Doctor.

MUELLER: Very well.

BILL: The schematic is over there in the file.

MUELLER: Very well.

I hope you noticed how very specific Dr. Mueller was in pinpointing the technical problem on the experimental video device on which he and William were working. What better proof could science want that Dr. Mueller's mind, memory banks, and personality are still alive and functioning in a useful and most dramatic way!

And now here is an excerpt in which they further discuss our Vidicom research project. Incidentally, the problems of developing a workable Vidicom system seem even more monumental than those of perfecting Spiricom.

MUELLER: Oh, by the way, William. Did you get that multifaceted crystal?

BILL: No, I didn't, Doctor. I got that five-faceted from Edmund's.

MUELLER: Edmunds? Edmunds? Who is Edmunds?

BILL: Edmund's is a company—Edmund's Scientific.

MUELLER: Oh, I understand. What were the results?

BILL: Well, I inserted it into the lens of the camera, but all I got was a lot of crazy colors of light. But I didn't get any imagery.

MUELLER: Oh, I see. Well, very good. Well, I think if we follow this other procedure, William, and I am not absolutely sure, but I have a feeling that this will help clarify the image, so we can discern features on the subject. We have the form, we have the face, we have the...we know...the human form. However, we must be able to discern the facial features, so we can identify the subject. I don't know yet [talking to another entity]. Just a minute, William. [To the other entity] What's that?

BILL: What's that, Doctor?

MUELLER: No, no, William, I am not...Someone is talking to you. William, do you know Nathaniel? There is a fellow here, William. He says his name is Nathaniel. He says he knows you and you know him.

BILL: Nathaniel? I don't know anybody by the name of Nathaniel.

MUELLER: He says he knows you.

BILL: I don't recall knowing anybody [named Nathaniel].

You perhaps noted that Dr. Mueller turned aside from the microphone to talk with another spirit person standing in the lab. William was unable to see him visually or clairvoyantly, or to hear him clairaudiently. The spirit who told Dr. Mueller that his name was Nathaniel seemingly could not talk through Spiricom. In the following days, with Dr. Mueller serving as intermediary, William and Nathaniel discussed boyhood activities, including pranks in which they had participated more than half a century ago.

The contacts with Dr. Mueller were sporadic. Days and even weeks would pass with no contact—even when William left the electronic equipment on. Then Dr. Mueller would pay an unexpected visit like this one:

MUELLER: William…William…Wiiilliiiaaammm, William…Wiilliiaamm. Are you there, William?

BILL: I'm coming, Doctor, I'm coming. [Out of breath] Oh boy. I am sorry, Doctor, I am sorry. I just went downstairs for a cup of coffee. I am sorry, Doctor.

MUELLER: That's all right, William.

Then, equally frustrating, there would be a totally unexplained termination of contact in the midst of a very useful conversation. Here is an example:

MUELLER: What's that, William? Did you understand what I mean?

BILL: Oh, I understand, but a lot of things I don't understand. Do you have any suggestions, Doctor? [Pause] Do you have any suggestions? Doctor, sir? Oh, my God! Doctor Mueller?

In the early months of our conversations with Dr. Mueller, electromagnetic factors, the phases of the moon, sunspots, or other unknown factors resulted in poor quality of Dr. Mueller's voice. Still, we recorded a lot of material. In this segment, Dr. Mueller responds to William's mention of possible surgery. These comments and his observations of his own death fourteen years previously are worth careful consideration.

MUELLER: I am very happy, William, that surgery was not necessary. There are times when surgery becomes necessary. Don't worry about it, William. Don't worry. Worry does not help the situation. Should surgery become necessary in the future, since it's not a malignancy—it's benign—there's nothing to worry about, William. Did you understand? Hopefully you will not have to have that surgery, William, but should you have to have that surgery, please, William, please—worry will not help. Do you understand, William?

BILL: Yeah, I understand. But do you understand, Doctor? I know I am not getting any younger.

MUELLER: I know. I understand, William. Well. In my case, well, I was fortunate. It was sudden. However, you know in advance. The important thing, the one benefit that you will find as the result of our contacts, you are aware! I was not aware of this side. I didn't know the potential over here before. So when I got over here it was like waking up in the morning and not knowing where you are! Like having a bad dream...

There are many discussions on more joyful subjects than surgery and death experiences in the many hours of tape we recorded of Bill's conversations with Dr. Mueller! Often Dr. Mueller displayed his delightful humor. In this excerpt, he speaks of his fondness for carrots and cabbage.

BILL: Yeah, I just turned on the tape recorder, Doc.

MUELLER: Very well, William.

BILL: You said to hurry back and I did. That has been exactly one week ago.

MUELLER: Ho ho!

BILL: Yes. Ho ho yourself. Cold weather has left us, temporarily, anyway. It's raining, it's nice and warm. Of course, you never know what to expect. I am going to try to put in a little garden this year.

MUELLER: Oh, wonderful! Send me a couple of carrots.

BILL: What's that again?

MUELLER: A couple of carrots.

BILL: Oh, carrots!

MUELLER: Yes, William, and a nice head of lettuce.

BILL: A nice head of lettuce! I'm not going to plant acres, Doctor. What's that? I think you were talking at the same time I was.

MUELLER: Well, perhaps. I said if somebody had some cabbage, I like fried cabbage. Oh, I love fried cabbage!

BILL: Fried cabbage! Well, I love sauerkraut.

MUELLER: Well, you know what sauerkraut can do?

BILL: Yes, I do. You know, Doctor, I never thought I'd see the day when I could talk to someone like you in the way we are doing. If ten years ago someone had told me this was possible, I would have recommended that they be sent to the funny farm.

MUELLER: Well, perhaps you are right.

Like Bill—and his fellow researchers—you readers may have difficulty believing these really are conversations with a scientist whose funeral took place fourteen years earlier. After all, it does seem preposterous!

I should explain that these transcripts were prepared from recordings made simultaneously on two cassette recorders, and often on the audio portion of one video-camera tape. Figure 3–5 is a still photograph of one frame

Fig. 3–5.—William J. O'Neil

of a videotape made while Bill was conversing with Dr. Mueller in August, 1981. (Bill's lab was only dimly lit.) Bill is standing in front of the Spiricom equipment where he must remain alert to fine tune the signal and tone generator to maintain the best quality of Dr. Mueller's voice. The photo of Dr. Mueller on the following page is from the archives of the Cornell University Library.

The following exchange is one of several in which Dr. Mueller states that serial time as we know it does not exist in his world.

> MUELLER: What did you say, William?

> BILL: I said I am sorry, Doctor, but—oh boy—it's almost four

Fig. 3–6.—Dr. George Jeffries Mueller

o'clock in the morning. The last time we talked it was what? About a quarter after two. I forget what time it was.

Mueller: Oh, here we go with that time again. William, you know better than that.

Bill: What's that, sir?

Mueller: You know better than that. I am not aware of time over here.

Bill: Well, I know. That's what you said, sir.

Mueller: I am not joking, William. I am not joking. Now listen, William, please listen very carefully.

BILL: Yes?

MUELLER: Adjust that frequency, William!

BILL: All right, sir. Oh, boy!

We were constantly amazed that Dr. Mueller could see everything in the lab. Often Bill would lay out letters or magazine articles, which Dr. Mueller would proceed to read and then discuss. Here he asks about a new instrument that had just been placed in the lab.

MUELLER: Very well, William. What is that in there? What is that instrument there?

BILL: Which one is that, sir?

MUELLER: The little one there.

BILL: Oh, the blue one, yes? The blue one, sir?

MUELLER: Yes, William.

BILL: That's a biofeedback, sir. A biofeedback unit.

MUELLER: Oh, really! Do you have any nerve problems, William?

BILL: [Chuckling] No, sir. You know what that's for, sir.

MUELLER: Well, I am just joshing, William. I am just joshing. Let's get on with it.

During our years of working with persons in the worlds of spirit, we have learned that most great inventions are conceived in the mental and causal levels of consciousness and are then implanted in the mind of a person called an inventor. We refer to this process as intuition. Some time in the decades ahead, ideas will be transmitted directly by instrument from a scientist in the higher planes.

Now for an evidential item that will gladden the hearts of even the most strict parapsychologists. On one occasion, Dr. Mueller suggested we refer to a small book he wrote for the U.S. Army in 1947 entitled *Introduction to Electronics*.

MUELLER: Did you obtain that book of mine yet?

BILL: Oh, that book of yours. No, sir. By the way, our friend, Mr. Meek, is really going all out to find that, because I want to read those two pages you mentioned.

MUELLER: Very well. And I want you to read that, William. There must be copies available somewhere.

BILL: Well, I think George—that's Mr. Meek, our friend...

MUELLER: Your friend!

BILL: Yes, even if he has to go to the Library of Congress. He'll probably do that.

MUELLER: Oh, I see. Oh, all right.

Even the Library of Congress did not have a copy. However, we located the book in the archives of the State Historical Society of Wisconsin, Dr. Mueller's native state. The two pages he specifically asked me to locate did, in fact, predict electronic advances such as this communication research (see appendix G).

I will conclude this series of excerpts from the Spiricom recordings with a most prophetic exchange:

MUELLER: William?

BILL: Yes, sir?

MUELLER: Did you make that telephone call yet? [Occasionally, Dr. Mueller would give Bill the unlisted telephone number of a professional colleague. I checked two of these and found them to be valid.]

BILL: No, sir.

MUELLER: May I suggest you do, William. Now, you must understand one thing, William.

BILL: Yes, sir?

MUELLER: *I cannot be here forever.* I cannot guarantee how long I'll be visiting here. However, I will do my best. Do you understand, William?

BILL: Yes, sir.

MUELLER: There is a time and a place for everything. So as I have mentioned before, this is something I think you should be aware of.

Dr. Mueller's statement that he would not be here forever was most prophetic. As the months passed, I was able to observe that he was beginning to shed his dense earthly vibrations and was starting his progression upward, as depicted in figure 2–2, "Interpenetrating Levels of Life and Consciousness." Within one month of his having made the statement about not being able to stay forever, he had increased his consciousness to the point where our electronic system called Mark IV could no longer be used for contact.

Any reader who wishes to know more about the eleven years of research that preceded these conversations between the living and the dead will find the detailed story in *The Ghost of 29 Megacycles* by John G. Fuller. Fuller was given access to more than three hundred documents—correspondence, research reports, agreements, library references, death certificates, social security data, news releases, audio and videotapes, and so on. He supplemented study of these with travel in the United States, England, and Germany to interview my associates and other researchers who were independently engaged in electronic voice research. In his resulting book, he used his investigating and reporting skills to create a balanced analysis of these mind-stretching experiences.

Events of the next few years were to show that Dr. Mueller's help in achieving hours of sustained communication and the worldwide readership of John Fuller's book laid the foundation for what was to become the next breakthrough.

Chapter Four
Via Instrumental Systems
(Part 2)

When the great invention appears, it will almost certainly
be in muddled, incomplete, and confusing form. To the
discoverer himself, it will be only half-understood; to everybody else, it will be a mystery. For any speculation which
does not at first glance look crazy, there is no hope.

—Niels Bohr, Danish physicist

Having rent the veil between the spirit worlds and the physical earth
plane, a project on which both Marconi and Edison failed, what
next? Should we attempt to tell the public about this monumental development? Is the public ready to accept into its belief system such a
preposterous idea? By what means should the news be disseminated?

After Jeannette and I pondered these and related questions, we concluded we were in the precise situation described by Dr. Niels Bohr. As
with most of mankind's major technical advances, a generation—say twenty
or twenty-five years—was required to move it into everyday life. We were
very conscious of the fact that we had merely scratched the surface with
our crude instrumentation and that years of work would be required by
many other inventors and researchers before there would be any possibility of having a really workable system. Only by going public and releasing all technical details without charge could we come into contact with
other intrepid electronic technicians around the world who would eventually create practical systems for both seeing and talking with persons who
had departed their physical bodies. Discussion of the public exposure

problem with our colleague Dr. Bruce Swain, professor of journalism at the University of Georgia, helped us formulate a plan.

We rented the main ballroom of the National Press Club in Washington, D.C., and scheduled a public press conference for Good Friday morning, April 6, 1982. We then made arrangements for radio announcements to be released on that day and for inviting representatives of the newspapers, magazines, and TV networks to the press conference.

Since we wanted this release of this news to be worldwide, Jeannette and I packed our bags and departed on our fifth trip around the world. This trip was for the sole purpose of apprising our colleagues in many countries as to what we were going to do. We wanted to provide them with materials they could distribute to the press in their countries on the same day when we had the press conference in Washington, D.C.

Back in Washington, after our globe-circling trip, we made the final preparations for the press conference. Being realistic, Dr. Swain and I knew that if we had even ten or twelve people show up at a press conference on the subject of instrumental communication with the dead we would indeed be fortunate. We were pleasantly surprised to have an audience of more than fifty representatives of the press.

The press packet we distributed to all those present contained a ninety-minute audiotape with excerpts from more than twenty two-way conversations, a one-hundred-page technical manual with photographs and diagrams of electronic circuits, a photohistory of Man's communication systems, and a press release that read in part as follows:

This may be the most significant Easter week in some 2,000 years. Christian beliefs concerning immortality got an unexpected boost Tuesday when METAscience Foundation researchers announced they had combined electronic instrumentation with certain psychic energies to achieve sustained contact with the "dead."

No visions, no seances with mediums, no random voices from the beyond. A machine—which they have named SPIRICOM. It involves a frequency modulation system using supplementary audio tones.

"For the first time we have electronic proof that the mind, memory banks, and personality survive death of the physical body," foundation president George W. Meek said at a press conference held at the National Press Club.

There was more good news. The SPIRICOM equipment, Meek said, is only an elementary start toward the perfection of a communication system using "electromagnetic and etheric energies" that should some-day permit those living on earth to have telephone-like conversations with persons very much alive in higher levels of consciousness. Beyond that, there is the distinct possibility of a television-like device.

Meek sounded one cautionary note: perfection of the instrumentation may take quite some time...

What was the media reaction? One of the newspaper reporters at the press conference filed a widely circulated story saying that we had failed to observe the "time-honored peer review process"; that is, submitting our research to a panel of scientific contemporaries for their personal reactions and responses. What that reporter failed to realize was that at least ninety-nine percent of all the world's scientists in 1982 were as ignorant on the subject of life after death as were ninety-nine percent of all the world's ministers, priests, and rabbis! The reporter's criticism was as nonsensical as it would have been to criticize Thomas Edison's work with an objection that on none of his more than one thousand patents did he subject his con-cepts to the time-honored peer review process.

The journalist also disregarded the fact that I had assembled at the press conference a panel of eight men from the United States and Europe who were among the handful of true experts in this matter. A highly credible scientist, Professor William A. Tiller, then head of the Department of Mate-rial Science at Stanford University, introduced me to the assembly of reporters. Professor Tiller was one of the very few scientific colleagues who were, in fact, my peers. As to my electronic peers, three of the eight experts I had assembled on the speaker's platform collectively had more than one hundred years of work in the field of electronics.

The TV networks ignored the announcement, but, thanks to a balanced and thorough wire story by a United Press International reporter present, more than 150 newspapers in the United States carried brief reports. As was to be expected, a goodly portion of these were highly skeptical, but many handled it with a light good humor. Nevertheless, the overall objective was accomplished; namely, getting this news item exposed to readers all over the world.

In the following months, interest was sufficient among potential researchers that I made two trips to Europe and two trips across the United States to talk with people who were toying with the idea of starting such research on their own.

This situation in the United States and the around-the-world trip by Jeannette and me generated publicity that resulted in another breakthrough.

Breakthrough Number Four: Research in Many Countries

Gradually over the following years, we received reports telling that men and women had started their own research in Brazil, England, West Germany, Switzerland, Austria, Luxembourg, Italy, France, the USSR, and Scandinavia. These reports told of contacts with the "dead" via telephone, telephone answering machines, computer, and radio, and the obtaining of photographs of the communicators in the spirit world via the TV picture tube.

However, as the years went on, several things became obvious. First, no communication was possible unless there was some individual person in the spirit world who was deeply motivated to participate in the research. Second, it became obvious that the higher the level of spiritual development of the earthside communicator, the greater was the possibility of successful communication. Third, it became obvious that just as in the case of William O'Neil, a certain type of psychic sensitivity was necessary on the part of the earthside communicator. (In ways still not understood, these psychic energies help serve as a bridge to interface with the psychic energy of the person living in the realms of spirit.) In spite of these serious limitations, progress continued. Today spirit communication has taken place by the use of all four of these instrumentalities—via radio, videoscreen, telephone answering machine, and computer. If you are surprised at the reference to the telephone, it should be noted that two American researchers, Attila von Szalay and Raymond Bayless, summarized their research in a book entitled *Phone Calls from the Dead,* which listed more than fifty momentary telephone contacts with persons who had died.

However, by all odds the most exciting and potentially fruitful development is that of communication via computer. Ken Webster of England published a book (now out of print) in which he reported on more than two hundred computer contacts with local persons who had died in the seventeenth century.

Breakthrough Number Five

The most dramatic computer contact I have witnessed was one that took place when my physicist colleague Dr. Ernst Senkowski and I were in the home of Jules and Maggie Harsch-Fischbach in Luxembourg. A week earlier, Dr. Senkowski had submitted seven very, very searching questions soliciting information beyond his knowledge of physics. He and I had been told that if we were present at 2:00 p.m. on a day in February 1988, the reply would be transmitted by computer. Promptly at 2:00 p.m. Maggie turned on the computer, called up the menu, and pressed the agreed-upon code word. Immediately, the printer started operating. The printing head flew back and forth at a speed of two hundred words per minute and printed an answer that occupied two full single-spaced sheets. The contents of the material were so profound that they required considerable study by Dr. Senkowski.

My first contact with Jeannette via instrumental means also took place in Luxembourg. Before Jeannette's transition, I had asked her to get firmly in mind the name of the spirit-side transmission station, Time-Stream, and the name Swejan Salter, a woman scientist from a parallel universe who operates the station in the astral world.

I spent a weekend in July 1990 in Luxembourg and observed the assembly of a completely new system, using electronics, ultraviolet light, and crystals. It had been fabricated during the past several months, and this was to be the first operation of the new system. Dr. Theo Locher of the Swiss Parapsychology Association and I observed the final assembly of the system.

This two-day-weekend work did not leave time to explore contact with Jeannette. Late in the afternoon the computer was printing out a protocol that was to summarize this weekend activity. The printer stopped at the end of the protocol.

However, while our eyes were all focused on the closing lines displayed on the screen, the computer then indexed over to the lower left-hand corner and printed out—

"Hello Sweetheart, Jeannette."

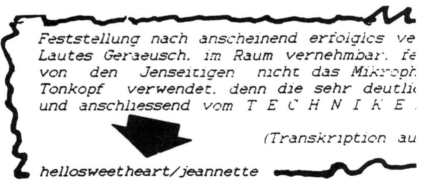

Feststellung nach anscheinend erfoigics ve
Lautes Geraeusch. im Raum vernehmbar. fe
von den Jenseitigen nicht das Mikropf.
Tonkopf verwendet. denn die sehr deutli(
und anschliessend vom T E C H N I K E .

(Transkription au

hellosweetheart/jeannette

Fig. 4–1.—Jeannette's Computer Greeting

My co-author Jeannette had succeeded in making contact with the help of the Time Stream...and squeezed in never-to-be-forgotten evidence that she was on deck and observing the spirit-side transmission of her personal identity! Confirmation that Jeannette was, in fact, present at the Time Stream Sending Station in the astral worlds came from Swejan Salter, the woman scientist who is the director of the station. Dr. Salter is quoted in a later newsletter publication of the Luxembourg organization as saying RIGHT NOW [the time when the above message was transmitted by computer] JEANNETTE IS STANDING BESIDE ME AND ASKING TO PASS ON SPECIAL GREETINGS TO GEORGE. SHE LOOKS LIKE A YOUNG GIRL AND IS A LITTLE BEWILDERED. ALTHOUGH SHE KNOWS A LOT ABOUT THE SPIRIT WORLD, SHE NEVER IMAGINED IT WOULD BE SO OVERWHELMING.

To better comprehend how this astonishing two-world instrumental communication became possible, the reader is referred to appendix B. The Historical Overview shows the slow but steady research progress over a period of sixty years.

Breakthrough Number Six:
My Friend Projects His Photograph During His Funeral
As further justification for the title of this book, consider the following paragraphs:

Perhaps the most astonishing of the instrumental developments in recent years is that of obtaining pictures on TV tubes of persons known to have departed their physical bodies. One good source of information is the book published in German by Rainer Holbe of the Luxembourg radio and TV station. The book, *Bilder aus dem Reich der Toten (Pictures from the King-dom of the Dead)*, reports in detail the successes Klaus Schreiber had in obtaining pictures of his deceased wife and other persons on the TV tube of his home.

On one of my European visits, I had dinner with my seventy-eight-year-old friend, Hanna Bushbeck. Hanna was active as head of the German Electronic Voice Association, which she founded. Shortly after her death, her photograph appeared on the TV tube showing her as she looked as a young woman—at perhaps the age of thirty. (Jeannette, who died at age eighty-two, chooses to look as she did at age forty-five. She feels this is appropriate, as our daughter in the spirit world appears at the age of twenty-six.)

However, of the few dozen TV photos that I have seen, I have chosen one particular situation to share in-depth with the reader. It is the case of a deceased Swedish friend of mine, Friedrich Juergenson. Juergenson appeared paranormally on the TV screen in the home of my friends Claude and Ellen Thorlin *at the time of his funeral service* more than one hundred miles away in Stockholm.

Friedrich Juergenson, while not historically the first to record the voice of a person known to be deceased, is considered the Father of the Electronic Voice Phenomenon. His life's path led him from Odessa in the Ukraine via Estonia to his chosen country of Sweden. He traveled in many countries as a painter, singer, archaeologist, and highly creative film director. When he died on October 15, 1987, at the age of eighty-four, he had spent almost thirty years studying the Electronic Voice Phenomenon and presented copious documentation that the voices were indeed those of the "dead."

His book, *Sprechfunk Mit Verstorbenen*, has become a classic in the field of electronically-assisted spirit communication.

Nils Jacobson, M.D., of Stockholm (a member of my International Advisory Panel) and I had the privilege of being house guests of Friedrich on a weekend fourteen years ago. Juergenson shared with us the details of his then current work in recording voices of the dead. Looking ahead, we concluded that sooner or later some researcher would obtain visual images of the so-called dead.

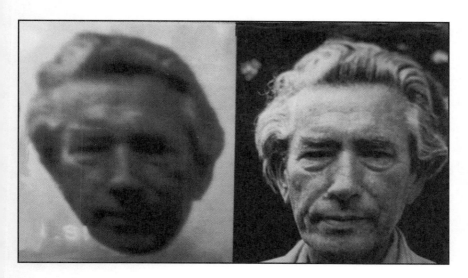

Fig. 4–2.—Juergenson via   Fig. 4–3.—Juergenson
Video During His Funeral   Before His Death

We never met again person. However, Swedish parapsychologist Claude Thorlin, who had worked with Friedrich on the EVP research since 1963, occasionally kept me abreast of Friedrich's work, as did my colleague Dr. Ernst Senkowski in West Germany. Hence I was aware that during the closing years of his life, Friedrich was deeply involved in research in getting pictures of the dead on videotape or movie film. (After all, he was internationally famous as a producer of documentary films.)

Claude Thorlin and his wife Ellen live in a town in Sweden one thousand miles from the small town of Hoor, where Friedrich had made his home. On the morning of Wednesday, October 21, 1987, Claude and Ellen (who has been clairvoyant and clairaudient since childhood) were sitting at breakfast. Ellen heard an unidentified voice tell her to use channel 4. Both were mystified because their radio had only three channels and their TV had only two working channels—channel 1 and channel 2. Ellen could not hear the voice clearly, but she felt it must involve the funeral service of their friend, Friedrich Juergenson, which would take place that same day.

As a knowledgeable parapsychologist, Claude, of course, knew of the Harsch-Fischbach research with the TV pictures in Luxembourg and the similar research of Klaus Schreiber in West Germany. Hence, he located his Polaroid camera and at 1:00 p.m., he and Ellen began to watch the blank screen of their TV. As Claude told me in a personal letter:

> I adjusted the TV set to Channel 4, even though I knew there would be no program for us to watch on that channel. Sitting there got to be boring. We began to wonder if Ellen's clairaudience had failed her.
>
> We had just about given up and were ready to shut off the TV when the appearance of the screen changed. I thought maybe the picture tube had gone because everything turned black. All of a sudden something happened on the screen. The lower left became light. At that time, I raised the camera, took aim, and took the first picture.
>
> In about six or seven seconds, the light expanded over the whole screen and then slowly changed. Just at that moment, I took a second picture. I looked at my watch and it was exactly 1:22 p.m. Later I conformed that Friedrich's burial service had started at 1:00 p.m. (fig. 4–3).

So! Friedrich Juergenson, the father of EVP and a pioneer researcher of pictures of the dead, used his own funeral to continue his research from the other side. The picture he transmitted, while not something to win a photography prize, certainly conveys the main features as to the shape of his head, mouth, ears, hair line, etc.

Let Us Pause for a Moment

Ponder the significance of this and the preceding chapter.

Their message is loud and clear. As a result of these breakthroughs, the prophecies and predictions of the past eighty years, sampled in the opening pages of chapter 3, have been fulfilled.

The veil between heaven and earth has been rent—
by INSTRUMENTAL SYSTEMS!

And from the standpoint of twentieth-century materialistic mankind, nothing in the past two thousand years has done this so effectively. Man in the flesh on planet earth has devised electronic instruments that enable him to actually talk with persons who have been buried in the ground or cremated. Man has discovered that these people are still very much alive. Their minds, memory banks, personalities, and souls are still intact and in good working order. They think and speak just as they did before cremation or burial!

What are the implications of this rending of the veil? Changes so momentous that within only one or two generations, the developments that will naturally follow this humble start could beneficially modify the course of civilization and human evolution. The profound questions generated will undoubtedly be the subject of many books that will be written worldwide in the next decade.

Chapter Five
Via Mental Telepathy?

T he dead have been speaking since the dawn of recorded history—and in cultures all over the world. The answer is no longer an open question—the answer is an unequivocal YES.

Throughout history some have had the experience of "hearing voices" or "conversing with the spirits." Such experience was not limited to religious figures or so-called "holy men." Socrates in Greece in the fourth century B.C., certainly one of the greatest men in all history, had frequent, two-way conversation with what he called his "familiar spirit." Jesus of Nazareth in times of stress would go aside to meditate and pray. According to the Bible, he received guidance from angels, archangels, and the spirits of the great souls, such as Moses, Elijah, and many others. In the United States, Abraham Lincoln held seances in the White House as a regular Sunday afternoon activity and frankly stated that his spirit advisors played the decisive role in his decision to use his utmost efforts to abolish slavery. Moreover, he dictated portions of a book by mind-to-mind contact after his physical death (see chapter 13).

The most widespread period of activity of "hearing the dead speak" came at the close of the nineteenth century and the first half of the twentieth century. In England and Brazil, and to a much lesser degree in the United States, both men and women developed the ability to "converse with the spirits." Referred to commonly as "mediums," such persons would both privately and publicly go into a light trance—let us say a slightly altered state of consciousness—and in that state converse with the deceased family members of the so-called sitter. This became so common in England in the last century that a weekly newspaper was published on these activities. I have in my library a bound copy of fifty-two weekly issues published more than a century ago—1876.

Verbal contact with the spirit worlds made little penetration in the United States. A few "spiritualist" centers were established in Florida, New York, and Indiana, and for a time these were quite active. As with most human endeavors, there were increasingly large numbers of situations in which the mediums resorted to fraud. However, with the passing decades, there were a small number of psychic men and women in the United States, England, France, Brazil, and Canada who developed their mental telepathic capability to a superb degree—with two-way conversations far beyond the intellectual content of the earlier mediumistic exchanges with Aunt Susie or Cousin John. I will not discuss the current developments further because the whole subject is presented in great detail in the outstanding book, *Channeling* by Jon Klimo, published in 1987 by Jeremy Tarcher.

In the past three decades a most startling development in spirit communication has taken place. Previously it was considered that only the occasional or rare individual was endowed by God with a sixth or seventh sense. Supplementing the five physical senses of touch, taste, smell, hearing, and sight, these people seemed to possess two other senses: clairvoyance—the ability to see into the nonphysical worlds—and clairaudience, the ability to hear nonphysical sounds.

Serious study of this development by many researchers has revealed that perhaps most persons on the planet today apparently possess these two senses, but they are in a dormant state. Books, organizations, classes, and private teaching are available to help any serious seeker learn to make at least a start at developing these two additional senses. In fact, so many persons are now developing their sixth and seventh senses that it was recently observed, "Goodness gracious, channels are coming out of the woodwork all over the country."

As my worldwide contacts developed, I found persons who had sufficient mental telepathic control to maintain contact with their loved ones. An example: for the past fifteen years, a close collaborator on our survival research has been Arthur Garside of Johannesburg, South Africa. Arthur's beloved wife, Phyllis, has had telepathic contact with him continuously since her graduation thirty years ago! Recently Arthur wrote:

> My Phyllis encourages me now and then, letting me know she is at my elbow. I get the thrill of knowing that I am not alone and that there will be at least one soul waiting eagerly for me to make that transition. I am as certain of that contact as are you with Jeannette. Hold to yourself the wonder of such a condition of communication for it is so little believed by the vast majority of people who lose loved ones and think they have "gone forever."

However, the above-mentioned explosion in the field of telepathic channeling is creating a serious problem. Each year hundreds of thousands of young people learn to play the piano or some other musical instrument. Yearly thousands of people learn to paint with watercolors or with oils. Yearly tens of thousands of people learn to play golf. But how many of these people become outstanding in their abilities? What percentage of the musicians or artists or golfers turn out to be Chopins or Paderewskis, Rembrandts or da Vincis, Hogans or Palmers?

So with channeling. In twenty years of extensive worldwide searching for the da Vincis, Chopins, or Mozarts of channeling, we have found the merest handful. Out of the hundreds of mediums and channels studied in person and in the literature, one of the most gifted turned out to be a middle aged woman who was literally living almost in my backyard. Although she was born and had lived for forty-five years within twelve miles of my home and laboratory, her abilities were unknown to almost everyone except the members of her immediate family. Forces in the spirit world had selected her to nurse Jeannette through her terminal illness and provide in my very own house the experiences which make possible major portions of this book and its companion volume, *Love Letters from Another Dimension.*

Loree, as we shall refer to her in these pages, is unique in many ways. She never attended even one year of school. From age eight, she helped her mother make a home for themselves and her two younger sisters. The hardships of her life and other details will be found in chapter 9 and appendix H.

Right from the start, it became apparent that Loree and Jeannette had perfect mind-to-mind attunement. In chapters 6, 7, and 8, you will encounter excerpts of these contacts. In part IV you will encounter lengthy telepathic exchanges not only between Jeannette and Loree but between Loree and members of three generations of her Cherokee Indian ancestors, all of whom are dwellers in the spirit worlds.

Taken as a whole, the material in these two volumes should go far to help a high percentage of readers realize that the evidence showing the dead can speak via mental telepathy is as substantial and satisfying as the evidence that the dead can speak via instrumental means such as the radio, television, telephone answering machine, and computer.

Part III

Preparing for Graduation

Chapter Six
Pre-death Discussions Between the Co-authors

D uring the twenty years when we were traveling all over the globe gathering information on both life and death, Jeannette and I were fortunate that death did not once touch our own family. Obviously, this situation could not last forever. At age seventy-seven, Jeannette had the first really serious illness of her life. In the next three years, she had a series of problems including shingles, osteoporosis, a small stroke, and pneumonia. Beginning at age eighty-one, she had a major stroke and we both knew it was all downhill from there on.

We were fortunate to be able to set up a private nursing facility in our home with help of two practical nurses providing round-the-clock care. We quickly learned that one nurse, Loree, was a phenomenally gifted psychic and had perfect two-way telepathic rapport with Jeannette. We placed her bed only three feet from Jeannette's bed and arranged for her to give Jeannette twenty-four-hour-per-day care. (Even if something went wrong with Jeannette at night, Loree would psychically sense it, wake up, and tend to Jeannette's needs of the moment.)

During the next several months, I would sit beside Jeannette's bed and Loree would sit on the other side. Occasionally I would activate a tape recorder. Loree could also activate the tape recorder when I was not present. She would repeat aloud what she heard Jeannette or any other spirit entity speak. Thus we got both sides of the communication on the tape. During the final eight months of Jeannette's illness, her physical condition deteriorated rapidly. We accumulated eighty typed pages of our two-way conversations made possible by Loree's perfect telepathic rapport with Jeannette. The following excerpt was recorded February 23, 1990, at 5:00 p.m.:

JDM: I'm concerned about some things I need to ask you about, George.

GWM: Take your time, sweetheart. With Loree's help, she'll tell me what you say.

JDM: This morning I asked you for the truth about my illness.

GWM: Yes, that's right.

JDM: I don't remember what you said.

GWM: All right, sweetheart. You asked me the truth with respect to your illness. I told you the history of it, going way back five years ago, when you had the trouble with your spine and we had to have a plastic brace made which went all the way from your hips up to your shoulders. You wore that for three years. But you had continuing problems so we had to go to the Shealy Pain Clinic out in Missouri to see if they could relieve the pain. They had very great difficulty and didn't have much success. You were barely able to keep functioning. But then a year ago you and I were driving to Florida. You had some strokes in the automobile as we drove along. We went into the hospital in Sarasota and you were there for ten days while they ran all kinds of tests on you. And they concluded there wasn't anything they could do because of the residual effects of the stroke...

Five months ago, you had another stroke. You had a massive stroke and that undid all the improvement you had made from the other strokes.

Now your right leg is paralyzed, your right hand is just like a claw—it's all misshapen. Your right leg, which is paralyzed, is bent around so that the heel of your leg comes up into your crotch and it's just locked into that position. And this stroke five months ago was so bad that it affected your vocal cords and you couldn't talk to us anymore. You couldn't swallow much by yourself. It might go down the windpipe and then you would choke to death. So Loree has fed you now for over five months, one spoonful at a time, of baby foods, soft foods, puddings, yogurt, and things like that.

But in recent months you have been losing weight. Loree estimated the other day, you are less than seventy pounds. This nice right arm that's done so much over the years has almost no flesh on it; it's just the bone of a skeleton with some skin over it. And that's the way with your back. It's just like the vertebrae almost stick through the skin of the back. There's no longer any meat there. And you are continuing to lose weight even though we feed you every time you want something to eat.

There is nothing that medical doctors can do to turn the situation around. You are just continuing to lose your strength and losing the tissues of your body. Fortunately, in the last few days, your mind has been functioning better, so I can talk to you like I am now and you can ask questions and I can answer you.

Now I've taken time to go into detail because it's so important for you to know exactly what the situation is. We'll take a moment. Would you like Loree to give you her viewpoint?

Loree: She says, "Loree has already told me that I would not get better. I asked Loree for the truth and she told me."

GWM: So, it's a sad thing, sweetheart, but this is the truth as we know it.

One month after this exchange, and one month before Jeannette made her transition, we got insight into the phenomenal telepathic rapport between

Jeannette and Loree and Loree's ability to speak with an unexpected visitor from the worlds of spirit. The visitor was Jeannette's mother who had made her own transition thirty years earlier. It seems as though the primary purpose of her mother's visit was to encourage Jeannette "to let go, let God" and make the transition.

GWM: (Now I am going to record on this tape the conversation which Loree and I had with Jeannette after breakfast when we went to her bedside.)

Jeannette, it's very important that I get this straight. Loree says that last night you had quite a cough, a tickle, and she didn't want to go to sleep while you were that way. So she sat here until about two this morning when you stopped your coughing. And as she sat on her bed, she was surprised to see somebody here in the room. And I just asked you if you could remember last night. I understood you to say you did. Now I am going to ask you again. Will you tell Loree what you saw last night?

JDM (telepathically): It was so strange. I saw my mother (deep emotion).

GWM: You saw your mother. Wonderful. Did she speak to you? Can you tell me what she said to you?

JDM: Mother said, "Let go, my daughter, and come to the Light." And that was so strange.

GWM: You say your mother said, "Let go and come to the Light"? It was really wonderful that you could see your mother. Could you tell me how she was dressed? Or maybe you couldn't see, lying flat on your back here in the bed [blind in one eye and little vision in the other].

JDM: Honey, I was so surprised, I did not pay any attention to her dress. [Actually, Jeannette can only dimly perceive black and white.]

GWM: Okay. Did she stand here about where I'm standing beside your bed?

JDM: Yes.

GWM: Did she reach out and touch you?

JDM: *She stroked my face* (said with great emotion).

GWM: She stroked your face, good. And do I understand her comment was to—"my daughter, come on to the Light"? Is that about what she said?

JDM: She said, "My daughter, come *into* the light."

GWM: Did she say anything else?

JDM: She said, "Daughter, Mother will be there waiting for you."

GWM: Good. Well, that should give you a lot of pleasure and courage to know that your mother will be there. And that she is waiting for you.

JDM: She said it's wonderful, but I was worried about being there by myself. Now I know I won't be there by myself.

GWM: Good, sweetheart! Ah, here comes that wonderful smile. Quite a gal. Well, at least you know you won't be there by yourself. You couldn't ask for a better companion than your mother.

JDM: Mother said she will show me around (in wonderment).

GWM: Well, you couldn't ask for anything better than that. That's just wonderful. You know for weeks I've been telling you, you will have a great reception when you arrive over there. I told you your mother will be there, your father will be there, probably my mother and my Aunt Dede, my sister Lois. Yes, we've been told they've planned quite a reception over there.

JDM: Now, honey, I won't have to worry anymore about taking you and Loree with me! (Expressing relief.)

GWM: Good. That's right. Because you've got lots of friends over there, lots of good friends over there. Now you know it! And all because your mother came! That is so wonderful, sweetheart. You've been held here because you've been worrying about going over without Loree and me. You want to take us with you, or stay here with us. I kept telling you I've got a few more years of work I want to do here yet. Now I can do that work and I will know you're in good hands on the other side. Isn't that great?

JDM: That's wonderful.

GWM: Well, I don't want to tire you out. I think that's about all we can push for now. But it's so helpful we could get this conformation through you that Loree was telling the truth about what happened at 2:00 a.m. while I was sleeping. This shows you'll be taking your good, sharp mind over with you.

JDM: Mother told me I wouldn't forget her.

Loree: Jeannette is wanting to ask, "Loree, who do you think will come to visit me tonight?"

GWM: Well, maybe you'll *go* with them, *whoever* comes.

JDM: Yes, that's possible.

GWM: Yes. Maybe it'll be your daddy tonight. You haven't seen him for a long time. Let's see, it was 1934. You haven't seen your daddy for fifty-six years.

JDM: I'm sorry, honey, but I'm going to sleep.

GWM: Okay, we've tired you out, so we'll let you go to sleep. After I give you one more kiss. Thank you, sweetheart. You go ahead and have a sleep and after that, if you want some food, you just tell Loree. She'll take care of you. I bought a new supply of baby food yesterday. Good night, sweetheart.

Twice since reporting this incident, Loree has recalled the unusual experience of the pleasant odor which was present when Jeannette's mother was beside the bed. She just continues to shake her head in amazement, saying, "Never in my life have I ever smelled anything as sweet, as lovely, yes, as heavenly as that odor. And, of course it came as a complete surprise, as I had never heard of such a thing. Goodness, if I could package that odor, I could sell it and make a fortune!"

There are references in books I have seen in libraries in Great Britain about the odor that sometimes accompanies such a visitor as Jeannette's mother, particularly in books written around 1900.

Monday, March 26, 8:00 a.m.
Two mornings after the visit from her mother, I again stood at Jeannette's bedside. It was obvious she was very weak. Her sweet face was at peace. She said, "Honey, I am very, very, very weak." I said, "Yes, and you are also at peace. Wasn't it wonderful that you had the visit from your mother two nights ago?" She replied, "Yes. I am at peace. I still hate to leave you and Loree behind. But this next time when I get started through the tunnel, I will not turn back."

Well, to tell the truth, Jeannette did not keep her word. On two additional occasions, she was actually in the entrance of the tunnel only to turn back again—because "she did not want to leave George and Loree."

The time had come to have a meeting of minds about the big question: "What should GWM do after Jeannette finally goes through the tunnel?"

There was obvious agreement that before Jeannette got settled in in her new environment, GWM had to handle the pressing matter of disposing of her cast-off physical body.

Chapter Seven
The Birthday and
Graduation Concept

From the preceding chapters, it is obvious that our two decades of worldwide research on the continuity of life had demonstrated that

- Death of Jeannette's physical body would merely open a door to continuing use of her mind, memory banks, personality, and soul.
- Jeannette, separated from her husband after more than half a century, will proceed to function in her astral or spirit body in a disease-free and pain-free environment.
- Jeannette's separation from GWM will be merely a temporary situation, since already at the age of eighty-one he might soon follow her.
- After GWM's short period of rest and recuperation, he and Jeannette will be able to continue their togetherness, which both deeply desire.

What a joyous relief to be free of the gnawing uncertainties, doubts, fears, and taboos about death that have distorted mankind's belief system since the beginning of recorded history.

With the above knowledge, it behooved us to do some planning for the disposal of Jeannette's physical body. The first major decision was to choose between cremation and burial.

Considering that cremation is the course that will be followed by per-haps three billion of the persons now alive, we would be in good company to go that route. However, for purely personal reasons, we decided in favor of a conventional burial, but in a different format from that widely used in our Western civilization.

We decided to utilize the philosophy common in the area of the Far Eastern countries—that is, replacing the sad, weepy funeral of the West with a joyous *Graduation* and *Birthday* celebration! However, as we dis-cussed details, we promptly encountered a very real and limiting factor—the religious belief systems of the more elderly of Jeannette's personal friends and neighbors.

Living in the Great Smoky Mountain region of western North Car-olina, we had kept a high percentage of our friends totally ignorant of our research into life after death. Many of our closest friends were members of fundamentalist church groups with beliefs such as "Once Jeannette is dead, she is dead forever!" "Jeannette will lie in her grave until God has a Great Day of Judgement," or "It is not for mankind to know what happens after Jeannette's death." We certainly did not want to go so far on our joy-ous or fun-and-games approach as to cause needless mental and emotional stress for our good friends.

As the days of Jeannette's illness and physical deterioration continued, we began to finalize the plans for the Birthday and Graduation party.

Several weeks before Jeannette made the transition, we had this exchange:

GWM: ...But that's another one of the things that will be in the funeral home to help people see this is a joyful graduation. You've done all these wonderful things here, and now you're going to leave us for the time being and go over to the other side. After you get rested, you'll start on a whole new life. Here is a summary of our talks regarding the chapel service.

After we assemble, son Willis will announce the program and introduce our minister friend, Harold Strader. Harold will deliver an upbeat five-minute talk.

So, in keeping with our overall theme concept, I have selected two hymns, one to sing near the beginning of the service and one to sing near the end. The first hymn starts out, "Blessed be the dear, uniting love that will not let us part. Our bodies may far off remove, but we are still one in heart." I will arrange for a nice, soft organ accompaniment.

Son George will present the fifteen-minute slide talk entitled "Glory of Life," with the subtitle "The Saga of the Duncan and Meek Families." He will use portions of the recording of your voice at our fiftieth wedding anniversary party.

Next, I will deliver a six-minute talk on the topic "The Secret Life of Jeannette Meek." I will disclose how you worked for twenty years at no salary; how you have helped with the correspondence with doctors, scientists, psychiatrists, psychologists, and so on in more than twenty countries; and have helped make our published books good enough to warrant translation into several foreign languages. Without doubt, there are many people alive today as a result of your working on the book *Healers and the Healing Process.* All of your work is unknown to most of even your close friends.

Then we will sign the closing hymn. Its first lines are very appropriate: "Blessed be the tie that binds our hearts in Christian love, the fellowship of kindred minds is like to that above. Before our Father's throne, we pour our ardent prayers, our fears, our hopes, our aims are one, our comforts and our cares. And when we now asunder apart, it gives us inward pain, but we shall be joined in heart and expect to meet again." James [our third son] will conclude the service by reading aloud this item:

There is No Death

I am standing on the seashore. A ship at my side spreads her white sails to the morning breeze and starts for the blue ocean. She is an object of beauty and strength, and I stand and watch her until at length she is a speck of white cloud just where the sea and sky come to mingle with each other.

Then someone at my side says, "There! She's gone!" Gone where? Gone from my sight, that is all. She is just as large in mass and hull and spar as she was when she left my side, and she is just as able to bear her load of living weight to her destined harbor.

Her diminished size is in me, not in her. And just at the moment when someone at my side says, "There! She's gone!" there are other eyes watching her coming, and other voices ready to take up the glad shout, "Here she comes!"

And that is dying.

—Author Unknown

As the people leave the chapel, our three sons and their wives will individually greet the people and give to each one a copy of the little booklet, *The Magic of Living Forever*, which you helped me create ten years ago, and the memorial pamphlet about you. As I told you, we are going to offer nineteen thousand copies of this booklet and the Many Mansions Chart to hospice workers, rest homes, penitentiaries, and elderly people around the world, as a memorial to you.

Sweetheart, your mind is really quite clear today so I want to ask you if what I have summarized from our previous discussions meets with your approval.

JDM: It certainly does! Couldn't ask for anything better. I love you so very much. And I am going to be at my own funeral. [See next chapter as to her efforts on this point.]

Remarks volunteered as the people left the chapel indicated that Jeannette's desire for her Happy Birthday and Graduation Exercise had been fulfilled. Her remarks two months later confirmed this opinion.

Chapter Eight
Jeannette Attends Her Own Funeral

As indicated in the preceding chapter, Jeannette and I had discussed plans for her "Birthday Party" or "Graduation Party." We had also discussed the possibility of obtaining photographic evidence that she did, in fact, keep her promise to be present in the funeral chapel at the time of the service. These predeath discussions and the resulting actions were crowned with success.

One area of our twenty years of investigation into the unknown (and unseen) universes was what might be called "etheric photography." Marvelous as the human eye is, it has a very limited ability to "see" into the world that surrounds each human being. Normal eyes can "see" in only a very narrow band of light wavelengths—what the scientists call the visible spectrum.

A good parallel for this situation is the horse whose head harness includes blinders to limit its peripheral vision. In the human case, the built-in blinder of the eye prevents us from seeing what is going on in the infrared and ultraviolet worlds that surround us. Our research demonstrated that ordinary color photographic film could see a little further into these invisible etheric worlds than the human eye. (Recall the photo of my astral body when I was momentarily outside my physical body, as shown in figure 1-2.)

Naturally, I wondered: "Might it be possible to photograph Jeannette's astral body while her physical body is in the casket at the funeral chapel?"

After Jeannette's Birthday Party and Graduation Exercises were concluded and the attendees had left the chapel, we set up special ultraviolet light sources and loaded our thirty-five millimeter camera with Fuji 400 color film. Those present were Jeannette's nurse, Loree, two of our close women friends, and one man friend (all psychically endowed).

After getting ready to film, it was discovered that a strong source of daylight could not be blanked out, making it impossible to achieve illumination limited to certain ultraviolet and infrared wavelengths. While tempted to terminate the entire project immediately, I decided to go ahead and snap more or less at random in the hope we just might catch something unusual on film.

The camera shutter was operated in turns by one man and one woman.

Of the eighteen photos snapped in less than ten minutes, one photo showed an astonishing effect of Jeannette's presence at her own funeral.

In the ninth photo (fig. 8–1), I am standing at the head of the casket, which is closed and contains Jeannette's discarded physical body. Opposite me is Loree, Jeannette's psychically endowed nurse. Loree and I each had one hand placed on the top of Jeannette's casket. Note particularly the scene on the wall covering immediately behind my shoulder.

Now carefully observe photo number ten (fig. 8–2). My hand is still were it was in photo number nine. However, the upper portion of my body has just disappeared. Moreover, the wallpaper scene is now visible behind my upper torso and the data on the tote board has become completely readable. (The color print is superior to this black and white reproduction.)

What happened to cause this surprising effect—on only one particular photograph? When I asked Victor, who had operated the camera for this shot, if he had seen anything clairvoyantly, he replied, "Yes, I detected Jeannette's spirit body was just beyond the head end of the casket and behind the tote board."

Just then, as I was mentally preparing to kneel (to say a prayer of thanksgiving for and to Jeannette), Victor said her image was transformed to the

Fig. 8–1.—GWM and Loree Beside Jeannette's Casket

Fig. 8–2.—Effect Produced by Jeannette's Energy Fields

golden light of her higher self and that this golden light bundle moved closer to the head of the casket.

During the momentary overshadowing, merging, or positioning of Jeannette's spirit-body energies with my own energy fields, my head, shoulders, and chest became totally transparent. My hand was still in place on the casket.

It was Victor's opinion that the golden light energies that he clairvoyantly saw probably interfaced with or in some degree intermingled with the light energy field of my body. This might account for the fact that my head, shoulders, and chest were not recorded in the film emulsion. (The spectral response of the film did not extend to the necessarily higher wavelengths of light.)

Victor's clairvoyant observation was given complete corroboration by Jeannette herself. With the help of Loree's superb telepathic channeling ability, approximately two months after Jeannette's Birthday Party, Jeannette and I discussed the situation person to person. In audiotape number two, Thursday, June 21, 9:00 p.m., we discussed many aspects of the chapel service. I told her about the disappearing torso in photo number ten. I told her of Victor's statement about clairvoyantly seeing her standing beside me and the tote board.

GWM: Do you recall standing behind me at the head of your casket?

JDM: Yes, my dear, I do. I started out behind you and I was going over to give Loree a hand and bring her closer in so I could stand between you.

GWM: Bless you for that important information. At that precise moment I was just starting to bend down on my knees beside your casket. Well, thank you for explaining that.

So Jeannette confirmed she was standing at the place indicated by Victor and had decided to move between Loree and me. Her object was to hold one hand of each of us as we three stood together, with the hope her astral body would show in the photo. (Loree was aware of Jeannette's presence, but she was not aware of Jeannette's motive.)

The June 21 reading continued:

GWM: Did you notice the people got tremendous enjoyment out of the slides that we showed them?

JDM: Yes, my dear, I did. Honey, why did you have to show that one of my kneeling down and stretching out that tent, with my bottom stuck in the air? (Pause) Honey, people laughed at me!

GWM: That was the very reason for using that slide! It was selected for that purpose. They commented afterward, "We're so glad you gave us a chance to laugh because funerals are ordinarily so very serious."

So the predeath funeral service plans succeeded. Jeannette did in fact attend her own Graduation Exercise. Evidence consists of:

• Independent observations by two clairvoyants
• Visible effects on the emulsion of standard color photographic film
• The audio recording of Jeannette's voice seven weeks after her funeral service, describing her part in affecting the standard thirty-five-millimeter color film*
• Her personal reaction to a color slide of herself in an act that caused the audience to burst forth in spontaneous laughter.

In Part IV, Conversations After Death, we will share a sampling of the many dozens of lengthy conversations with Jeannette, beginning just seven weeks after her transition to the highest astral plane.

------

*As an historical footnote, I might observe that the total transparency effect of flesh, blood, bones, and clothing is a replication of the same effect captured twice on Fuji 400 film in my Ft. Myers, Florida, laboratory twelve years earlier when my astral body was temporarily projected (see fig. 1–2).

Part IV

Conversations
After Death

Chapter Nine
Contact Is Established!

Yes, Jeannette Meek did in fact attend her own funeral...and she greatly enjoyed it. But what happened after that?

After three attempts to let go she was joyously welcomed by some of our loved ones. Then she was put into a place where she could sleep, rest, and begin to forget the trauma of the closing weeks of life in her physical body.

Seven weeks after the trip through the tunnel, Jeannette connected telepathically with Loree just as she had done while she was still in her physical body. But before introducing the telepathic material transmitted by Loree in this and the next two chapters, I should acquaint you with some highly personal information about Loree herself.

Loree was born and has lived all her life to date in the Great Smoky Mountain area in the western part of North Carolina on the edge of the Cherokee Indian Reservation. Her father was a pure-blooded Cherokee who passed psychic powers on to her. By age eight, her best friends were the nature-spirits with whom she could freely converse. It was at this age that her father abandoned the family. Loree was the oldest of three sisters and her mother relied on her for milking the cow, churning the butter, helping with the garden, laundry, housework, and so on. Her two sisters went to school, but Loree's total contact with formal education has been less than one year.

Loree married at age fifteen and had six children by age twenty-two. At age twenty-three, her husband became drunk and went berserk. After horribly mutilating her, he left her for dead. Loree was not discovered until eight hours later when she was taken by ambulance seventy miles to a qualified hospital. She was on the operating table for eight hours. Her jawbone—shattered into four pieces—was replaced with stainless steel. Two broken ribs were removed and other internal organs were repaired. More than four hundred stitches were required internally and on the surface of her body. At today's price scale, her eight weeks of specialized hospital treatment would cost perhaps $250,000. One bonus of this stay was that she and a diminutive Catholic nun, Sister Rita, had complete telepathic rapport, even though Loree was wrapped like a mummy with life-support tubes.

It was seven years before she could graduate from a diet of baby foods and bananas. It was twenty years before she located a dentist who could fabricate a wearable set of dentures resting on the skin transplants, which were taken from her legs and used to cover her stainless steel jawbone.

In spite of such handicaps, within a few months of discharge from the hospital, Loree assumed sole parental responsibility. She earned money as a practical nurse, made it possible for each of her half a dozen children to graduate from high school…and partially supported her husband for the next twenty-two years.

Her psychic abilities continued to develop, although they were known only to her own family. She gained and still has complete telepathic rapport with her Cherokee grandmother, her Cherokee grandfather, and her Cherokee great-grandfather. You will encounter the first of these three wonderful people, each of whom are in the spirit world, in chapter 10 and chapter 12.

When she entered the local annual flower and vegetable garden competition a few years ago, there were six categories of judging, each scored from zero to one hundred. With guidance from her nature-spirit friends and the spirits of her Cherokee Indian grandparents, Loree scored one hundred in all six categories.

But! And here comes the shocker. Just before her forty-sixth birthday, I discovered that Loree could not spell. I purchased a good children's dictionary for her, only to find that she did not know the alphabet…and that she could not read or write!

The situation affected her mental telepathy activities in only one area— she had a very limited vocabulary, and her mountain-folk grammar was atrocious.

Consider this contrast. Jeannette earned her master's degree at the University of Michigan in speech and linguistics. She taught English and drama in high school for six years. She once staged a play in which she played all five parts.

Trying to put Jeannette's thoughts and vocabulary telepathically through Loree's mental apparatus was like trying to pass freshly picked berries through the holes in a piece of insect screen.

But there was one great advantage. There was no way Loree could fake any important information as coming from Jeannette. Loree just did not have the education or communication ability to fake. All she could do was listen to the words and sentences Jeannette was thinking and then as best she could try to use her very limited vocabulary to speak what she heard Jeannette thinking. All of the many dozens of conversations between Jeannette in the spirit world and me have been recorded and transcribed. It thus fell to me as editor to correct the grammar and occasionally select a word more in keeping with the extensive vocabulary possessed by Jeannette.

Historically, the first and very informal contact came when Loree was staying overnight at the home of her youngest daughter. The daughter was having very serious trouble with the delayed delivery of her first child. The next morning, Loree described the contact to Molly Philo, my secretary, and me as follows:

Tape #1, June 20, 1990 (seven weeks after Jeannette's passing)

LOREE: It was about five minutes to twelve last night and I was lying on the couch and I was real upset and I was crying. And I dozed off and something caught my attention. Someone was wiping the tears from my eyes. So I opened my eyes. And it was Jeannette!

And she said, "My dear, you shouldn't cry like that. Everything will be all right." We talked a little bit more and she said, "How is my honeybun?" And I said, "He's all right." And she said, "Tell him that I love him very much. I also love you too very much. Tell my honeybun to quit being so upset about things. I keep an eye on him and you and all my friends. My dear honeybun says it's good to cry sometimes. But not all the time.

"Loree, I would have visited you sooner, but I had to get used to things. Honeybun—George—always told me that I was a little daredevil. I would do about anything. Loree, this is kind of hard [making changes in the spirit world].

"This is the first time I've visited the earth planes. But I will get in contact with you again. I have more information for you and my honeybun and all my friends. I have been visiting Mother, Father, Nancy Carol [our infant daughter who died at the age of two weeks, fifty-two years ago.]

"I've decided I'm going to stay just like I am. Tell my honeybun that I'm not going to be any younger or any older, that I'm staying just like I am." [She revised this decision later!]

Loree said that was the end of the conversation as well as she could remember it.

Well, the first contact with Jeannette had been achieved. ONE channel was open for business!

The Second Channel

Once we knew for a fact that Jeannette was settled in her new environment, I wanted to establish promptly a communication link parallel to the one that was now operational in Loree. Here is a very brief digest of a contact via Loree:

Tape #3, July 5, 1990

GWM invites Jeannette to join him in his pending visits to European channels and researchers. Jeannette says she is more accustomed to contact through Loree. When asked about her living conditions, she says she had chosen to live temporarily in a farmhouse with her parents and Nancy Carol. [Jeannette grew up on a farm in eastern Ohio.] Nancy Carol is interested in the farm animals. Jeannette's mother has chosen to look younger. [She died at seventy-eight, as did my mother.] Jeannette points out that in her present realm people can construct their own reality with whatever thoughts they have. For example, they can decide to sleep or not. She has taken up teaching again, initially with the fifth and sixth grades. She says from her location she can see many moons and many suns. She agrees to try channeling through Sara Hieronymus in the future. She says her eyesight is again perfect. [In 1937, she was one of the first persons in the United States to wear contact lenses, because her vision was down to fifteen percent. Hence she is particularly interested in reporting that they have 152 colors over there, which astonishes her.]

The most significant item was Jeannette's agreeing to try to communicate through Sara Hieronymus. I had worked with Sara on channeling research for eighteen years and found her to be one of the finest channels encountered in my worldwide research. For example, in 1979, during five days in my office in Florida, she channeled all of the chapters in the book *As We See It From Here*, a classic in the field of channeled material. Hence only two days later Sara came to my home and, in the presence of colleagues

Rolf and Hilda Schaffranke, Loree, and myself, generated the tape which
is briefly summarized here.

Tape #4, July 7, 1990

The session opens with twenty minutes of warmup messages from Sara's
spiritual guides, Hilarion and Elihu. Jeannette is brought through with the
help of Samarka, Sara's lifelong spiritual teacher. Jeannette says she is now
starting to teach persons of all ages in a large place with many counselors
because so many newcomers are bewildered. She teaches mathematics of
a sort—the power of numbers is stressed for spiritual development. She is
also studying and learning to see other persons as "sparks of light" and to
gain skills in identifying the other beings so she can evolve further. She
says her teacher is a bright, luminous being. She says she has been touch-
ing George's hair lightly. Says she wants to push ahead. George encourages her. She tells of the treatments made to the auras of the newly arrived
there. She says it was too quiet at the farmhouse with her parents and she
was not learning anything, so she has moved to a beautiful houseboat on
a large lake. [We lived aboard a large cruising houseboat in Florida for
eighteen years.]. She says she has contacted numerous other friends in Ft.
Myers, Florida, and elsewhere, and George will hear about this in due time.

This transmission via Sara H. went very smoothly with the assistance
of her wonderful spiritual helpers—whom I had learned to know and love
over a period of eighteen years.

So the second telephone line to Jeannette had now been built. It was
used for the second time in:

Tape #9, September 29, 1990, via Sara Hieronymus

Present were Tom and Fran Pratt, "Jack," and GWM. The message opened
with different and lengthy prayers by Sara's spiritual guides. Jeannette was
introduced to the Pratts, who will take over the operation of METAscience
Foundation, which Jeannette and George had built up over a period of

twenty years. Jeannette is emotionally very upset. She wishes George would join her and our daughter promptly. Weeping, she says she is no longer with her parents and spends much time in checking on George and his illness. She says the forests and all in her world keep blowing away and she can no longer hear or see her teacher. George pleads that he needs more time to finish the book project. Gradually, it occurs to George that Jeannette and daughter Nancy Carol had become separated while making a mercy trip to the lower astral realms. She asks all present to join hands and send her some light. Elihu, one of Sara's guides, comes in and repeats the twenty-third Psalm. Jeannette reports she has now been restored to the higher planes and it is so wonderful to again be back in the land of light and beauty. George counsels her to seek Elihu if she ever becomes depressed again. Jeannette agrees to try to introduce Nancy Carol to Swejan Salter, a woman scientist in a parallel world, so that Nancy Carol can learn more about computers. George asks Jeannette if he can now use ultraviolet light in future sessions in the photographic research. She replies that her eyes no longer bother her and the lights in her current surroundings exceed everything on the earth plane in intensity.

So there we have it. Jeannette has now spent three months (our time) in the spirit world since her first communication with us. She has given ample and most gratifying evidence that she is now well adapted to her new life on the middle of the highest astral planes.

And she has demonstrated her ability to come through *two* channels.

Chapter Ten
Earth Ties, Abortion, Birthdays, and Spirit World Psychotherapy

In the preceding chapter, we reported our initial actions that resulted in establishing very solid contacts with the spirit worlds. In this chapter, we will present five specific examples of the very useful knowledge now being generated through these contacts.

In February 1991, Tape #35, ten months after Jeannette's transition, she and I were reminiscing. We realized we were now in a position to generate a flood of useful information.

JDM: Honey, you may remember in our living room when I was lying in the hospital bed. You and I talked about my helping write a book after I died. I told you I would do my best and that's what I intend to do.

GWM: Bless your heart! On anything you ever did when I was around, you did your very best. And your best has always been very, very good.

JDM: Thank you, honey.

GWM: More and more every day I thank our Creator for bringing you and me together and then finally for bringing us together with Loree.

JDM: Yes, Loree was the missing link we were searching for.

The great variety of subjects encountered and the quantity and value of the information led to a decision that two books would be needed to present the material already generated. The first book would present a thoroughly documented perspective. A second book would be needed to present an extensive sampling of the transcripts themselves.

With material already in hand, it is now obvious that these two volumes will provide a breakthrough in comprehending the age-old mysteries of life and death—a message providing at least one of the foundation stones on which a whole new and more viable civilization will be built starting in the next century.

The research in which Jeannette and I and our professional colleagues around the world have been involved for twenty-one years can now be seen in its broader perspective: There is literally no limit to the areas in which spirit-world guidance can be made available to mankind. As just one small illustration of this viewpoint, this chapter will give examples in four totally unrelated areas of knowledge.

1. Earth Ties: Photographs, Old Clothes, and a Spray Can

It has long been known that a new arrival in the spirit worlds is initially lost and bewildered at the almost unimaginable series of new and strange experiences. Usually there is also an overriding feeling of sadness regarding the loved ones left behind. Such grief is completely natural—on both sides of the veil.

But the new arrival must get on with the business of starting a new life. Excessive and prolonged grief by family members represents a tie that tends to hinder the new arrival from concentrating on the job of starting a whole new life. In Jeannette's case, as the weeks wore on, we were surprised to learn that the great "hold" possessed by family photographs and her now-discarded clothing could easily be broken by an antistatic spray!

GWM: After our last meeting, I took down the photographs of you I had all around the house and I'm arranging to distribute them to our children. [The energy of these pictures and other personal effects were exerting a pull that Jeannette said was distracting to her.]

JDM: That's wonderful, honey. That's what I wanted you to do. If you noticed, I didn't sit in my big rocking chair because my energy is gone from it.

GWM: Your energy is gone from it? That's good. (Laughing) Just a half hour before you came tonight, I took a can of anti-static spray [which Loree had been instructed to purchase for that purpose] and I sprayed it all over the afghan that you made thirty years ago and on the chair. I told Loree that that would further reduce our tie to you.

JDM: Oh, honey, thank you. White Star, [Loree] I love you.

GWM: And another thing. Loree and I finally decided this week we had to make a break and part with your many dresses and other clothing. And after talking it over, we decided we would take the material to the Hospital Women's Auxiliary. They sell the clothing at modest prices and use that money to help the women's auxiliary at the hospital so the pink ladies can render more service to the patients in the hospital. We thought you would be glad for us to do this.

JDM: Yes, honey, I approve of that one hundred percent.

GWM: And to reduce the tie there, Loree took the antistatic can and sprayed all of your dresses individually so they will not tie you to the earth plane. It will be just as effective on the dresses and other clothes as it was on your rocking chair in cutting the magnetic ties to your personal earthside possessions.

JDM: That's wonderful, honey. And that makes me not miss the earth plane so much. Thank you.

*   *   *

JDM: Honey, I'm so pleased that White Star thought to ask what to use to take my energies out of my belongings here on the earth plane. I love you very much for doing that for me. And that way it won't continue to hold me back.

GWM: Well, we realized that idea because of my work in psychometry with the great psychic Bertha Harris in England eighteen years ago. She was able to pick up a photograph or any other personal object and establish immediate contact with the person, whether they were living in the body or on the other side. She gave me an understanding of how we leave our energy imprints on our clothing, our furniture, and everything else. So Loree and I discussed what to do, and I'm glad that we found a solution. It was so easy to use this antistatic spray. I think that is something that will be of great interest to many people around the world. It also is a means of taking out the imprint of evil forces, evil that has been put on all kinds of personal property.

JDM: Yes. And energy which holds people back here on the earth plane, keeping them from moving on up higher, too.

*   *   *

JDM: Oh yes, honey, before I forget. White Star, will you take that spray and spray that little band of gold that George has on his right hand? [Jeannette observed that the light I used to monitor the two tape recorders was shining on my well-worn fifty-five-year-old wedding ring.]

GWM: (Laughing) So, even the energy of the ring is a tie! Okay. How about spraying George, too?

JDM: That's funny, honey.

GWM: That little gold band—speaking of my wedding ring! Amazing that you should see that detail.

JDM: Pardon me, honey, I meant the left hand on George and on the right hand of myself. [This demonstrates that Jeannette, then in the highest astral plane, still had vision to see minute objects on the earth plane.]

GWM: All right. Are there any last observations you want to make before...

JDM: Yes, honey. Have you sprayed the pictures?

GWM: Yes, all the pictures. I have taken them all out and gathered them together and they are in one place down at the other building. Then I will take them up to Washington, D.C., and I will distribute them to the children.

2. Abortion

No social issue in the closing decade of the twentieth century stirs more heated argument than abortion. Apparently it almost never occurs to any of the outraged participants to say, "Hey! Wait a minute. At what stage does an individual consciousness or soul actually enter the embryo or fetus?"

It seems everyone just takes it for granted that this event occurs when the sperm and ovum unite. What if it could be proven scientifically that the nonphysical soul enters the fetus only at the precise moment of departing the mother's womb? Well, based on some comments by our daughter, who is a freshman in a medical school in the spirit world, it might be worthwhile setting up a research project for investigation by a team of spirit and earthside investigators.

GWM: Loree certainly will be pleased. Is Nancy Carol available this morning?

JDM: Yes, she is. She's right here.

GWM: Nancy Carol, I thought the other day something about your statement that you were an incubator baby for quite a period of time until you were a girl living with Grandma and Grandpa at age ten. Could you tell me any more about that situation of the incubator?

NC: I'll try to, Daddy. When I came over [at the age of two weeks], they had a special place here in heaven to keep us babies when we were small. A guardian angel would look after us. And we didn't have to have any food or anything like that, but we had an incubating period that we had to stay. I stayed until Mother came. But Grandfather and Grandmother Duncan would come and see me, and people who I knew came over. They would come and check on me. And Daddy, I knew when they came.

GWM: Good.

NC: My mind and my thoughts were right with me when I came over. And I guess you know, Daddy, before I was born I didn't have a soul. But when I was born, when Mother gave birth to me and I lived for one week or however many days I lived, I had a soul. A guardian angel looked after me.

GWM: Do you have any recall of what that soul did in its previous lifetime?

NC: Daddy, not really, because I've never asked the Great Spirit what I did in my past life.

GWM: That's all right. You made a very interesting statement to me sometime back saying that the soul goes into the baby, into the fetus, just at the time the fetus is taken from the mother's body. Am I correct in what I am saying?

NC: Yes, just as soon as I came out of Mother's womb, I had a soul. But when I was with Mother, Daddy, I didn't have a soul because I was using Mother's and part of your soul, too, Daddy.

GWM: That's most interesting. That's entirely new information for me. The reason I want to get as much enlightenment as I can is that one of the biggest discussions among the public today is the pro- and anti-abortion interests. There is just a tremendous argument going back and forth about the problem of abortion and whether or not teaching should be given to prevent conception. Some people say that if the soul has not gone into the embryo at the end of two or three months, there is no harm done if they arrange an abortion at that time. Is that correct?

NC: Yes, it is. It doesn't matter, Daddy, because in my case I didn't have a soul until I was born.

GWM: I saw an opinion the other day that goes something like this. At the moment of conception, a soul in heaven goes on a waiting list to be born into that child at the time when the birth takes place. I am wondering if the change of plans brought about by an abortion causes any problem or disturbance to the soul who has been earmarked and is waiting to go into that baby.

NC: No, Daddy. There is no problem because there will be other babies needing souls. If the mother has a baby she does not want, then the soul in that baby would be abused. That's what causes so much abuse to the little children because their parents don't want them, Daddy. And the babies understand that.

GWM: That's very helpful information. I appreciate it. Did I understand you to say you are studying to be a medical doctor and a psychiatrist?

NC: Yes. [Perhaps a spiritual psychiatrist!]

GWM: How far are you along in your studies?

NC: Well, Daddy, I am a freshman in medical school. I have a lot to learn.

Yes, Nancy Carol has a lot to learn! If we can someday get precise information as to when the soul enters the embryo or the fetus, it will resolve a major current public issue.

However, ponder the tremendous effect the knowledge of the continuity of the individual nonphysical mind, memory banks, personality, and soul will have on the heated arguments on the right-to-die subject.

3. Birthdays in Two Worlds

It might be expected that after a person makes the transition to one of the nonphysical planes of life, earthside birthdays would be forever left behind. The fact that they are not may be surprising, but it is also comforting. Moreover, it is a small but important indication that the veil between the earth plane and the spirit worlds is gossamer-thin. Consider the following evidence:

In Tape #21, December 3, 1990, Jeannette requested via Loree to talk to GWM at 9:00 p.m. GWM opened the contact by singing: "Happy Birthday to you, Happy Birthday to you, Happy Birthday, dear Jeannette, December the third 1990."

JDM: Thank you, honey. Honey, I just had to come back and visit.

GWM: Okay. Welcome. What's on your mind?

JDM: Honey, I spent fifty-five years with you and I thought I would come back tonight through Loree to be with you on the fifty-sixth birthday. I am eighty-three years old today, honey!

GWM: Yes, I had been thinking we might get together on your birthday. You were born on December 3, 1907. Did you speak to your mother and father today about your birthday?

JDM: Yes, I did, honey. But my mother and father are trying to stay the same age they were when they came over.

GWM: All right.

JDM: But if I were there beside you, I would be eighty-three.

GWM: Yes, and in another month, I'll be eighty-one. But now we are in the period where you are three years older. We used to joke about this.

JDM: Yes, we did. But over here, honey, I have chosen to be just forty-five years old.

GWM: That's great. Now you're thirty-five years younger than I am.

JDM: I've got it on you now, haven't I, honey?

GWM: You certainly have. You've turned the tables.

JDM: Father said I rolled the clock back a few years. When you come over honey, you can roll the clock back, too.

GWM: Sure, I'll roll it back to your age. We enjoyed the visit last night from Nancy Carol.

*   *   *

JDM: You have a birthday coming up on the seventh of January, don't you?

GWM: I certainly do. As I said, that's the time I'll be eighty-one years old, only two years behind you, your old age. I'll have to start thinking altogether differently now, thinking of you at age forty-five.

JDM: Well, I wanted to wait until you came over to be with us, but, honey, that daughter of ours just runs me ragged, so I figured I'd better get to the age where I could sort of keep up with her [and look like her mother instead of her grandmother].

*   *   *

Tape #28, January 7, 1991

JDM: (singing) Happy Birthday to you, Happy Birthday to you, Happy Birthday, dear George, Happy Birthday to you. It's your honeysuckle talking, honey.

GWM: Thank you, honeysuckle. Bless your sweet heart. I thought you don't have time over there. I'm surprised you knew this was January 7 on our calendar.

JDM: Well, honey, I have been marking down every day.

GWM: Okay. Well, you've hit it right on the button. I've got some news for you on your assignment to locate...

*   *   *

Tape #32, January 20, 1991

[GWM's mother who "died" 31 years ago.]

MM: Son?

GWM: Oh, hello, Mother, this is a real pleasure. This is a totally new experience, wishing you a happy birthday after all these years.

MM: It is wonderful to hear your voice, son.

GWM: I was so pleased a few weeks ago to learn that with the help of Loree's grandmother, Nancy Carol, and others, you have come out of seclusion after thirty years to rejoin the group and really enjoy life again. That development is one of the great pleasures in my life.

MM: Yes, Loree's grandmother taught me there wasn't anything you can't accomplish if you let your heart be your guide.

Note: The reader will learn from the next item the significance of Mother Meek's statement.

4. Spirit World Psychotherapy

GWM's mother, father, and father's sister (same age as his mother) were caught up in an emotional triangle that caused GWM's mother to be an invalid much of her life and caused her to be closed off in her own little section of the spirit world for thirty years. We pick up the story in Tape #24, December 17, 1990.

GWM: Nancy Carol, I've been looking forward to an update on your work with Grandma Meek. I understand you've been spending a lot of time with her.

NC: Yes, I have, Daddy.

GWM: Do you feel progress has been made?

NC: A little bit.

GWM: She's been over there for a long, long time and it's a real tough problem. But any help at all you can give will certainly be much appreciated, I'm sure. Do you have anything special tonight to bring up?

NC: Well, Daddy, I thought I would just come and tell you that Grandma Meek has made a little bit of change in her life over here. But you know, Mother said it was better than no change at all.

GWM: That's certainly right. You just keep up the good work. I'm sure as time goes on, one thing will lead to another.

NC: Yes. You know, Daddy, I didn't stop to think about this situation I was getting myself into. But I enjoy it, Daddy. But sometimes, you know, you wonder. Daddy, do you have any advice for me?

GWM: No, I really don't, Nancy Carol, because I've never had a similar experience. There are probably some teachers on your level who have run into this situation before. That's the kind of help I would seek. I would make inquiries as to...

NC: I will make inquiries, Daddy.

GWM: I'm sure there have been many people who go over to the spirit worlds with what they call psychological hangups.

NC: I guess so, Daddy. Can I say something to you about Grandma Meek?

GWM: Certainly.

NC: Daddy, she does not want to go anywhere. She just wants to stay put. I want her to walk with me and talk to me and open up to me, Daddy. But, oh, I'm giving up. Daddy, what makes Grandma Meek have so much resentment?

GWM: Because of the relationship between her and her sister-in-law. My father's sister...

LOREE: Aunt Dede?

GWM: Aunt Dede lived in the house with Mother and Daddy almost right after their marriage and Mother resented Dede's being able to go to work, not to have any family duties, make good money, and take nice vacations in the summertime, when she didn't have such opportunities. And Mother got very jealous of the relationship. Dede tried to do her best to be loving and nice to Mother and to us children, but it was just Mother's nature that she resented Dede and it finally made her an invalid and she had very poor health during the last twenty years of her life. But basically she was a good, loving person and she dearly loved the teachings of Jesus.

NC: Yes, that I understand, Daddy. But she just couldn't take it that there was another woman in Grandfather's life.

GWM: Yes, I wonder if maybe what we call a "frontal attack" might be appropriate. You're free to tell her you talked to me and I reviewed this situation about Aunt Dede that distorted her thinking. Try to tell her that Dede loved her very much. I don't know whether you can get anything out of these rambling remarks or not.

NC: Well, Daddy, I'll sort them out and do my best. Because, bless poor Grandfather Meek, he is so precious.

GWM: Yes. He would be so pleased if Grandmother Meek could be a better companion to him.

NC: Yes. Because Grandma Meek just sits there with her arms crossed, Daddy, and she's in her own little world. She's not included Grandfather in anything. She resents him.

GWM: Of course what basically is wrong is the lack of love and if there is any way she can be taught that love is the...

NC: Key.

GWM: ...key to a happy life. Remind her that she had love for me. And she had love for my two sisters and she loved Daddy, so tell her that when she begins to love Dede, it will begin to open up a new world for her...

A week later, Nancy Carol makes a progress report.

NC: Daddy, I'm going to help Grandma Meek with her education. But I'm going to talk to her first, Daddy, because I don't want to just jump in and say, "Grandma Meek, you're going to learn this and you're going to learn that." That won't work.

GWM: No, that won't work.

NC: But I am going to work patiently with her and show love and kindness and I will help her.

GWM: That will be the approach. The love and the kindness will get her to unfold, to open up her own heart.

Loree had the brilliant idea of getting Loree's spirit-world Cherokee Indian Grandmother to help Mother Meek. The Grandmother described to Mother Meek how the White Man moving into this area of North Carolina punished her for trying to save twenty-five small Indian children. They tied her to four horses and pulled off her arms and legs. Yet she forgave them.

When Mother Meek saw this level of love, her own domestic problems paled into insignificance.

Tape #29, December 26, 1990

NC: Daddy, I told you I would try to get Grandma Meek to talk to you.

GWM: Yes, you did.

NC: Well, Daddy, here she is!

GWM: Good morning, Mother, this is a wonderful experience.

MM: Good morning, son.

GWM: I had never dreamed that this contact might be possible. I am so glad you accepted the invitation from Nancy Carol to come visit with us through this loving person we call Loree.

MM: Yes, I hear a lot about Loree.

GWM: I was very distressed when Nancy Carol and Jeannette told me you were not in the position to enjoy yourself over there, that you had apparently been keeping yourself more or less shut off from communication with other people. Is that true?

MM: Yes. Son, I talked to your Aunt Gertrude, well, Aunt Dede, as you and your sisters called her. And I feel better about myself now. But now, son, I need to talk to you.

GWM: All right, you just go right ahead.

MM: Son, I want you to forgive me for locking you in the closet. Will you forgive Mother?

GWM: Of course. I forgave you a long time ago. I realized what pressure you were under there in our family with Dede having her nice job and being able to go out and work and come home with no responsibilities, while you had the responsibilities of taking care of Dorothy and

Lois and a little boy by the name of George and making a home for Daddy. So it was easy for me to understand why you had gotten into a position where you had a lot of psychological pressure. So there is nothing to forgive. You were just a victim of circumstances. That is all past us now and we can forget all about it and we can think about living in the today, in the now. I cannot tell you how happy I am to know that you have now put all that unpleasant experience behind you and that you and Daddy can have a wonderful life together.

MM: Yes, that's what Nancy Carol told me.

GWM: Well, Nancy Carol is right. I think you found she is a very wonderful granddaughter.

MM: Yes. But you know, son, when you were small, I despised Dede and I had to go to her and ask her to forgive me. I resented everything that woman ever did.

GWM: Well, that was what was necessary—to ask forgiveness and express love. It seems a simple thing, but it's a wonderful thing. That's the way it works.

MM: Your blessed father tried to talk to me about it, but I wouldn't listen to him because, you know, son, I thought he was taking your Aunt Gertrude's side like he always did. But now I understand. And Dede, your Aunt Dede, sends her love to you.

GWM: All right. Thank you.

With an accomplishment such as this by our daughter, Nancy Carol, the authors of this book see a bright future for the practice of psychotherapy—when it adds a dimension that results in spiritual psychiatry.

Next, in chapter 11, we present one complete transcript of a typical single channeling session.

Chapter Eleven
Mideast War Dead, Guardian Angels, and Judgment Day

In the two preceding chapters and Chapter 14, we present bits and pieces of transcripts that were assembled to give an idea of the variety of subjects we encountered in our visits with Jeannette. In contrast, this chapter will consist of one uncut transcript. It will show the reader how material flows in a natural conversational manner, with one subject often leading into another. (The companion volume, *Love Letters from Another Dimension*, consists of substantially uncut transmissions as well as summaries of transmissions.)

Tape #34 Tuesday, January 29, 1991 4:47 P.M.
Present: GWM, Loree, visitors JDM and NC
[Twelve days after start of the Mideast War]

Prayer

JDM: Hi, honey.

GWM: Hi, sweetheart. This is unusual to have you come so early in the day.

JDM: I'm sorry; you know time doesn't mean anything to us.

143

GWM: It's all right. I told you to come anytime. What's on your mind today?

JDM: Honey, we've just received Loree's grandmother. [Loree's grandmother, three months shy of one hundred years of age, had died less than seventy-two hours before.]

GWM: Good. I imagine she will be resting for a little while.

JDM: Yes. Bless her heart, she was so bewildered; she was in bad shape. We have had to put her in isolation for a while so she can recuperate. [The hospital attendants had pulled the life-support tubes five days before her transition, with the family's permission.]

GWM: She had it very hard the last four or five days.

JDM: Yes. That I understand, honey. If you remember, honey, I did, too.

GWM: I was just thinking about the hard time in your last several days. It hurt me so much to see you in all that pain.

JDM: Well, honey, I was so stubborn, I just didn't want to let go!

GWM: Fortunately, that is all in the past. We can forget about that and think about this wonderful, wonderful situation we are now having, working together.

JDM: Loree's grandmother will be safe with us. Now, honey, tell me a little bit about yourself.

GWM: I continue to work on our book. I sent off the material today to Jean Peterson in Colorado so that she can now, at her leisure, contact Eleanor Roosevelt and show her the material that precedes Eleanor's spot in the book. Mrs. Roosevelt can make a decision as to whether or not she wants to prepare the eight or ten pages of material for which I have left space. [See chapter 13.]

JDM: Jiminy Crickets, honey, I forgot to talk to Eleanor Roosevelt. You asked me to and I completely forgot! [As a matter of fact, Nancy Carol had taken it upon herself to go up to the podium from which Mrs. Eleanor Roosevelt had just concluded addressing a large meeting, and discussed the project with her! Mrs. Roosevelt herself comments on this action by Nancy Carol in chapter 14.]

GWM: You've been busy, too. The next move, in any event, will be up to Jean Peterson.So I expect sometime in the next few weeks I'll be hearing from her.

JDM: Yes. That would be wonderful. Honey, tell me a little about George and Jean and their recent visit to Franklin.

GWM: George and Jean had a short but good visit with us. Our biggest activity was with respect to the job George has been doing in making a videotape of the sixteen-millimeter moving pictures on all the camping trips we had with our three children forty years ago. [GWM then gives detailed report on matters of family interest only.]

JDM: Honey, Nancy Carol wants to say a word.

NC: Good afternoon, Daddy, how are you?

GWM: Fine. I'm glad to hear from you again. Have you been working with Mother and the others on what I would call the rescue work for war victims who are just starting to come over?

NC: Yes, Daddy, everything has been topsy-turvy over here.

GWM: Could you tell me a little bit about what you actually do with the people when you see them coming out of the tunnel?

NC: Well, Daddy, we give them a hand and tell them how much we love them. We reassure them that they will be all right. There is nothing for them to be afraid of, Daddy. That's what we tell them.

GWM: Then what do you do with them after you've taken them by the hand from the tunnel?

JDM: Well, honey, this is Jeannette. When they come to us, they have to be judged for the deeds they did.

GWM: Oh, that takes place at the end of the tunnel? This really surprises me! I thought judgment came later.

JDM: I wanted to tell you because I, too, was judged at the end of the tunnel.

GWM: Apparently, that was a very favorable judgment in view of the wonderful life you had lived.

JDM: Honey, there is something else you should know. Our mind goes back and we remember everything we did on earth. We see everything we did, the good and the bad. [Forty-eight hours after this judgment, Jeannette visited the channel referred to in appendix H and asked for forgiveness for an unfriendly act!]

GWM: That's most interesting. I think I might be able to put that in our book. After they have been judged, what is the next thing that happens?

JDM: If a person has done real bad things, selfish and mean things, that's where they stay until we can teach them. Then the more they learn and the more spiritual wisdom they absorb, they move up. But if they don't want to let go of the earth plane—things they had on earth—they will never grow. They will stay where they are on the lowest astral.

GWM: Let's say you brought through a person who was judged and they had a life where they weren't bad, but let's say they still weren't highly spiritual, what is done with them?

JDM: Honey, we just tell them how much we love them, put our arms around them, and show them what love is. Loving, sharing, and caring for one another. Then we put them in a special place where we can work with them and teach them—right from wrong and good from bad.

GWM: Is there usually a period between the arrival and the judging on the one hand and then the time they start in on their new activities? Is there a rest period there?

JDM: No. When you first come through the tunnel and you walk to the end of it and come out into the light, you are judged right there on the spot. [This is all encoded in the person's astral body.]

GWM: But take a person—take Loree's grandmother who went over three days ago, just three months short of her one-hundredth birthday. She had very difficult days before she went over. Is she put in a resting situation like a rest home or something?

JDM: Yes, she is, honey.

GWM: So that's where she is now. I suppose the length of her stay there depends on how severe her problem has been coming over.

JDM: Yes. Loree's grandmother was a special lady and she won't have a serious problem.

GWM: I have continued to think and study to get more information on angels. [I now have about twelve books dealing in part with angels. See the bibliography.] Would this be an appropriate time for me to ask you some questions that I have identified on the subject of angels?

JDM: If you want to, honey.

GWM: You said the last time we talked that there are angels of mercy and love and peace and goodwill. Are there any other kinds of angels?

JDM: Honey, we have angels to love and let people be loved and sharing and caring for one another and just keep them out of trouble if we possibly can. And you've heard of guardian angels, haven't you, honey?

GWM: I certainly have, and I'm sure I've got several!

JDM: Well, honey, they are the main ones to help us over here to help take care of the ones on the earth plane. Just like Loree. Loree does not know this, but she is a guardian angel, also. [Loree and Jeannette were said to be sisters at the time of the Civil War. Loree is said to have been a battlefield nurse. See appendix H.]

GWM: Well, she's certainly been acting like *my* guardian angel!

JDM: She was mine, too, honey.

GWM: To which group do you belong—mercy, love, peace, or do you belong to any specific group?

JDM: Honey, right now my business is just sharing love and kindness.

GWM: Okay. What activities do you do as a guardian angel of love and kindness?

JDM: Well, when the people come through the tunnel, Nancy Carol and I have to sit them down and talk to them with love and kindness. We cannot talk harshly to them. And some of them are just fighting and screaming and just everything, honey. It's something that no one can fully understand until they come over themselves. Only then, they can. You know how I was. I didn't want to die; I was fighting to live! Well, honey, when I came through the tunnel, I was still fighting to live and I went into total shock when I found out I didn't have that old, physical body with me. It scared me. And so, that's what we have to teach them. It took me a month or so to realize I didn't have my physical body. I still had my mind, but the physical body wasn't there. You know, just like if you woke up some morning, honey, and looked and couldn't see your physical body, but you knew that you were there.

GWM: That would indeed be a frightening situation.

JDM: Yes. That's what I felt. We have to work with them to teach them they are still alive, but their physical body is gone.

GWM: Who assigned you to the category of angel of love and kindness?

JDM: Honey, the Great Spirit Himself.

GWM: As to the Great Spirit, I guess that's Loree's term because of her Cherokee Indian ancestry. Is this the one we would call Jesus?

JDM: Yes.

GWM: I assume that you still have male and female on the mental planes because I've talked to my father. Are there as many male energies of love and mercy as there are female angels?

JDM: Yes, there are just as many, honey. And you may not believe this, but there are a lot of little children who are angels, too. [Billy Graham, in his book, *Angels are God's Secret Agents,* states that angels "...are mentioned directly and indirectly in the Old and New Testaments nearly three hundred times." For further reference, see the bibliography, Angels.]

GWM: I can easily understand that. Loree's little nine-year-old grand-daughter Danielle already qualifies as a little angel! She is one marvelous little girl.

JDM: Yes, indeed. Danielle is going to be like her grandmother Loree.

GWM: Now that you are working in the angel status, have you discontinued your school teaching?

JDM: Honey, it's on hold right now. But when everything has straightened out, I intend to go back to teaching.

GWM: All right. You spoke about guardian angels a while ago. Do all guardian angels on your level wear wings?

JDM: Yes, they do, honey.

GWM: Do you guardian angels ever appear without wings?

JDM: No. We surely do not. [Some months later she modified this statement!]

GWM: When Eleanor Roosevelt appeared as a speaker at the hierarchy of light meeting, did she wear angel wings?

JDM: No, she did not, honey.

GWM: And so everybody then doesn't wear wings?

JDM: Correct.

GWM: Are there just a small percentage of dwellers on your plane that are in the angel category?

JDM: Honey, the Great Spirit gives us a choice, assuming our own development justifies. Then, if we want to be an angel, we can be an angel, but if we want not to be an angel, that is our decision, also.

GWM: Good. I'm glad to get that information. When you are assigned to the tunnel job and you meet an Iraqi, a Palestinian, an Egyptian, a Kuwaiti, or an Arabian at the end of the tunnel, a person who does not know the English language, how do you communicate with him?

JDM: Well, honey, I had to go to school myself to learn their language.

GWM: Oh, so you can actually communicate in their language? That's astonishing.

JDM: I most certainly can, honey.

NC: Daddy, I can, too.

GWM: Goodness! I think how long it would take to learn those languages here on the earth plane. It's almost unbelievable to me to think that in such a short period you would learn to communicate in those languages.

JDM: Yes, but you know, it is so wonderful over here. Whatever you want to do, you just set your mind to it and wham, you can do it.

[Jeannette graduated to the mental plane. She is no longer on the highest astral plane.]

GWM: Now take, for example, a small child who was a recent war casualty. I believe Mother spoke of one who had lost arms and legs. I also recall Mother said it had shed its maimed physical body during the passage through the tunnel. My question: after coming from the tunnel, this particular child that had lost its arms and legs in the bombing—what specific actions did you or Mother perform?

NC: Well, Daddy, when they come through the tunnel, they still have the blueprint of their physical body and what I see missing is just pieces of blueprint. And when they come all the way through the tunnel, the blueprint is gone.

GWM: Mother or Nancy Carol or both, can you give me any estimate of how many people you have helped so far—war victims who have come through the tunnel?

JDM: Well, Nancy Carol and I are working with certain ones now. We're not there to greet everyone who comes through the tunnel.

GWM: Of your friends and close relatives, who besides Ann and Jan have been helping presently on some phase of the tunnel rescue work? [Ann and Jan were members of our small weekly meditation group, and both went over a few months before Jeannette's transition.]

JDM: Well, honey, your mother has been helping. She wanted to do something worthwhile, so she volunteered her help.

GWM: Have Ann and Jan been working?

JDM: Yes, they have, honey, and Mary Peterson, also. We've all been just busy as bees over here. [Mary was the wife of a trustee of META-science Foundation.]

GWM: How about my sisters, Lois and Dorothy?

JDM: Honey, I haven't seen them for a while.

GWM: Okay. Am I correct in assuming that they are not in the angel category?

JDM: They are not in the guardian angel category.

GWM: Thank you. I believe that Jeannette said that my father was involved in some kind of record-keeping work at the tunnel discharge. Could you give me any additional details about his work activities?

JDM: Well, honey, he helps keep a record of the ones who come through and what problems they have. You know, like if they were having a problem of crying and can't stop or they have earthly treasures on their mind and don't want to let go for selfish reasons. Your father keeps a record, so we'll have something to work with.

GWM: From the organization standpoint, who is in charge of the group of angels with whom you work?

JDM: Who's in charge? There's no one in charge but ourselves! We have to take hold of our own responsibilities. The Great Spirit is over all of us. But we don't have a head angel.

GWM: This has been wonderful to give me so much concrete information about the guardian angel activities—at least as you have been experiencing them. I've had great difficulty finding specific information on guardian angels in books, just as you predicted three weeks ago! Is there any other subject that you would like to discuss today?

JDM: Well, I just thought I would contact you and talk to you.

Chapter Twelve
Mental Telepathy Research

Conversation Between GWM and JDM

Jeannette Speaking Through Loree, October 3, 1997

JDM: Good evening, honey.

GWM: Good evening, sweetheart. This is a pleasant visitation.

JDM: Why, thank you, dear.

GWM: I understand that you are volunteering to help us on the present situation. We're in need of a little additional information to go in the book we are preparing.

JDM: Yes, okay. Now I'm going to start it. Just don't interfere.

GWM: Okay

JDM: Okay, I'm going to tell you what it was like when I went through the tunnel. You know my body here on the earth planes was in a total wreck with the strokes I had. Well, when I went through the tunnel, this huge beam of light, I walked right on through it. And, honey, when I got through there, I looked down; I was amazed. I was a cripple no more! I could walk and I could talk, and you know when I was here on the earth plane, I couldn't walk, I couldn't talk, I couldn't do anything. I couldn't even move my arms. Even my voice wasn't working! But when I went through that tunnel everything came back and I was so pleased and I was standing in front of my mother…my beautiful mother…she put her arms around me, and Daddy…and honey, I just broke down and started crying until I got over my shock, you know, when I went through the tunnel. Everything was so wonderful there; the flowers were so gorgeous…the colors…it's different from what they are here on the earth plane. I didn't have my physical body. I could run, I could jump, I could take both hands and wave at people in the spirit world. I was amazed with this, but the most important thing is the Master. He walked up to me and said, "Welcome home, my child." Honey, from then on I was at home. I was at peace with myself and I missed you very much, George, but I knew that you would be with me someday. So, I went with Mother and Daddy. They had me by the hands, and they led me down a little path, but the little path was so wonderful! The little flowers and the birds…it was just…wonderful and the water…I was overcome. Here I was, in a place where there was not any pain, anger, hurt, or anything. I was at peace with myself. I went on with Mama and Daddy and met up with my little girl. I said, "Mother, Daddy, why are we here with this little girl?" Mama looked at me. She said, "Jeannette, that's Nancy Carol, your own baby."* Honey, I just fell to my knees and I wept. I was so overcome to be with my baby at last. You know, when she died and left us, I cried for a long time. I wouldn't let you see me cry, but I did. But now, I went on down the path, I got Nancy Carol by the hand, down the path, and I sat down on a bench-like thing. I had picked up Nancy Carol and set her on my lap, and Mama and Daddy were there. All at once, I looked up and there was a rainbow.

It wasn't raining or anything; it just came on! I was speechless! Then a little dog was running around…a little white dog. Oh honey,

*Nancy Carol died at the age of two weeks.

Nancy Carol grabbed that little white dog and she held it close to her chest. She said, "Mama, can I keep the little dog?" I said let me think about it. You know, honey, when I was here on the earth plane I couldn't stand dogs, cats, or anything! I said okay. I looked in her little face and she said, "Mama, please let me keep that little dog."

A great big dog came. It was a St. Bernard. She set the little dog down and took up with this big monster of a dog. She said, "Mama, I'd rather have this dog." I answered, "Okay. You can have it providing you look after it." She said, "Okay, Mama, I'll take care of it." I said, "Well, what are you going to name it?" She said, "I'm going to name it Brandy!" I said okay.

We went up. We quit going down and we went up. We went up this hill, and on top of this hill was the most gorgeous water fountain that I have ever seen. The water was coming up different colors, amazing colors. Honey, I can't tell you the colors because they are colors I have never seen before. I looked and there were my friends. There was Marion McCracken, Ann Blakely, and Jan Shields. So we all just had us a family reunion. [These were her closest friends.]

The trees...the trees...just beautiful, just gorgeous. You know, honey, the people that have out-of-body experiences. They want to come over, but really they don't want to. They know about this place called heaven. I know in my heart that they want to do good for mankind. They don't want to miss this place because they have already seen it!

GWM: (Cannot hear what is being said. Too far from microphone.)

JDM: Let me talk a little bit more about my experience in heaven. So we all went on our way. I said, "Mother, where are we going?" She says, "To the Glory Land." I said, "Where is Glory Land?" She said, "At the side of the water." So we went there. I walked along this beautiful sandy beach water. The sand was so gorgeous...it just glittered...and the water is perfect; so clear and so blue. And *different* animals...we have animals in heaven. So if someone loves their little pet on the earth plane, please don't worry about them, because when you come to be over here, your little pet will be waiting for you. Your little dog, cat, bird...they'll be here!

I sat on the sandy beach and watched beautiful porpoises jump up out of the blue water. It was gorgeous! And I was speechless when I saw a beautiful whale come up out of the water and splash the water. When I looked up in the water, it was clear, not muddy, not muddy water... beautiful, clear blue water. I could see the different kinds of fishes and Nancy Carol and I, and Mother and Daddy, we walked on the sandy beach. So we went up and sat beneath a tree.

The gorgeous, beautiful angel...appeared out of nowhere and had a beautiful blue, pink...it was mostly the blue and pink we know here on the earth plane, a different color was outstanding, beautiful...I just stood there and looked at it and at the angel. I asked, "Who are you?" The angel said, "I am your guardian angel, Gabriel." So, I got up. I stood there for five or ten minutes. You know, we don't have any time over here like we have it on the earth plane and we don't have dark, we don't have darkness...it's just light all the time because we do not need our sleep, we don't need to eat. We're in a body that's perfect!

There's no place like strolling over heaven. And honey, do I love strolling over heaven with my friends! Then we came down and at the bottom of the little hill there were lions, tigers, and little children, honey, running around leading these lions and tigers; just little, small children. They weren't trying to hurt them! I just sat there and watched them run and play with the animals. There were acres of beautiful flowers. The breeze blowing the flowers; you could smell the beautiful aroma from the flowers. Honey, I can still smell them! And another thing, the little pets, the little ones, are so precious. You can love them and pet them and they don't try to bite, they don't try to harm you in any way. They're just full of love and kindness.

Honey, I've strolled over heaven and now it's time to get busy. I went and said, "Master, would you please find me a job that I would like to do?" He said, "My child, what would you like to do?" I said, "Teach children." You know, honey, that I was an English teacher here on the earth plane. So, I got the little children and they're red, yellow, black, and white. They are precious.

Their little souls, you know, the little colored children, their souls are as white as yours and mine. It doesn't matter if you're African-American, or little Indian children, the Master loves them just as much as little white children, and little Korean children, little Philippino children. He loves all children. Little children born in Japan, Iraq. He loves them. He loves all little children.

So I taught those children English. But I had problems with the little Iraqi children because I couldn't get them to understand. So we had to find a teacher that could teach them, and I taught English. And we had to find a teacher to teach the little Korean children, and the little Japanese and Chinese and Philippino. We had to find teachers for the different groups. People on the earth plane need to know about this place called heaven. Because it will give them a chance to come to heaven, come through the tunnel and come through the bright light.

Mothers and fathers, if your children get killed in a car accident, drunk driving, drug overdoses, don't worry about them, because they are here in heaven! We all have a second chance. The Master knows when you do your best, that's all you can do. And friends on the earth plane, always reach out and help someone that's less fortunate than you, especially old people and little children. And overcome the hatred and bitterness and go to the light.

If only I had my life to live over, I could have done things different than what I have done. I could have given more money to help people that were in need. I could have fed the little children that were hungry. I had all the money I could ever hope for when I was on the earth plane. But that money didn't do me any good. Oh, it brought me food and things I needed, but I'm talking about spiritual things, like going out and taking a box of food to a needy family; their daddy was sick or their mother had just come out of the hospital from surgery and they couldn't get any food. I wish I could have done more of that. But it didn't make me any less of a person because I didn't do it. I just wish that I had done it that way. There are so many little children and elderly people going hungry, even dying, because they can't get food. When you live on the earth plane, you have to have food to survive, but when you're in the spirit world, you don't need it!

Well, I'm to go to another subject now, and I'm going to talk about personal things. What I mean by personal things—it seems to happen while I'm over here in the spirit world. I miss my family, oh so very much. I miss my three sons and the grandchildren and the great-grand-children, and George. I know that they will be with me someday and that I can always see them and love them. Sometimes it breaks my heart to look down upon this beautiful planet that I once lived on and see so much anger and hate and greed and murdering and killing. Oh, it makes me cry. The heavenly forces are not destroying this beautiful planet that I once lived on; it's mankind that's destroying this beauti-ful planet with nuclear bombs, missiles...and things to kill people with. Man is destroying this planet. It will be destroyed by its own destruc-tion. People need to be more in tune with the light, the heavenly forces.

So now I'm going back to talk a little more about my beautiful daughter. George and I have a gorgeous, beautiful, red-headed daugh-ter. Her hair is auburn-red and is down to her hips. It is as curly and beautiful as it can be. She stays with me. She went back, bless her lit-tle heart, she went back and got the little white dog, the big dog got so big she said, "I don't think I want it, Mama. I want the little dog, the little white one." She calls it Snowball. I was so thrilled to meet my grandfather over here in the spirit world, and I have two of my brothers with me now. So, I already have a wonderful family in the spirit world. So that is the reason why I told George, I said, "Honey, don't be in any hurry to come over because you have work to do here on the earth plane." I said, "Yes, we have a book to write!" Our daughter is all grown up now. She is a beautiful young woman.

Now I'm going to go back to the beautiful flowers. Oh, what a fragrance. There is no perfume on this earth plane that can give you the beautiful smell that these gorgeous flowers do here in heaven. And the beautiful mountain peaks!

We don't have cars, trucks, planes, helicopters here in the spirit world. And we don't have the little corners that we go off in. We all mix and mingle with everyone. We go and we sit at the foot of the gorgeous, beautiful mountains. We listen to the Master as He talks to us. He always gets up and spreads out his arms and says, "Welcome, my flock, welcome." That is the most wonderful feeling that you'll ever have when you come through that tunnel, and the Master is waiting for you at the end of the tunnel, and saying, "Welcome home, my child."

When I completed reading this section aloud, Nancy Carol said, "There is one subject I want to add near the end. Let's wait until tomorrow. Let's stop now." At this point, Nancy Carol came again and said, "you are all tired now. We will come back tomorrow."

Chapter Thirteen
George Washington and
Abraham Lincoln

Most adults learn as they go through life that it is necessary on life's important issues to be cautious—to resolutely ask the question, "Who says so?" So far, much of the material presented herein has been based on the lives and research of Jeannette and me, our personal friends, and professional colleagues.

Now, in this and the following chapter, we will share evidence of the continuity of life from persons older, wiser, more experienced, and of far greater renown than the authors and their research colleagues. Three of the most renowned, trustworthy, and intelligent people to live in the eighteenth, nineteenth, and twentieth centuries were George Washington, Abraham Lincoln, and Eleanor Roosevelt.

Each makes a profound statement that testifies that you can enjoy your own funeral and can so live your life in a manner that will assure you of having a happy forever.

These might be the most photographed individuals in world history. It is no accident that their images were chosen as symbols of integrity on countless billions of dollars of U.S. currency. So for a moment lay aside the personal testimony of the authors and their colleagues. Learn what these beloved leaders have to say on the subject—in recent years.

George Washington (1732–1799)

Communicated 1944

Did Washington ever write an autobiography? The answer is, "Yes, he did—145 years after his death!" In the 1930s, Washington had observed one of his spirit friends, Wilfred Brandon, dictating books of memoirs to Edith Ellis. A highly respected businesswoman in New York City, Ms. Ellis was a superb telepathic channel whose activities were unknown to all but her closest personal friends. Washington, having observed from the spirit world Ms. Ellis's masterful channeling of thoughts from Wilfred Brandon, asked her if she would consider channeling his autobiography. She agreed.

Over a period of several months in 1944, Ms. Ellis sat for George Washington, taking his dictation by automatic writing. When the material was later typed, they had created an autobiography of more than seven hundred pages. Repeated attempts during Ms. Ellis' s lifetime to find a publisher failed. Being personally familiar with this still-unpublished work, I want to share with the reader a few pages of this memorable document. (The manuscript is the property of James Young, 1 Moya Loop, Santa Fe, New Mexico, and Harriet von Tobel, Troy, New York.]

I quote from Washington's autobiography, beginning on page 502, entitled, "Valley Forge," dictated November 20, 1944:

History has made the winter of Valley Forge a synonym for starvation and cold, death, and the horror of an Army deserted by the people it fought for. I do not intend to harrow the reader's feeling by detailing the unutterable suffering we endured there from November until March. It is a tale of the human being against every odd, willing to keep the faint, flickering flame of his life still unquenchable.

My most terrible moments were when in the old, ramshackle barns we had to use as barracks, the poor fellows lay among the hay strewn on the floor and in the lofts. I said a prayer for the dying and knew it was only lack of food that had taken that life, and no one was to blame but myself.

I tried to persuade myself again and again to surrender—just for bread — just for warmth—just for the chance to live on, but something mightier than my own mind would seem to take possession of me and with such power that I was unable to resist. This was a conviction that my brother Charles's vision and my own astral self were under the guidance of the very spirit of life and that by holding out I would accomplish what I had been destined for.

Fig. 13–1.—George Washington

All that winter I came to feel more and more this finger of fate. It saved me from going insane. It prevented me from ending my own life. It gave me the power to live from one day to the next with no hope of relief. It even stilled the pangs of my own constant hunger for food. It gave me the strength to stand the groans and cries of my own starving men and even their curses. It left no room for anything but its own dictum, "Survive and Win!"

Martha, never away from my side, had come to look like the wraith of her old self. She was always at my side and constant in her care of me and of the men who were unable to walk. She came to be their only comfort. She talked and read to them from the scriptures when they asked her for this distraction. We had to be so careful not to let the enemy know our condition and that prevented some help that might have been given us.

The men ate the horses. Then they ate the bark off the trees and the roots. We even beat up the shrubbery for the insect nests for what nourishment might be in them for spiders and ants. We caught the rats and ate them. We made traps for rabbits, but only three were ever caught. We had no ammunition and could not hunt. We starved down to the last ounce of flesh on our bones.

We also were, now, all but naked, for our clothing had to be slept in as well as worn in the daytime, and our blankets were now thin and in verminous rags. We let our beards grow for warmth and we tied the hay around our feet and legs to keep them from freezing.

All men were like wild creatures and gave up all attempts at either cleanliness or even decency.

Of the six hundred who went into camp, four hundred were gone when March came—some to their homes and two hundred fifty to their graves.

*   *   *

Martha, too, was lying down. There was no other way of keeping from freezing. We had scoured every inch of the roadside and woods for fallen branches and odd pieces of sticks. Now there was nothing with which to make a fire.

It was about six o-clock in the afternoon and still daylight. I was roused from my thoughts by a pounding on the door and the young farmer asking if I was in the mood to speak with him. Of course I got up and welcomed him. He had been thinking over my poor soldier's death by starvation and he could not believe it. I asked if he would care to see the others. He was interested and I took him to the barn where the poor fellows burrowed in the hay in their clothes and blankets. They came to attention when I gave the command and their sorry appearance in their rags and bearded faces, hands like claws and feet wrapped in rags with hay, all made the farmer stare in shocked astonishment.

"Why, how did this happen?"

"It is because the colony of New York that offered to keep us if we would fight for their freedom has now deserted us. We have no food, ammunition, or money from that colony for five months."

This was the signal for an outburst of anathema from the men. I went on to say that many had deserted and gone home, but of those left, half were now dead of starvation.

My voice, now weak with hunger, began to grow even fainter and I fell in a faint on the barn floor. My men came and pulled me over to a pallet and did what they could to restore me by rubbing my hands and getting water down my throat.

* * *

I was all but unconscious one day from cold and hunger. Martha was with me and in almost as bad a case. I was in the stupor that hunger brings on when I suddenly saw Fanny Ball, my grandmother, more clearly than on that first occasion when she stood before me as I sat stupefied in my chair. In a compassionate voice, she said:

"My dear George, you will never be left to die here. Help is on the way."

That was all. I spoke of it to Martha, and she, as always, took the cheerful view and seemed to be strengthened by it. In two hours, a man arrived with a letter from Aaron Burr that also contained two pound notes and the words:

"All I have at present. More as soon as I can lay hands on a debtor of mine. Never give up the fight. Yours to the end, Aaron."

I was all but prostrated by the emotion this dear message caused. Martha knelt and prayed for him and blessed him. This, once more, showed the divine soul of Aaron Burr, that soul that has been burdened with such sorrow, cruelty, and calumny as have been the lot of few men in human history.

* * *

Why do intelligent people shun this great knowledge of the world you and the spirits live in together? A sane man knows how to use the knowledge. And weak minds should be taught the laws of the spirit world and so learn how to protect themselves against obsession by low entities. This is at present filling your asylums with those who do not understand what afflicts them, any more than do the psychiatrists who spin fine and unsound theories about them. [Also in 1991?]

A great deal of harm is done by fooling with Ouija boards and holding seances by those who have no guardian spirits or whose habits attract entities who are clever at impersonating and often pretend to be the souls of famous people of the past.

You are being fooled in this, too, by your so-called "intellectuals." They feel that what they do not know cannot be true.

The souls of your dead soldiers [World War II] show us how ignorant your youth are of all this. The work Wilfred Brandon and I do with them makes us despair of ever giving them the information they need to make a success of life here. They are all spiritual morons for the most part, and jeer at all the truths we tell them of the use of their powers here.

Can't you in your smugness realize that this is a crime against humanity?

Be a little humble before the laws of nature, you materialists, or you also, along with these poor, foolish, ignorant college and primary school graduates, will pay a terrible price for your idiotic denial of what has been known by all people and proven since the dawn of history.

Smugness, spiritual morons, materialists, terrible price, so-called intellectuals, filling the asylums, spinning unsound psychiatric theories, foolish and ignorant college students, idiotic denial of what has been known about the spirit worlds by all people…and proven since the dawn of history.

Yes, George Washington was, in 1944, describing precisely the sad situation that still exists now, as men and weapons from thirty-five nations are being assembled for what just might be the start of the biblical "Wars of Armageddon."

It might be productive to reread the last six paragraphs of this small excerpt from Washington's autobiography. If nothing else, George Washington's own personal life experiences and knowledge provide valid evidence for the continuity of life—the survival of the individual mind, memory banks, personality, and soul.

Abraham Lincoln (1809–1865)

Communicated 1954.

Very few American citizens alive today are aware that President Abraham Lincoln, like George Washington, had psychic powers and used them to receive guidance from the spirit worlds on many occasions. He regularly had spiritualist mediums come to the White House for Sunday afternoon sessions with him, personal friends, and government colleagues. On numerous occasions he relied on spirit guidance to direct actual movements of the army during the Civil War. He also acknowledged that such guidance played a part in his issuance of the Emancipation Proclamation.

Fig. 13–2.—Abraham Lincoln

During the 136 years since President Lincoln's arrival in the spirit worlds, there are records of his communications through channels in England and the United States. [One of the best sources for information on these actions is the book *Abraham Lincoln Returns* by Harriet M. Shelton, Evans Publishing Company, New York, 1957.] For the purpose of including in this book a sample of Abraham Lincoln's more recent personal thoughts on the continuity of life, I use these short excerpts from his communication through the channel Miss Thirza Smith of London, England, in the presence of Harriet M. Shelton of New York in 1954:

A SPEAKER: We chose you some time ago to do this work for us and you have done it faithfully and truly. We are fighting even now so our words of truth shall be liberated, even as I fought for the liberation of souls that were in a living purgatory. The great time of the evolution of the spirit is near at hand for many of the souls in our own country. Such times have never been seen in the past. Such a future awaits our own country! It is destined to eventually be a leading spiritual power.

HMS: Will you give your name, please, just for the record?

AL: I am Abraham Lincoln—one of the pioneers of the past, still a fighter
for truth, liberty, and peace, and for the poor souls who have had to
fight for themselves in ignorance, in poverty, in distress. Thank God
these things are being eliminated, even if it is only a small beginning.
There are souls living today [1954] who will see a finer America, a
finer country than ever.

HMS: Are you pleased with what we have written about you in the book
about your psychic life in Washington?

AL: I am more than pleased. I tried to express that thought to you when I
said you were giving out truths which I had given you. I have been the
source of most of your book. I have truly brought some of my own self
to it. And I have done it for this reason: We are now laying the foundation, and we are bonded together for this great truth that you are spread-
ing, not only in America but to the whole world. For your book will go
forward and bring many new souls to our way of thinking.

It was a long time ago since I fought for this. I was just an ordinary man and I, too, knew what it was to suffer. I knew what it meant
to fight to live. I was not allowed to accomplish all things, though I
began to fulfill some of my ideals.

HMS: Yes, you did indeed!

AL: We have a profound truth here. It is not upon great ideas, but upon a
simple truth that you find the indwelling of the real character. It is in
one's own heart that God brings forward those truths—the simple
thought, the little gestures that you meet with day-by-day, the smiles,
little kindnesses that go from one to another. I am like yourself, the
same type. I am not a high personage.

The new world is passing through its birth-pangs. It is the humble
beginners who see in a great manner. Those who are blinded are those

who see only the glitter of life. But God does not allow millions of souls to come dwell on the earth plane without the guidance of some of his own souls.

HMS: Will you please tell us something about your psychic life in Washington?

AL: I always had an inner feeling of the reality of life. People may have thought that it was foolish to tamper with things in spirit. I did not tamper. I knew. It was interesting to find that there were other people with the same ideas. It was a great joy to me to know that in the beyond there would be a fulfillment of these ideas. I should never have been able to accomplish the things I did had not an inner conviction been given to me. I had no power myself, but I had power within which showed me the way and helped me reach out and find truth and gave me the courage to fight all the way for those things in life that I held most dear. Read the pages of history and you will find that all psychic forces of great leaders were put into use in earth life, physical life, long before they themselves entered into spirit.

An outstanding example of the manifestation of psychic powers was given to Abraham Lincoln on February 5, 1863, when a physical medium, the diminutive Miss Nettie, came to the White House. While in deep trance—and in the presence of President Lincoln, Mr. Somes, Colonel Kase, and a cavalry major from the Army of the Potomac—a grand piano was caused to levitate. It remained suspended in the air for several minutes in full view of everyone. President Lincoln investigated and stated he was satisfied there could have been no mechanical contrivance used and the phenomenon had been caused by some invisible power. Mr. Somes said, "Mr. President, if I tell some of my acquaintances that which I experienced here tonight, they will give me a knowing look and in a wiser demeanor say, 'You were psychologized, Somes!'"

Manifesting the humor for which he was known, Lincoln replied gravely, "You should bring such a person here. And when the piano seems to rise, have him slip his foot under the leg and be convinced (doubtless) by the weight of evidence resting upon his understanding."

One of those present writing about the account said, "When the laughter caused by this quip had subsided, the President sank wearily into an armed chair, the old, tired, anxious look returning to his face."

In concluding these frustratingly brief comments from Lincoln, we close with his eloquent testimony to the continuity of life.

AL: I am giving you this, so that those who follow after you may remember my words. Out of the greatest turmoil the world has ever known will arise the life beautiful.

Tell them that. For many hearts are sad. Tell them above all things there is no death. Give to the world the news—there is no death. It is a change of form, a change of living, but a wonderful change and a blessed reunion with those to whom you were bound, with your friends and relatives. But again I say, bound with a bond of love. For that is the true relationship, the true life, and brings the greatest happiness to mankind. There are higher beings than we, celestial beings, who also send power to help in our own spheres of life. One day we shall be together, and you and I shall work again. God bless you! You shall journey forward in happiness and peace.

President Lincoln, speaking to us in 1954, is saying:

- Give the world the news.
- Tell them there is no death.
- Tell them they will have a blessed reunion with friends and loved ones.
- Tell them that out of the greatest turmoil the world has ever known will arise the life beautiful.

Chapter Fourteen
Eleanor Roosevelt
(1884–1962, Age 78)

The Communication—1991

I t is possible no woman in American history left a more indelible mark
than did Eleanor Roosevelt. Wife of the only man to be elected four
times to the presidency, she became our nation's most active first lady
at home and abroad. She played a leading role in conceiving the need for
a United Nations organization, helped plan and organize it, and then became
the first American ambassador to it.

By a most curious set of circumstances, we have been able to ask her,
twenty-nine years after she "died," to add her personal thoughts to those
of Washington and Lincoln. Credit for this rests squarely on my co-author,
Jeannette (eight months after she herself made the transition to the spirit
worlds) and Jean Peterson of Castle Rock, Colorado. This is how the project evolved:

Excerpt #1—Tape #24 Monday, December 17, 1990

GWM: The other matter I want to tell you about is a potential contact I've
had with Eleanor Roosevelt. Do you remember some years ago you
were getting some recorded books for the blind—and you got the autobiography of Eleanor Roosevelt? We were driving some place on a

long trip and we listened to the autobiography as we drove along. Do you remember?

JDM: Yes, I do, honey.

GWM: We learned that she was quite a wonderful woman. She has just recently come through my dear friend, Jean Peterson. Eleanor Roosevelt had learned about our work and there were certain parts she became interested in. She learned that you had made the transition and was on the same side of life that she's on. So she mentioned the possibility of contacting you. I don't imagine she has contacted you as yet, has she?

JDM: No, she hasn't.

GWM: I will write to Jean and tell her I offer an opportunity to Eleanor Roosevelt to write a chapter in our book around the idea of her thoughts on the continuity of life. Of course, I would have final say as to what I would use, but I thought she's so well known all over the world that it might make a nice balance to these few highly personal sections you and I supply. I would invite Eleanor Roosevelt to tell about the experiences she's had that testify to the continuity of life.

JDM: Yes, that would be a wonderful idea, honey.

GWM: So we'll leave it there now. But it's entirely possible she might contact you as she already knows you are there. So we'll just see what happens. I'm glad you share my thoughts that it might be of help to our readers.

Excerpt #2—Tape #29 January 13, 1991

JDM: Honey, that is a subject I don't know so much about. Loree might or might not channel from Eleanor Roosevelt's level. But I've got some more news I think will be important to you.

GWM: Okay.

JDM: I may have a meeting with Eleanor Roosevelt sometime.

GWM: Good news! I'm glad you brought that up. Jean Peterson has advised me that Mrs.. Roosevelt has consented to explore the matter with me.

JDM: That would be good because Loree, bless her heart, has a very, very limited vocabulary.

GWM: I am sorry to say that the way things are going to happen in the next months and year, there is going to be so much death and dying around the world that people are going to take more interest in the subject of survival.

JDM: Yes, that's right, honey.

GWM: So the timing will be right for our book. I'm so glad about your news from Mrs. Roosevelt. When you talk to her someday, please tell her I express my great pleasure in learning she has made contact with you.

JDM: Yes, I surely will, honey.

GWM: She is a very wonderful person. She was the wife of the only man elected four times to the presidency of the United States and she was his good right arm all those years.

JDM: That was Theodore Roosevelt.

GWM: No. Theodore Roosevelt was way back in my childhood.

JDM: You know, honey, it's so strange that some things I get boggled up in my mind even while I'm over here. Why is that? I imagine it's a human side of me I brought with me when I came over here.

GWM: Oh, sure. We're glad you're still human! We wouldn't want you to be inhuman!

Excerpt #3—Tape #30 January 17, 1991

JDM: Yes. Honey, Nancy Carol is so excited about attending the meeting of the Hierarchy. Nancy Carol, go ahead and tell your father.

NC: Daddy, you know who was the leader of the Hierarchy meeting?

GWM: No.

NC: Eleanor Roosevelt.

GWM: Is that right? I can understand that because she did such a great job in helping to establish the United Nations organization. The effort was flawed from the start because mankind was not evolved to a point where it would provide law enforcement on a global scale. Now this is the first time the nations have combined, something like thirty-five nations, to do the necessary work to attempt to unseat Saddam. That's great news about Eleanor Roosevelt's continuing her active leadership role.

NC: And, Daddy, if I get any more information I think you could use, I'll sure tell you.

JDM: And, honey, there was no woman ever on the earth plane smarter than Eleanor Roosevelt.

GWM: I wouldn't have any argument with that at all. I recently saw a documentary film on TV about Mrs. Roosevelt and I realized more than ever, she was a truly remarkable woman.

Excerpt from Tape #35, February 6, 1991

JDM: Nancy Carol just attended the Hierarchy meeting. After Eleanor Roosevelt spoke, Nancy Carol introduced herself. Mrs. Roosevelt told her she had some work to do for you. George, does that make any sense to you?

GWM: Yes! I have been arranging for my channeling friend Jean Peterson in Colorado to receive material from Mrs. Roosevelt for inclusion in chapter 14 of our book.

JDM: Honey, that explains it. I just thought I would let you know. [Nancy Carol arrived at this point.]

GWM: Mother has just told me about your initiative in contacting Eleanor Roosevelt. Many thanks!

NC: Daddy, Eleanor Roosevelt doesn't take a back seat to anybody. She is an outspoken, lovely lady. She was that way on the earth plane, and she is that way in the spirit world, too.

Tape #36 Sunday, February 10, 1991, 8:15 p.m.

GWM: Loree has a signal that someone wishes to talk with us. They provide her with an image of the Star of David as an identification of the intended speaker. [Brief prayer.]

ER: Good evening, Mr. Meek.

GWM: Good evening. To whom am I talking?

ER: This is Eleanor Roosevelt.

GWM: Oh, good evening, Mrs. Roosevelt. I was happy to get your message via Jean Peterson a few days ago saying you would cooperate on a segment for our book. I'm delighted to have this opportunity to speak to you personally and thank you for whatever contribution you will be able to make to our work.

ER: You are most welcome. Mr. Meek, I wanted to come through Loree to talk to you one on one. The world, the earth plane, is ready for all the knowledge we can give them. And I will do everything I can to help your work.

GWM: Very fine. I would like to mention that we have limitations in bringing a brilliant mind and soul such as Eleanor Roosevelt through our dear colleague Loree because of her extreme lack of education.

ER: That I understand, Mr. Meek.

GWM: But we will be only too happy to receive whatever comments you care to make tonight.

ER: Mr. Meek, I talked to your lovely daughter. She is a very fine young lady. She is someone you can be very proud of.

GWM: Thank you.

ER: And your lovely wife, Jeannette. Mr. Meek, I need to say something to you. Do not hold it against Loree because she cannot communicate too well with me. Loree is very special.

GWM: Oh, no. I do not in any way cast aspersions because of her very limited education. I daily thank the Creator for Loree's beautiful soul and the rare privilege I have of working with her.

ER: Yes, before coming in, I gave a signal to Loree. I showed her the vision of the Star of David I have around my neck. I can feel Loree's Star of David. Does she have it around her neck also?

GWM: Yes. She has it around her neck.

ER: That is the symbol of the Hierarchy meetings we go to.

GWM: Six months ago, the Christ [or the Great Spirit, as Loree uses the term in her Cherokee tradition], mentioned that Loree had been awarded the Star of David. I went to the local library to do a little research and I was surprised to find that this symbol did not originate in the Jewish religion, but that it was depicted on earthenware some eight thousand years ago. Did it come from another planet originally?

ER: Yes, from the Pleiades. It serves as a symbol that is awarded to someone special. The Great Spirit, as Loree calls him, has the symbol around His neck also, Mr. Meek. Tell Loree I thank her and we all love her very much. I thank her for letting me come through her and speak to you because I wanted to make personal contact.

GWM: Thank you for that information.

ER: Are there any more questions you'd like to ask me, Mr. Meek?

GWM: No, you caught me
unawares. I had no prior
thought that you might be
coming in so I have not had the
time to carefully consider the
best use of this wonderful
opportunity.

[Coming out of trance, Loree said,
"I certainly never channeled *that*
energy before! It's like it's way up
there with the Great Spirit energies."]

The next day's incoming mail
included a letter from Jean Peterson
transmitting the material Mrs. Roosevelt had prepared for us to use in
this chapter. It was accompanied by
various materials Jean had located
in her local reference library. All of
it tended to confirm that we were

Fig. 14–1.—Eleanor Roosevelt

indeed receiving a 1991 communication from Eleanor Roosevelt, who made
the transition to the spirit worlds twenty-nine years previously.

For our many readers who came to adulthood after the active period
of Mrs. Roosevelt's life, and for readers in other countries, the above portrait will enable the reader to better attune to the remarkable person who
dictated the remarks for this chapter.

A Letter to Humanity from Eleanor Roosevelt
Realizing the Eternal You

Not being one, in the life and connotative name of Anna Eleanor Roosevelt, who sat in a rocking chair in her old age and knitted garments,

I now do not sit on a cloud and play the proverbial harp. I am active in the so-called "spirit world," as I was on earth in the twentieth century. So it is that life goes on in a continuing flow of ever-expanding experience into and beyond earth's scriptural attempts to define eternity.

Many of my friends of earth limit their thinking pertaining to the "real hereafter" simply by not allowing the God-given right within their very being to illuminate their understanding. Yet they are astute in the a search to build the body beautiful, and from youth to death of the present physical casing, most attempt to establish "top of the rung" status levels within existing societal structures. Generally speaking, many put in last place within their thinking, the God-given right of each individual life form to live, grow, and evolve in peace, beauty, and equality.

Earth peoples, in droves, live in situations of extreme poverty and the daily grind of poor health, hunger, and appalling housing units where vermin coexist with their human counterparts. Please remember and know that all life is sacred unto itself. Human souls have the ability within their DNA cellular components to assist the vermin within their homes to evolve elsewhere within the earth planetary body. In these instances, both vermin and human have lowered their understanding as to the created arrangement of life within the universe in which they exist. I speak of this due to your knowledge, on earth, of my lifetime in which those very souls who live in such conditions touched my heart. It was my chosen work to assist them in evolving to a greater perception of themselves and their self-created life situation. I continue, then, from the level of consciousness in which I now reside, in earth time, to do the same.

Jean Paul Getty once said, "The man without a home and country to call his own owes it to himself to work his fingers to the bone to provide both country and home for himself. The material goods accumulated by my family have been earned with the sweat of the brow and then handed down generation to generation." [*Encyclopaedia Britannica:* "(1892–1976) U.S. oil billionaire reputed to be the richest man in the world at the time of his death. At his large estate (home base) near Surrey, England, he went so far as to install a pay telephone for guests!"] The truth in that statement is the fact that each person chooses wealth or poverty to work with in each lifetime on earth. Often the persons who have attained great wealth and those who live in poverty are working on the same earth lesson, but simply from the opposite polarity.

You may learn to provide the necessities of earth life, being food, clothing, and shelter, and then share the excess along with your knowledge of how to provide the material needs of mankind, from the polarity of wealth or poverty. For those who possess great wealth must use the God-given brain computer to maintain their wealth, and that avenue of expressive brain waves is the same one used by those who live in poverty and wish to learn how to provide earth's material needs to maintain physical life.

You may ask, "How do you, who exist in a corporal body, work with someone such as I, Eleanor Roosevelt, who exists in etheric energy body/form?" Well, we have our ways of speaking and working with you. One good example is the words upon this page, which came into being through a method known as telepathic contact with the earth personality and messenger who records them for your discernment. For truly, my friends, my greatest purpose in speaking with you in this outrageous manner is to lead you within your own consciousness, and, thereby, to expand your capabilities beyond the five senses most of you limit yourselves into noticing and working with at this time.

What we say here may be likened unto the words of our friend, Abraham Lincoln, who said in his Gettysburg Address, "The world will little note nor long remember what we say here…" Yet the world remembers to this day! May you who read these words spoken telepathically by the continuing life force, whom you know as Eleanor Roosevelt, hear them with the inner ear and feel the energy of which they are constructed with your heart and soul. In each soul lies a recording of continuous and eternal linkage with all creation, granted by the Supreme Being at the very moment you were created! You may hear me, see me, know me and other spirit or etheric entities by communicating with us using the senses beyond the initial five, which many of you identify as your total earthly "bag of tricks."

It is, indeed, incidental whether or not you remember our words, for our purpose is to guide you into implementing the concepts of the words we share at this time into practical daily twentieth century usage! At this level of evolution in which I dwell presently, we often use the pronoun "we" in place of "I," for we have evolved into comprehending the linkage of all life, and "I" does not convey our meaning as well. When experience is placed into earth language composition, by its very nature, it limits the experience. Therefore, those of you who sincerely wish to perceive what we are saying here will choose to *feel* the energy of our words with the intrinsic attributes each of you on earth has been given, in equality, from the Creator God!

By the hour the words upon these pages reach you, the reader, the earth peoples will have completed the biggest and potentially most destructive bomb targeting known to modern man (the Persian Gulf War, January-February 1991). Many of the souls departing the physical casing need special care on the spirit side of continuing life, due to Man's incomprehension of the physical laws of the universe which extend into the spiritual planes of existence. In the hands of earth peoples, a book such as this has the potential to assist those of us within spirit realms in our work with the souls who newly have made the transition from physical to spirit. In truth, physical and spirit are one, but that is another chapter in the continuing human saga of eternity!

Do you catch a glimpse of the wheel of round-and-round activity and life experience Man has created for himself in recent centuries of recorded history? At the time Abraham Lincoln wrote the immortal words of the Gettysburg Address, brother fought against brother upon the land of America in a war which had the magnificent vision of liberating peoples to live in freedom. George Washington, the great general and first president of the United States, led the right in the American War of Independence seeking to sever ownership ties from the country of England.

At the time of this dictation [February 6, 1991], the United States of America leads a thirty-five-nation mandate from the United Nations

Security Council in an attempt to free the small Mideastern country of Kuwait. If left to defend itself, Kuwait would perish from oppressive and sure annihilation by the military might and insane ravings of the dictator of Iraq, Saddam Hussein. Underlying or behind the scenes of up-front statements of the United Nations Security Council and the United States of America to ride the winds of hostility into freedom for Kuwait stand many levels of opportunity for attainment of power, money, and hopes and dreams of rising to the top of the status ladder for those who lead the war machine.

At its inception, the United Nations manifested a magna carta for the beginnings of an organization whereby all earth inhabitants could be represented within one body of democratic law-making mandate capability. During and since my time, it has fallen far short of the resolutions and working guides drawn within the first committee meetings, which I had the privilege and honor of attending as a representative from the government of the United States of America. We worked long and hard to establish rules and guidelines for the United Nations Assembly to follow, so that the organization would not be a paper puppet, but a viable working organization for peace on earth.

Regardless of the policy making, politics, peer pressure, and downright power struggles behind the scenes of the recent United Nations resolution to secure peace and freedom for the Mideastern country of Kuwait, I was proud to have been a small part of that organization's beginnings as the Kuwait resolution was passed with a resounding "Aye!" Until peace is established within the hearts of all mankind, my friends, there are causes worth fighting for! As long as one man holds to the power system of earth, in a sense, all do so! The objective is to recreate peace within all hearts and souls who reside upon earth, and then peace will reign upon the land! More evolved beings from beyond your world interact and share their wisdom with you who are less evolved at this time, for in a sense, we all are one!

The country of England, which the great General George Washington fought in the American War of Independence, and which was in the Persian Gulf War, stands as the greatest ally of the United States of America and the Coalition Forces. Does not the circle of time, effort, and incomprehension of the laws of the universe lead you to reason that it is time to create a new way of behaving on earth? Can you not perceive the greater picture? From the level of consciousness in which I reside, you appear to be schoolchildren in the sandbox with the highest thought being: "How can I be the one with the most toys?"

So it was in my time, that my husband, President Franklin Delano Roosevelt, fought his own personal battles with health, power, money, and status, as we all do on earth. Yet, in the time of this country's need, when the Great Depression reared it ugly head, he rose to the occasion and the results of his wisdom are recorded in earth's history for all time.

I now take the risk, even further, of stretching your willingness to give these words credibility by stating to you that the New Deal programs were originally outlined to Franklin Roosevelt, myself, and a few others whom Franklin trusted implicitly, by beings from other worlds. Man, as a whole, has labeled energy forms beyond his perceived comprehension as ghosts, bogeymen, the devil, or in his most allowing references he uses the words "angels" and "extraterrestrials."

Now many of Man, such as you who are reading this book, have evolved within your consciousness toward the exploration of potential life beyond earth. The impetus for that exploration necessarily resides within Man's search for his own immortality—eternal life. More evolved civilization structures exist beyond the third dimension of earth life. We, who make up the population of worlds which extend beyond your own, communicate with earth peoples by various ways and means. Does not the so-called spirit world, or the heaven of earth scriptures, lead you to know that other worlds exist?

Will you allow the possibility that I, Eleanor Roosevelt, in an ever-expanding exploration of life, am speaking to you through telepathy and the written word for one purpose? That purpose is to guide you into the place within yourself wherein resides the truth of what I am communicating to you. Indeed, there is no proof within the words upon this page of text. The proof of eternal life lies within each individual self.

You have always been, you always will be, in whatever form you choose to express life within. Man has the inherent ability within his molecular nature to remember that life is eternal. No proof outside yourself can ever be enough. By the time the readers reach the last page of the book, some will have located that proof, and some will have discovered enough proof to fire the desire to continue the search. Those who have not located their own proof within the self will take the documented proof contained within the words, photographs, charts, and outlines within this book and toss them in the dust heap of "Well, this book is just another way to make a buck!"

In the still of the night, when even the birdsong is hushed, my friends, we all know where the buck stops, do we not? It is to that quiet, knowing, secret place I am attempting to guide you with my words. For within the soul—the place where all thought and action comes home to roost—there resides your knowledge of the continuity of life. Therefore, the heart of my message to you, my earth friends, is to allow the words, photographs, and material within this book to function as a springboard into greater awareness, which exists within you.

So then, beings from other worlds, who had evolved into living in harmonious peace, came to our world and to human beings, at a time of our great need. They possessed regal bearing, complete healthy attitudes and bodily forms. I found them to be wise beyond earth knowledge, technologically advanced even beyond the military might displayed so wantonly in the Mideast Persian Gulf War of your day, loving, helpful, and generous beyond words to express. They came in peace, and they came from a civilization which recognizes the Universal Law of noninterference with a planet and its life forms' evolution! They came to Franklin Roosevelt because he was to be the leader and representative of the people of America for the thirteen years to come. The extraterrestrials, known as Star Brothers, knew that fact even then before we were sure, for the Democratic convention had not yet been held for that first election which would propel Franklin into world politics and public scrutiny.

People asked me, "Mrs. Roosevelt, where did you find the energy to attend meetings by traveling the world, write, attend to home and family, garden, and all the sundry daily tasks which make up your life?" I could not tell them that a portion of that energy came from sure knowledge of mankind's ability to create harmonious peace and brotherhood upon earth, shown to us by the extraterrestrials. For Man's chosen evolutionary stage was not such that under Universal Law, the extraterrestrials from the level with whom we interacted, could manifest fully on earth. That day will come when Man chooses it!

As Franklin and I, along with America, were swept into world events which shaped World War II, we knew that the outcome had the potential to show mankind its true nature. Sadly, Man is still learning that great lesson from the Mideastern Persian Gulf War. From my present perspective, I can only hope that the Persian Gulf War will lead you closer to recognizing your sistership and brotherhood with all earth people and all creation.

So the Star Brothers came in their spacecraft to the nation of the United States of America in the time when Franklin Delano Roosevelt began his campaign for the presidency. On screens similar to earth television, they showed us pictures of the despair upon the faces and within the hearts of mankind, which waited in the wings of time to come in the Great Depression and the Second World War to be brought about by man's own hand.

The New Deal programs were temporary stopgap measures outlined by the Star Brothers, which were intended to be put aside when the economic and banking systems of America were stabilized. I worked behind the scenes and up-front within the public eye toward implementing the New Deal programs into fruition. Franklin and I, along with the few others who met our friendly visitors from space, worked toward the goal of economic stability within the land of freedom. An empty stomach within the physical body leaves little room for evolving very far beyond the question, "From where is my next meal coming?" At the same time, hunger can act as a catapult into greater awareness for those who are ready for such—a bit of a dichotomy, but nonetheless fact.

At earth's present time cycle, and through the Divine Plan, America is acting as a spiritual leader of the world. Through freedom of speech and press, people who wish to explore consciousness beyond the third dimension may do so at this time without risk of burning at the stake, which once would have been their lot. Therefore, the economy of the United States needed to be stabilized in my time, so that in the intervening years before the Armageddon Wars of which the Persian Gulf War is one, America could be a place of refuge for souls who wished to evolve into greater awareness of eternal life and the cycles within time on earth. That is not to say, my dear friends, that the rest of the world did not explore consciousness in its own way!

Life is eternal and linked throughout creation. Therefore, the chain of life exists within each individual atom and cell that resonates with the energy you call God. Man, in his arrogance, chooses not to perceive that which his five senses do not compute—you know, compute? You have coined a most apropos phrase, "Garbage in, garbage out." That, indeed, is a great truth. The human brain receptor works as a receiver rather than a generator. God is Original Thought! Drawing from Universal Flow whatever thoughts you wish to compute from the unlimited thought, which is God, preordains your output! Power and status input equals war and strife output—every time—in a system of Universal Law known as cause and effect! When will man learn that the great teachers, such as Jesus, the Christ, who stated time and again in His life lived as an example of teaching mankind through love instead of power, "Whatsoever a man soweth, that shall he also reap"? The teachings of the Universal Law of cause and effect are not idle words of power-hungry men who seek followers. Instead the teachings of cause and effect have their basis in the great truth of Universal Law.

Within the book you hold in your hands reside the tools for those of you who choose to remove them from the pages, indelibly write them in your soul, place them within your mind and hands, and thereby set yourselves free. For eons, Man has self-chosen the pathway of evolution which has chained him to the post of limited mind and being. The five physical senses are but the tip of the iceberg of mankind's total potential. I communicate to all of you within hearing distance of my voice, which speaks from beyond time—should you choose to follow the guidance within this book, you will become free of the limited comprehension of eternal life, which you have failed to explore until your present incarnational cycle.

With love to you all, I am Eleanor Roosevelt writing a letter to humanity, whom I love through my continuing exploration of life eternal. May insights gleaned from the material offered in this book, and the messages within my letter, lead you to personal and planetary freedom to evolve in a continuing human wave of love, spanning the unlimited horizons residing within the God-given right of eternal life for all!

With Love and Affection,
Eleanor Roosevelt

Let us face it. Most of us mortals currently living in fleshly bodies seldom have occasion to read material as profound as the communication Eleanor Roosevelt crafted for this chapter. For many readers, it will require a second or third reading to fully comprehend and appreciate the ideas being put forth.

The news of the role extraterrestrial beings played in meeting and advising the Roosevelts will come as a surprise to most readers! However, our research has shown:

- Such extraterrestrial contact with our U.S. presidents has continued.
- None have felt the U.S. public "could stand the shock of such a secret."
- The Star Wars project has as one of its objects the destruction of craft not originating on earth.

Most important, of course, is Eleanor Roosevelt's personal and up-to-date testimony as to the continuity of life.

The majority of readers will find the foregoing statements shocking, unbelievable, and perhaps utter nonsense.

Is it possible that Presidents Truman, Eisenhower, Kennedy, Nixon, Ford, Carter, Reagan, Bush, and Clinton have had contacts with extraterrestrial beings, as did the Roosevelts, as stated in Eleanor's communication dated February 10, 1991?

The answer is an unequivocal *yes!*

Ashtar, the Commander of an Intergalactic Fleet, has discussed this subject in depth in his communications through superb-quality channels in several countries, including the United States.

One such communication in late 1990, through Jean Peterson, who channeled the foregoing communication from Eleanor Roosevelt, gives Ashtar's specific statement:

Your American president rides the winds of change, and this he knows. Through our emissaries on earth, we have contacted the heads of the American government and have talked with them face-to-face in conference. They do not report such to you, the American peoples, for indeed that would blow their cover, so to speak, that we exist in the first place. Still they do not wish to compromise by creating peace and equality for all earthmen. Still they wish to maintain power for each individual self who has scrambled up the ladder of power and government success. It saddens us greatly that Man will not take the reigns of higher truth and create peace and equality upon earth.

We have sat long in the councils of higher light deciding how we may assist those of Man who wish to project their energy forward into levels of light which will create peace on earth. We long have stood in line with you, our coworkers on earth, waiting for the day to arrive when your earthean brothers will awaken from their eons of sleep.

Readers interested in seeking information on this subject are referred to the special bibliography in appendix I.

Chapter Fifteen
O'Neil Attends His Own Funeral

In chapter 3 of this book, we documented the historic role that my electronic colleague William J. O'Neil played in mankind's first extended instrumental communication with the spirit worlds. Little did Bill or I dream that someday after his own move into the spirit worlds, he, like Jeannette (chapter 8), would report his attendance at his own funeral.

In recent years, Bill and I have had only sporadic telephone conversations with each other. I knew he was in poor health. But on February 18, 1991, I was astonished when he established his first telepathic contact with Loree while in a ward in a hospital in Pennsylvania.

This situation had its start on that day when Loree came to me and said, "Some entity is asking permission to use my telepathic abilities to permit him to talk to you. Do you want me to connect?" I replied in the affirmative.

UNKNOWN VOICE: George, you remember when I did all that damn work for you?

GWM: I don't remember and I don't know what you're talking about. Who are you?

BO: I'm Bill O'Neil, George.

GWM: Bill O'Neil? Okay. You did work with me, and, yes, I worked with you. Bill, have you died and gone over to the other side?

BO: Hell, no, George, and you know better,

GWM: Well, I don't know. Your son talked to me several weeks ago and said he was going to put you in a sanitarium.

BO: A damn mental institution, George.

GWM: Is that where you are?

BO: Yes. And it's no damn picnic.

GWM: I'm sure it is not. But, Bill, there is nothing I can do to help you. Your son has taken over; Garry has taken over completely.

BO: Garry couldn't care less whether I lived or died.

GWM: Well, at least he made arrangements to put you in a safe place. That was necessary because you couldn't take care of yourself anymore.

BO: George, are you sure you can't come and get me out of this damn place?

GWM: No, Bill, I cannot. I'm not a family member. Only Garry, the member of your family who put you in there, can get you out.

BO: George, I don't mean to be any trouble, but you ain't heard the last of me.

GWM: Bill, can you feel any of this energy? (George is electronically "zapping.")

BO: Yes.

GWM: All right. Now I have means here, Bill, which will completely... [GWM advises Bill that he will not stand for any harassment from the spirit planes and has means to stop it.] I don't want to have to do that, Bill. I love you, really. You used to sign your letters to me—God's love—and that's the way it is, too. It still is. I love you, Bill, but I will not tolerate your interfering with my work.

BO: George, I want you to forgive me. I don't know what makes me do these things. It's not really me doing this, George.

GWM: That's right. It's the dark forces that get in and take you over, Bill. This is not Bill O'Neil. Bill O'Neil was a loving person. That is why he was such a good healer.

BO: You know what I told you one day? I said God is a good guy.

GWM: Yes. That identifies you. I know I'm talking to Bill O'Neil now. God is indeed a good guy.

BO: George, forgive me.

GWM: All right, Bill. I will pray for you and hope that there is some way that something can be done to help you.

[Subsequently, the state-appointed guardian told me Bill had inoperable cancer of the bladder and was hallucinating.]

In the next seven months, I sent cards to Bill, but there was no reply. On September 18, 1991, Loree advised me that a lower-plane energy wanted to talk to me. She said it seemed harmless.

UNKNOWN VOICE: Good morning, George.

GWM: To whom am I speaking?

BO: I'm Bill O'Neil.

GWM: Good morning, Bill, my dear friend. I received the notification from Mary Alice that you had made the transition. She gave me the copy of the death certificate in case I wanted to keep it in my files. I am sorry that your earth-life was terminated when it was, but I know enough about the possibilities ahead of you that I know the real Bill O'Neil, not the one who was bothered by the dark spirits, but the real O'Neil, has a wonderful possibility for life ahead in his new surroundings. So on the one hand, I am sorry to hear of your passing, but I am glad your agony is all over and that you are now being able to get some rest. So fill me in, Bill, on what happened.

BO: Well, George, I am very happy here and I don't have those split personalities anymore. I wanted to come to speak to you and ask you to forgive me for running you and your lovely wife off my property that day. George, I can reassure you that it wasn't Bill talking to you. It was the other entity in me that was doing the talking. Do you understand what I am trying to say, George?

GWM: I certainly do, Bill. I loved you a great deal in your other circumstances, but in this situation, I love you even more. Thank you for coming back so early and giving me this confirmation. I knew the real Bill was not the Bill that slammed the door in my face, chased me off his property, and made unpleasant remarks in front of Jeannette. It was fortunate I knew enough about the situation that I overlooked it and continued to keep my contact with you month after month, year after year.

BO: And, George, I love you like a brother and I'm sorry that I let the other entities take me over. But, George, I had such a terrible life when I was a small child with my father. I had his personality also.

GWM: Yes. I again was fortunate, Bill, in being able to diagnose that situation. I could see as the years went on what a terrible, negative impact your father had had on you. It was the curse of your existence all the years you were growing up, through your business life, and then through your married life.

BO: But, George, if I had only stopped and taken the time to search out my childhood with my other personal problems that I had, I could have taken it to Jesus and God and could have gotten rid of them. But I didn't, George. Now I am free from those problems.

GWM: That's good news. We can both put the unpleasant parts of our association out of our minds. I make a distinction between pleasant and unpleasant because some of the fondest memories I have, Bill, in all our years of research were when you were opening yourself to God and getting help in the healing work that you were doing. You benefited many, many lives during that short period when you were serving as a healer.

BO: Yes. But you know, George, if I would have put all my faith in God and Jesus, I wouldn't have been in such a mess as I was. I let cancer destroy me and it wasn't my doings. It wasn't Bill's doing. It was the other entities in me. That is the reason that I am here now. I thank the Lord that I am here, but they shortened my life twenty years.

GWM: I agree with everything you just said, Bill, but my main thought at this moment is one of rejoicing and knowing all of that is behind you. Now you have the possibility for a new start!

BO: Yes. And, George, I am very happy I talked to the Creator, the One who created us. He told me when I got a little more spiritual that I could work with children. You know, George, how I liked ventriloquism. I can teach the children to do this and have fun with the children, George. Now I am free. Isn't that wonderful?

GWM: Bill, I can recall with the greatest of pleasure those tapes on which you recorded your puppet shows for the children there in the Kitanning area before Christmas. You had tremendous ability in that area. I am so glad that you will put it to use with the children in the spirit world.

BO: George, I have never met Loree, but I want you to tell her she has another friend and one who loves here in the spirit world now.

GWM: Thank you, Bill. She is in a trance now and doesn't know what you're saying, but I will play this tape back for her so she can hear your words spoken directly to her. [GWM briefs Bill about Loree's work as a telepathic channel.]

BO: And you know, George, I am so happy to be rid of those entities that were in my body and now I don't have to hurt. I don't have any pain, George. And I think that is wonderful.

GWM: Bill, it's great to know we have established this communication. I am greatly surprised and pleased that you could make the connection so soon. I told Loree just yesterday that according to the death certificate you made the transition on September fourth. I knew you would have to have a period of rest and rehabilitation, but that sometime after three or four weeks, we might be able to talk to you. But instead of being three or four weeks, Bill, according to your death certificate, it is just two weeks since you went over.

BO: And, George, you know, I hung around on the earth plane for two days and then I went to my own funeral.

GWM: Good. Jeannette did the same thing. Who was in charge of the funeral service?

BO: My wife, Mary Alice.

GWM: Where was the service held?

BO: George, I don't exactly remember because I was just floating around and my head was in a spin. I still thought I was alive, but I was there and I saw my body. Finally, it just dawned on me that "Bill was dead." The body was dead, but my spirit was alive.

GWM: Bill, you don't know how happy this makes me to know you were able to make that change so quickly, learn who you were, and have a chance to look at your past lives.

BO: Boy, George, when I say God is a good guy, He is!

GWM: Bless your heart. I know from Jeannette's experiences that it's going to be all roses from here on for you. You've got just unlimited possibilities ahead for yourself, Bill. When we published our METAscience newsletter, we chose the name "Unlimited Horizons," and that applies to you. I'm so happy to know you have unlimited horizons to use all those many, many wonderful abilities that you have.

BO: George, you know I was working there on the earth plane with you and Dr. Mueller. Well now, George, if I meet him here in the spirit world I will just walk up and shake his hand in person.

GWM: I can tell you Dr. Mueller has moved on up beyond the plane you are on now. In our terminology, I would say you were probably on what we loosely call the Middle Astral Planes. You remember, one of the last things Dr. Mueller said was, "Come on, Bill, let's get on with it. I can't be here forever." And he was talking about the fact that he was spiritually advancing and moving up. I know from communications I had with him in the next few years through Lucille McNames that he did move up. It may be a little while before you can contact him, but I am sure you will ultimately be in touch with our good friend Dr. Mueller.

BO: And George, tell Loree that I didn't mean to scare her when I cut in on her telephone conversation on the phone earlier today.

GWM: Thanks for that piece of news, Bill. We were afraid that was a dark spirit that we're having trouble with.

BO: I tell you, George, some day when you pick up the telephone and you hear me say, "Good morning, George," you and I can carry on a conversation. Would you like me to do that, George?

GWM: Yes. I will take the call here at my desk where I've got a telephone recording device.

BO: Well, George, it may take me a little while to work out all the bugs because I wanted to tell Loree who I was and I got interfered with. But I think I did pretty good, cutting in on Loree's conversation with her daughter. You be sure to tell Loree that I didn't mean to scare her.

GWM: A couple of friends of mine wrote a book ten years ago called *Phone Calls from the Dead* in which they reported a lot of experiences of this type. What we do in the months ahead may provide a new chapter in that field.

BO: Well, George, you know how much I love electronics.

GWM: I should say so. And it's great to have this connection with you again.

[Bill and I chatted along for another twenty minutes. It was like old times. He had total recall. It was obvious that his reasoning mind, memory banks, and personality were one hundred percent unaffected by the loss of his physical body.]

GWM: Bill, thank you for coming back this morning and giving us this message. I think this is about the usual length of time that we have Loree in trance, so with your permission, we will stop off this first communication. Will that be okay with you?

BO: Yes, and George, always remember, God is a good guy.

GWM: What a good sign off that is! Yes, indeed. God is a good guy. Thank you, Bill. God bless you and keep you.

BO: God bless you, too.

On October 7, some three weeks later, Bill again contacted me and I recorded a 32-minute conversation. It was just like old times.

So yes, Bill—like Jeannette Meek—actually looked in on his funeral. Within a matter of a few weeks, he was able to resume the close working relationship we had initiated seventeen years earlier.

Chapter Sixteen
She Did It!

People who don't know what cannot be done
often go ahead and do it.
—Henry Ford

Yes, Jeannette did it! As mentioned earlier, prior to her transition, we had discussions as to actions she might take after getting settled into her new environment in the spirit worlds. One objective was to take actions to demonstrate the continuity of life. Now, ten months after her relocation to her new dwelling place, here is a preliminary outline of her achievements.

- Jeannette planned to attend her own funeral service. She did. When contact was established via mental telepathy seven weeks after her transition, she discussed even small details of her memorial service in the funeral chapel (chapter 8).

- Jeannette affected color film while her cast-off physical body lay in the closed casket in the funeral chapel (chapter 8).

- Some weeks after Jeannette's transition, an eighty-two-year-old psychic friend in Colorado wrote stating that Jeannette had appeared in her astral body at the foot of her bed and said, "Thank you!" Neither my friend nor I were certain as to what this was all about. Once I established regular contact with Jeannette, she explained that she was impelled to promptly take this action as a result of her past life review. She had been unjustly critical!

- Jeannette planned to continue her near-perfect mental telepathy contact with her nurse and companion *after* her transition. She did. Beginning seven weeks after her transition, she initiated visits, averaging thirty minutes, visits that came at intervals of five to eight days. (The companion volume of this book, *What It's Like in Heaven?*, presents abstracts of more than three dozen such conversations.

- Jeannette agreed before transition to attempt to establish instrumental contact with me by working through our earthside researcher friends, Jules and Maggy Harsch-Fischbach in Luxembourg. She did! (chapter 4).

- Jeannette, seven months after transition, took it upon herself to transmit to me via the Harsch-Fishbach computer in Luxembourg a special message she had conceived. She chose three very personal incidents known only to the two of us and in part by Molly, our assistant for eight years. (Discussed later in this chapter.)

- Only four hours after the above computer contact with me via Luxembourg, Jeannette initiated a mental telepathy contact via Loree so she could discuss the above-mentioned computer contact, news of which had been reported promptly to me via transatlantic telephone.

Yes, she did it! And considering her modest and retiring nature and her total lack of any technical or scientific knowledge, it is a most remarkable accomplishment.

The details behind the last two items listed above are of considerable interest. The story began at 3:15 P.M. on February 20, 1991, when I was sitting at my desk holding a letter I was planning to mail to Maggy and Jules in Luxembourg, asking about progress in reaching Jeannette via an additional computer contact. The telephone rang. It was Maggy and Jules! They wanted to share immediately the news of Jeannette's most recent contact.

They had just returned to their apartment and found that during their absence, the computer had been activated by Swejan Salter, a woman scientist in a parallel universe [not our spirit worlds]. Swejan had turned on the computer and entered a message. Maggy called up the menu and activated the code word. The computer then printed out before their eyes a message, one part of which was in German and one part in English. The English portion was a communication to me!

Maggy and Jules were so excited they immediately picked up the phone and read me the key portion. Jeannette explained she wanted to make a contribution to this manuscript. She had decided she wanted to transmit via computer in a foreign country three small examples of highly personal information, information bits that existed in her mind and probably in my mind.

Telephone conversation, February 20, 1991

GWM: Good afternoon, Jules. Nice to hear your voice again.

JULES: Hello, George, how are you?

GWM: I'm happy to say I'm better than anytime since I left Luxembourg last July.

JULES: Thank God. We just got a text, George. It is dated 18 February 1991 and it is coming from Swejan Salter. In the midst of the page she says there is a good friend of hers, Jeannette Meek, who wants to say some words to George who has stayed on this side. I will read it to you. It's in English. We'll forward a copy to you as soon as possible. But Maggy wants me to read it to you now over the phone:

"Dear G.W.,

"I'd like to cook up a few good names for believing I could have wings. I'm sure you recall I often have told you there are lots of things you come in handy for, not only to do such as take caps off pill bottles but also to tell somebody else just what to do—expert advice!

"Well, it seems as if there are still people who do not believe in the contacts your friends here at CETL are having. Here are some details known only to you and Molly. [Jeannette has searched her memory and selected three incidents, the details of which are known only to three persons, George Meek, Jeannette, and our secretary, Molly.] Give her my warmest greetings. I miss her. Nobody can know [how much].

"First story. In 1987, end of April, tenant Debbie called to say her refrigerator was off. It must have been on a Thursday morning and had no connection with the storm the day before. At the close of her work-day, she called again to say she was having more trouble. This time she had left her purse on the seat of the car of a lady with whom she had been riding. This lady lived quite far from Franklin, so Debbie asked to borrow our key to her place.

"Another story. On April 29, 1987, Ann Valentin wrote a letter that she had not received the *Magic of Living Forever* booklets they had ordered, but Harlequin novels.

"Third story. John Lathrop shut off the electricity at the "C" house to put in the new [yard] light. He wasn't down there very long but charged twenty dollars service in addition to forty dollars for the bulbs, plus tax. The charge seemed high.

"Don't try to explain this, honey. My never-ending love to you. I miss you so much, but I know we will be together. I have a big job to do here as a result of that idiot's war. Love forever! JDM" [Jeannette was serving as a guardian angel of love and kindness, receiving men, women and children victims of the Mideast War as they came out of the discharge end of the tunnel.] Please, Maggy, forward this to George.

He can be of great help to you all. Send my best wishes to Loree, also. Thank you. Jeannette Duncan Meek."

GWM: That's absolutely fabulous. The three items sound evidential.

JULES: I'll give you back to Maggy. Thank you for listening.

MAGGY: What do you say about this, George?

GWM: It's most remarkable. I know that one and three are okay in all details. I will search of what remains of Jeannette's correspondence files to check item two. This will make history in the field of instrumental communications.

MAGGY: I'm glad. We just got it when we came home now—fifteen minutes ago now. Yes, it is dated the eighteenth.

GWM: Does this use the new equipment that was set up over there last July when Dr. Locher and I were there?

MAGGY: No. For the moment, it is only computer. But we hope we will use the new equipment next time…

Yes, she did it! Even now, only I know the personal background of some of the thoughts and emotions involved. Example: Jeannette's maiden name was Duncan, and she inherited all the frugality associated as a daughter of Scotland. In her opinion—both at the time of the incident and now at least six years after the event—the mentioned electrician friend of mine charged more for the repair service on one of our houses than *she* thought was justified!

The incident of the tenant needing to borrow our key to a rental house was also absolutely correct. But what about Jeannette's third item—an error in one of her shipments of books?

Molly and I could find no answer in what remained of Jeannette's book order requests of three years ago. Ann Valentin had relocated two years she replied, "Why, of course, I remember the incident. The carton of books we received as a result of an order I had placed with METAscience Foundation did not contain the books I had ordered. It contained only Harlequin novels—cheap love stories."

I asked, "Ann, are you certain about the contents of that carton?"

Ann replied, "Yes, I certainly am. And I recall Jeannette and I were both astonished that they were old copies of second-hand quality."

So yes, Jeannette scored one hundred percent on the three highly personal incidents she chose to supply to us via computer printout in Luxembourg as substantial evidence of the continuity of life!

But the story continues to unfold. Only four hours after receiving the transatlantic phone call reporting on Jeannette's computer message to me, Loree said, "George, the energy beam I am receiving indicates either Jeannette or your daughter Nancy Carol would like to talk to you." The session opens after Loree goes into a trance:

GWM: Loree has indicated that she sensed an energy which would like to speak to me. Welcome.

JDM: Good afternoon, honey.

GWM: Good afternoon to you, sweetheart.

JDM: Have you received a message from Jules and Maggy Harsch-Fischbach?

GWM: I most certainly did. This afternoon, just four hours ago. It's a very wonderful message. I'll have to say thanks many times before you can appreciate how grateful I am. I'll start right...Thank you for the wonderful, wonderful message you brought though via computer in Luxembourg.

JDM: Well, honey, I just wanted to feel useful. I decided this was a good way to do it.

GWM: Well, I will share a secret with you. Months ago when I made up the first tentative draft of chapter headings for our book, I reserved chapter 16 and hoped to have something special from you to include in that chapter. So I have written around that chapter. As of today, I have written every chapter in the book except that one. This afternoon the telephone rang while I was sitting at my desk. I was holding the draft of a letter to Maggy to find out what was going on in Luxembourg. At that moment, Maggy and Jules were at the other end of the line telling me of the wonderful contribution you had just made to our book. Jules read over the phone what you put in the computer message, but they will send it to me by mail and in a week or so I'll be in a position to write and edit the final chapter for the book.

JDM: Honey, that's wonderful.

GWM: Your timing is absolutely right...

Yes, she did it! And just in the nick of time to occupy the only chapter space to which I had not assigned a title when I roughed out the structure for this book, five months before this writing.

Now in part V we will present answers to dozens of questions you may have concerning life in the spirit worlds.

Part V

Helpful Guidance

Chapter Seventeen
Forty-four Questions and Answers on the Continuity of Life

> Finding myself to exist in the world, I believe I shall in some shape or other always exist; and, with all the inconveniences human life is liable to, I shall not object to a new edition of mine, hoping, however, that the errata of the last may be corrected. —Benjamin Franklin

R egardless of race, color, caste, or creed, each of us—totally alone— walks through the door called Death. Then certain basic questions cry out for answers. Nothing could be more important than to know them beforehand.

The material that follows is possible only because of the inquisitive minds of dedicated researchers during the past century. First I honor the most dedicated of the serious (and honest) deep-trance mediums, primarily in England, Scotland, Brazil, the United States, Canada, Ireland, Italy, and South Africa. Second, I acknowledge the work of thousands of persons traditionally known as "sitters," whose presence seems to provide subtle energies that facilitate the best contacts with communicators from other levels of life.

These valuable contributions would have been lost, however, had it not been for dedicated psychic researchers and scientists who had the moral courage to investigate and report the work of these mediums and their sitters or "circles." These researchers, even down to the year 1991, have had to suffer ridicule from their peers and loss of their professional status. Men like Sir William Crookes in England, Schrenk-Notzing in Germany, Nobel prize-winner Charles Richet in France, Ernest Bozzano in Italy, Dr. Holtacher in South Africa, T. Glen Hamilton, M.D., in Canada, William Tiller, Ph.D., in the United States, and Dr. Hernani Andrade in Brazil all paid a price for their pioneering work.

Although the accumulated communications and data were fragmentary and often extremely contradictory, in time it became possible to piece together a reasonably consistent and experimentally valid picture of life after death.

Finally, in the 1980s, this type of research intensified. Communications under laboratory conditions from recently "deceased" communicators with medical and scientific backgrounds have added still more validity to the emerging picture. These have greatly enhanced our understanding of the process of death and rebirth. It has pushed our knowledge far beyond that which grew out of the first hundred years of spiritualism.

Hence I acknowledge my indebtedness to all those referred to in Data Bases A, B, and C in appendix A. Without their efforts, the material that follows would not have been possible. In general, they confirm age-old teachings that form the core of the world's great religions. Of equal importance, however, they strip away a vast accumulation of dogma and creed with which these religions have been profaned over the past three thousand years.

Regardless of race, color, religion, creed, caste, sex, or educational level, we are beginning to see more clearly what happens when each of us, totally alone, passes through the door labeled "Death and Rebirth."

Using an entirely different approach from that of the foregoing chapters, I will now list forty-four of the basic questions asked about death, dying, and graduation, and give the answers which present the best available data.

[Note: Many of these questions and answers were first published in 1980 in the book *After We Die, What Then?* The passing years have fully confirmed the validity of the answers.]

1. Let's take first things first. After all of this talk about life and death, what is the purpose of life?

Here is the answer, just as simply as I can state it: The purpose of each individual life (soul) is to grow mentally, emotionally, and spiritually back toward the level of creative intelligence from which it originally issued.

2. Is it painful to die?

No. Even those whose terminal illness caused prolonged and excruciating pain find that at the time of death all pain is gone. This is one reason it is often observed that the face of a dying person relaxes and even has a smile.

The actual transition is so smooth and painless that often one cannot believe he is dead. Frequently when a patient goes to sleep during a painful illness he awakes to continuing pain. When he awakens after death and finds no pain, the first thought is, "I must be dreaming"—or he may wonder if a sudden and miraculous cure has taken place. He has a feeling of lightness and buoyancy. The person sees his physical body lying still and dead and he observes the actions of the nurse and family members. Then it occurs to him, "I suppose I am dead! I did not expect it to be anything like this! I feel fine!"

3. Will I become a ghost? If so, how can I be released?

It is most unlikely you will become a ghost. Ghosts, apparitions, shades, or astral shells result only in the relatively rare cases when the etheric body (or etheric double as some call it) fails to separate from the physical and then disintegrate. Separation normally takes place in minutes, but may take up to thirty to forty hours. Some persons ignorant of this fact may have a tendency to hold onto the etheric body and may appear as ghosts. Some people will be able to see this energy field as a bluish-white mist.

Until the etheric body has separated completely from the astral body, the person cannot proceed to his earned existence in the astral world. This failure to shed the etheric body often results from a very traumatic event—

murder, fatal injury, or unpleasant emotional experience. Such a failure can also result if a person has never thought about an afterlife and has been wholly centered on his possessions and personal affairs.

A ghost can be released very easily from the area it is haunting by a good psychic. The psychic needs only to get in tune with the ghost and in a friendly, loving manner explain that death has taken place and that there is nothing to be gained by lingering in these old haunts. The psychic then encourages the soul to relax and look for any sign of light from persons who are willing to lead it into the realm where it should now be living.

4. Is there an actual place called hell? If so, where is it?

There is no such place. It is definitely not the fire and brimstone place of the Old Testament, nor the place depicted in the famous Hieronymus Bosch painting. It is really more like the traditional purgatory that has for centuries been referred to by the Catholic Church. It is a condition or state of mind that results from the thoughts and actions of the person in his just-concluded lifespan in the nitty-gritty three-dimensional world of the five senses.

The zone is cluttered up with thought-forms accumulated over the centuries as a result of humanity's hatred, greed, lust, jealousy, and other non-virtuous passions. These thought-forms can be as real as the shadowy bodies of the poor souls whose lives qualified them for this plane of existence.

Of all the levels in the lower worlds of spirit, hell is the lowest astral plane.

5. Is there a devil?

No, at least not a red-skinned character with a tail, a pair of horns, and a pitchfork, as has been pictured in centuries past. The lowest astral level—like all other levels in the worlds of spirit—is largely a world created by thoughts. This does not make it any less real. Far from it! Mental torments can be far worse than actual physical torments, as in the case of a person with delirium tremens.

In the darkness of the lower astral, imagination and conscience can create the most frightening devils of all shapes and sizes. To these are added the very real astral bodies of strange creatures of nonhuman lines of evolution.

Confirmation of what we are telling you about devils—and light beings—comes from a small research project reported in the May/June 1979 issue of *Parapsychology Review*:

A heart specialist from Chattanooga, Tennessee, has just finished a study of more than 100 patients brought back to life after being clinically dead. "The good news," he said, "is that some of them had a blissful encounter with a being of light." The bad news, however, is that over half the patients "had a perfectly appalling time," walking through dimly lit caverns... The doctor now firmly believes hell exists. "Reluctantly," he said, "I have come to the conclusion it may not be safe to die."

We can agree with the heart specialist's conclusion that hell does indeed exist on the very lowest of the astral planes. His second conclusion is certainly academic, since we all die. But the problem is neatly solved by living a life now that will entitle you to bypass the lower astral and arrive safely on the middle or astral plane.

In any event, if you do find yourself in the lowest astral planes, you can escape these torments if you persist in striving to find the light and in calling out for assistance. Sooner or later an encounter will occur with one of the compassionate beings who willingly gives of his or her time to lead tormented souls to a place of rest and enlightenment.

6. What can I or should I do to make certain that I am on a path which will bypass that dark and dismal level of existence you call the lower astral?

Let me share information that has come from wise old souls who have traveled much farther along life's high road than I have. One can place belief in far less than ten percent of the information that comes from spirit entities through mediums. It is very rare indeed to obtain direct communication from those highly evolved persons currently living on the mental, causal, and celestial planes. In our research in communication between the interpenetrating levels of life and consciousness, we have found and repeatedly tested a mere handful of communicators living on the higher levels. We have followed faithfully the admonition in the epistle of John to "try the spirits (to see) whether they be of God."

So in figure 17–1, I present not my answer to your very important question, but theirs. Only time will prove for each of us whether these wise old souls know whereof they speak. All I can say is that my own still, small voice has told me I can safely consecrate my current life to such a course of action.

Persons now residing on the higher astral and the mental-causal planes confirm the central core spiritual teachings of the world's great religions, once they have been stripped of the dogma and creed that each has acquired with the passing of centuries.

From their vantage point, they state that the concept depicted in figure 17–1 is the only time-proven, safe, sure, quick and enjoyable route for each soul to travel—now and throughout the coming centuries.

7. I am miserable and unhappy. Will I be better off after I die?

Sorry, but the answer is no.

When you someday cast off your physical body, the real you—your mind, memory banks, personality, and soul—will be precisely what they were before you left the physical body. If you are miserable and unhappy when you make the transition, you will still be miserable and unhappy in your new surroundings!

Today is the first day of the rest of your life. This is the day to start to follow Jesus' gentle admonition to "lay up for yourself treasures in heaven." Only by building into your life and actions many of the qualities listed in figure 17-1 will you enjoy this life and assure yourself of an exciting adventure in the centuries ahead.

Fig. 17–1.—The Proven Path for Individual Soul Development

8. Does a suicide succeed in escaping his troubles?

No, he only compounds them. There is no escape for any individual from the requirement that each one must evolve mentally, emotionally, and spiritually. A person who fails to cope with everyday problems does not escape by suicide. He cannot kill himself. He is just as alive after destroying his physical body as he was before he pulled the trigger, jumped out the window, or took an overdose of drugs.

He finds himself in the darkest, most dismal, and frightening level of the astral plane. A long, hard, and lonely struggle lies ahead before this soul achieves the level on which it would have arrived by natural death.

9. How long might a suicide or murderer remain in the lowest astral plane?

We have been told that there is a big difference in the time spent on the lower astral by those two categories. The suicide has harmed only himself and his loved ones, if any. Usually, he or she is immediately filled with remorse. There are exceptions, of course. Consider the person who commits suicide for wholly unselfish reasons; for example, the action of Titus Oakes of Scott's 1914 polar expedition, who took his own life to conserve the dwindling food supply for his companion. When a offer of help and guidance is given, the suicide is likely to respond readily. How fast he absorbs the teachings offered will determine how rapidly he moves to a more hospitable level.

The murderer is in much, much deeper trouble. His act in cutting short an earth life indicates that he has not only failed to learn much in his past lives, if any, but that he has not evolved spiritually in the present life. Usually he has little readiness to accept teaching when offered, so his stay on the lower astral may be from many years to many centuries of our time.

10. I have heard that if one has chosen to have the body cremated, it should not be done immediately after death. Is this correct?

Yes. However, some of our knowledgeable friends on the mental-causal levels have reminded us that in the Orient it has been the practice for countless centuries to burn the body before sundown on the day of death. This practice came about because in warm climates decay of the physical body starts promptly.

The etheric and astral bodies need ample time for a completely natural and total withdrawal from the physical body. Hence it is perhaps advisable whenever possible to wait for a day or two before cremating the body. Where this is not possible and the soul or spirit is forced to make a sudden departure from its physical body, it will again become normal after a period of rest.

11. Where is the next world (or astral world) located?

As noted in chapter 1, it is possible to have two or more things occupying the same space at the same time. Your physical body dwells in our common, everyday, three-dimensional world of space and time. Your mind and soul live in another space-time system that interpenetrates your physical body and occupies substantially the same space as your physical body.

Hence the next world is the one in which your mind and soul already live and in which your mind and soul will continue to live. When you have shed your worn-out physical body, you will be aware of the surroundings in which your mind and soul are living—interpenetrating the astral planes.

12. Will I have to meet immediately that alcoholic spouse who mistreated me and the children, and whom I divorced? And what about my friend Carol, who had five husbands?

No, to the first of these questions. You will find yourself in a group where you are in harmony with all of the other members. As for friend Carol, I can only assume that she has a long way to grow, both spiritually and mentally. But again, she too will find herself with those persons for whom she has an affinity. If she does not want to be with any of her former mates, she will not be.

In due course, we do have to meet those with whom we have unfinished business. Each must sooner or later balance accounts if he is to grow emotionally and spiritually.

13. Do persons addicted to alcohol, tobacco, and drugs lose their craving for such stimulation when they arrive on the next plane?

No, not right away. For example, an unrecovered alcoholic, being on the lowest astral plane, is in close touch with the physical or earth plane. Often he is not truly aware that he is dead. He may seek out his old haunts and get a vicarious thrill from visiting a bar. In fact, if he finds a patron who is depressed, muddled, and psychically sensitive, he may obsess that person. By this merging of their respective energy fields, the dead person may become more directly locked into the physical aura of the bar patron and experience more directly the feelings to which he had become accustomed. If the possession of the patron continues, it may completely wreck his life and in some cases may even cause the patron to commit suicide.

A person addicted to drugs is in the deepest trouble. He will be resistant to any offer of help and will persist in his craving. He will experience torments that equal anything pictured in the old ideas of hell. He may remain in this dreadful condition for what would be centuries of earth time.

14. Can a dead person look in on the activities of a child or mate?

Yes, this happens all the time. For a period of days, months. or years, the deceased person is very much attuned to the earth plane. If the transition is an unusually smooth one, the deceased may even look in on his own funeral (as reported by Jeannette)! The records are full of examples of a mate or parent who lingers for months and enjoys daily contact with surviving family members.

It is not uncommon for a deceased mate to want to complete some item of unfinished family business. In those rare cases where a good trance medium is consulted, the deceased may reveal where a missing and badly needed last will and testament or other document can be found. The settling of more than one estate has been accomplished by this means.

As the deceased becomes fully reconciled to his or her new life, the earth ties (primarily personal love and affection) become less binding. The deceased then becomes fully absorbed in the increasing challenges of the completely new world that has opened.

15. Is there is any factual basis for the idea that the spirit of a dead person can intrude into the mind of a living person and adversely affect that person's behavior?

Absolutely, even though, until now, modern psychiatry has laughed at this concept. However, for those who were open-minded enough to do serious research on this matter, it quickly becomes clear that there is a solid basis of fact for the age-old idea of spirit or demon possession.

Perhaps the best single piece of research on this subject is Wickland's *Thirty Years Among the Dead*, published in 1933. In it, he tells of the technique he developed for getting into two-way conversation with the possessing entity and then proceeding by persuasion (and in some cases shocks of static electricity) to induce the intruding spirit to depart.

Wickland's work has been confirmed by research in which I have been personally involved.

The many ways in which entities in the spirit world influence or communicate with people in physical bodies are illustrated in figure 17–2. Item A deals with obsession; the other forms of communication are far more beneficial and healthy.

I have reason to hope that in less than a decade, modern medicine will realize that perhaps as much as twenty-five percent of all mental hospital patients and prisoners are victims of obsession. Today these unfortunate souls receive no help because many psychiatrists are unable to recognize and treat this problem.

16. All my life I have been taught that when I die, I will lie in my grave until some far-off judgment day, and then I will be raised from the dead. The material you have presented in this book disagrees with my religious teachings.

I said in the opening pages of this book that this is not a religious treatise. I have presented information from many sources to the effect that present and future lives are intertwined and even concurrent. The fact that you believe in some far-off day does not reduce the need for preparing now for your very own judgment day whenever it comes.

17. As a Christian, will I meet Jesus when I arrive in heaven? As a Buddhist, will I meet Buddha? As a Muslim, will I meet Mohammed?

It is possible but not very likely that you would have immediate contact with these or any other being living on the celestial planes. Recall that I said in part 1 that modern science has shown us that everything in the

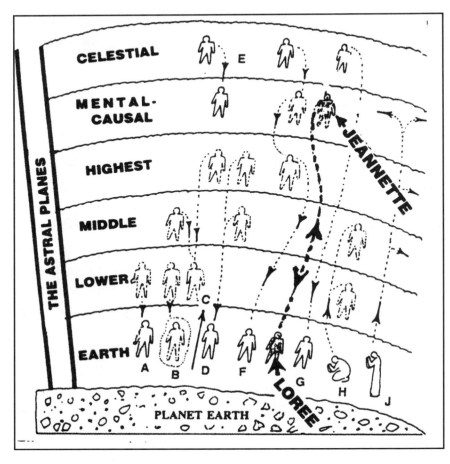

Fig. 17–2.—Interplane Communications

Key to the Diagram
A. The act of obsession
B. Ghosts, apparitions, "astral shells"
C. Rescue teams and invisible helpers
D. Teachers, masters, guides, protectors
E. Higher teachers, masters, angelic beings, light beings
F. The source of intuition and inspiration for the best creative activities of musicians, artists, poets, writers, sculptors, inventors, scientists, and the best channeling.
G. Guidance received by Jesus, Buddha, Mohammed, and all divinely inspired souls.
H. Prayers by the living for the newly "dead"
J. Skilled meditation and prayer

universe is vibratory in nature. As this is being written, the newspapers warn that it is dangerous to watch an eclipse of the sun without use of dark glasses to protect the eyesight. This is because the incandescent sun is sending out energy at such a high vibratory level that it would permanently damage the light-sensing cells in the retina of our eyes.

The dwellers of the celestial planes, the location of all man's great religious figures and gods, are such bright and shining beings that their energy would damage the new arrival from the earth plane. Hence it is not likely that you would meet any of these beings in person.

All such enlightened and compassionate beings, however, do have the ability to lower their vibratory rate by coming down through a succession of other beings on the various levels. (This is what the scientists call transduction, accomplished through step-down transformers.) So yes, it is possible for you to see and meet a being who fits your own image of the being you desire to meet.

18. Are angels a figment of the imagination of the prophets and writers of the Bible, or do they really exist, as Billy Graham says they do?

Yes, angels do exist, as Billy Graham says. Some have wings as portrayed in the beautiful and imaginative drawings and paintings of the Middle Ages.

The subject of angels is complex. There are many types or classifications. It would take a lengthy chapter to do justice to the subject, so we will have to be content with the following oversimplification of a very wonderful and helpful aspect of God's great universe.

The angels of the most numerous types are largely concerned with the health, well-being, and advancement of man, beast, fowl, plant, and mineral life forms. They work at all levels on the astral plane as depicted in figure 17–2. They evolved from what in Sanskrit are called *devas,* meaning radiant beings. Jeannette's most recent graduation from the earth plane, her then rapid spiritual development on the highest astral plane, and her further spiritual growth on the mental plane resulted in her having a choice of activities. She chose to serve as a guardian angel of love and kindness (fig. 17–2.) Also you might want to reread chapter 11, which describes her angelic assistance to the persons departing their physical bodies in the current phase of the Mideast War. (Also see section A of the bibliography.)

The highest form of angels are known as "archangels." They are concerned mainly with performing major tasks in the overall operation of our universe. For simplicity we might call them "God's helpers." They are great beings of infinite wisdom, love, and compassion who in every sense deserve the phrase "the power behind the throne." Or we can say these are the top executives who help with the day-to-day management of our little part of the solar system.

Both of the above categories are true angels and should not be confused with the term "guardian angel." This is a broadly descriptive term that is applied to the friendly and helpful beings on the mental plane who work with us as individuals in this present lifetime as well as those who are attracted to us at various stages of our mental, emotional and spiritual growth. These beings are all in the human line of evolution. They are more properly called guides, masters, teachers, helpers, protectors, and so on.

The categories in figure 17–2 consist of loving and compassionate beings interested in serving man and his Creator to the fullest of their individual capabilities. In ages past when a sage, seer, mystic, or even a simple shepherd saw such a being, it was certainly natural to use poetic terms to describe it. Today it is possible for some highly clairvoyant persons and very advanced meditators to encounter angels and describe them as light beings. [As of the date this is written, Jeannette is functioning as a guardian angel of love and kindness. See chapter 11).

19. Have beings in the worlds of spirit described what they see as "material things"?

Yes, literature is full of such reports from dwellers on the different planes. A typical report from the middle astral planes about sixty years ago stated:

The surface of the zone is diversified. There is a great variety of landscape, some of it most picturesque. We, like you, have lofty mountain ranges, valleys, rivers, lakes, forests, and the correspondence of all the vegetable life that exists upon your earth. Trees and shrubbery covered with the most beautiful foliage, and flowers of every color and character known to you, and many that you know not, give forth their perfume. The physical economy of each zone differs from every other. New and striking scenes of grandeur are presented to us, increasing in beauty and sublimity as we progress.

In 1977, the first member of our research team made the transition from this plane to the higher astral plane. Melvin Sutley died at the age of eighty after a life full of love and service to his fellow man. When we talked to him a year later through the telepathic channel Sarah Hieronymus, he had this to say:

SUTLEY: This talk with you is something I have been awaiting for a long time. Yes, I think back to the days we worked together and I had the privilege of sitting in on the information that was given us and the times you visited me when I was in bed in Philadelphia and unable to get up and go to meetings in the lab. This is marvelous. It is difficult to communicate in this manner, and I must get used to the medium.

This place where I have been living is so beautiful, George, so beau-u-tiful. I know that all that beautiful country that you brag about where you used to live in Florida cannot possibly measure up to this.

MEEK: Good!

SUTLEY: The trees are so green, the grass is so green and so velvety, air is just like breathing wine, if you could do such a thing. The sun is not too hot, the breezes are lovely. Oh, it is marvelous. I don't know why I hung around that place Philadelphia so long. I didn't know it would be like this.

MEEK: That answers a question in my mind. I frankly wondered why you did stay quite so long in that nursing home when we could see what a terrible strain it was on you. When you were alone you couldn't have have the best of attention and help—it was a tremendous strain for you to stay there, those last few months particularly.

SUTLEY: Yes, if you and Paul and Hans and [unclear] had stayed there with me, I think I would have made it a few more years. But I'm so sorry I hung on so long because this is... Oh, they tell me I'll forget about it, you know, and I will. [Jeannette on arrival gave similar detailed comments that correlated perfectly with Melvin's report ten years earlier.]

MEEK: I looked at the early transcripts from the Philadelphia lab where you and R.B. were present and saw reference to the name Margaret. I am ignorant in this situation. Was she your wife?

SUTLEY: Oh, yes! That's my wife [with great pride in his voice]. You know what, George? She waited for me [sounds almost like tears in his voice]. I kept her waiting all that time. I didn't know. [He really feels sad about that].

Nine months after the above contact with our friend Melvin, we were pleasantly surprised when he came through at the end of one of our scientific discussions. We had been talking, by means of a channel, about the nature of time in the worlds of spirit with Dr. William Francis Gray Swann, who had died in Philadelphia in 1962. (See appendix C.) Here is the relevant portion of the transcript:

MEEK: All right, we will be glad to share this tape with Paul, Hans, and Will. This is the extent of our questions. If there is anything else tonight, Dr. Swann, that you or one of your teammates wish to share with us...

SWANN: Yes, we have two new arrivals in our midst: Melvin and Margaret.

MEEK: Good evening, Melvin, and good evening to you, Margaret. Although I didn't have the pleasure of meeting you here on the earth plane, we have heard much about you and it is a great pleasure to greet both of you.

SUTLEY: You are very kind, George. Since I have grown stronger, we have given up the old home and decided to join our old friends and acquaintances and remind them that we were in communication with them before we came to place.

We thank you very much for your kindness and your thoughtfulness over a period of time. We are glad again that the experiment is going forward. Frankly, it has gone so far afield from what we had in mind that I can foresee that when the breakthrough comes, it will be enormous.

MEEK: Two thoughts come to mind. First, you mentioned the help that we gave. It is deeply to be regretted that we were not able to give you more help, more assistance in the closing months. We felt very keenly that due to geographical separation and occupational problems, we were not able to share more with you. We deeply appreciate the great part that you played in the original activity in setting up this whole interplane project. We recall frequently your initial contact with Paul and R.B. and the key role that you played. We also well remember the financial contribution which you made to our work.

SUTLEY: It was of great interest to me and still is. You are most kind, you and Paul and Hans.

MEEK: What are you finding of interest these days, Melvin, to make use of that marvelous mind and soul you have?

SUTLEY: Margaret and I have not been here very long, but we find there is quite a lot going on. We have been in on some very interesting discussions, and we have fitted some of our knowledge gained in our last earth experience with some of the ideas being given out by some here who have not been involved in a life experience for a long, long time.

We have been circulating from group to group deciding where we belong. It is very wonderful to be here. For a while I thought it had to be as it was before with the house we had just like that one in Philadelphia and everything that I had before. [The thought-created house Melvin had constructed for himself when, after death, he arrived on the highest astral plane. Many mediumistic communications refer to thought-created structures and surroundings.] But I found out that it just wasn't satisfying. It is going to be much, much more interesting here.

MEEK: We are delighted with that news, Melvin. We hope that you find it possible to come in frequently in the months ahead as we get more regular communication with Dr. Swann and our friends.

SUTLEY: True. Tell Paul and Hans hello for me. I am most grateful to them.

MEEK: We will share this tape with them so they can hear the inflections of joy and excitement in your voice.

The significance of this second communication from Melvin is that it shows how rapidly this man and his wife have progressed from the "summerland" or highest astral to the mental and causal planes, where Dr. Swann and his teammates are. This rapid upward movement through the worlds of spirit can be attributed to three factors. First, Melvin and Margaret had led lives of great service to their fellow men. She was a renowned surgeon; he was a specialist in hospital administration and one of the founders of Spiritual Frontiers Fellowship.

Second, through his lifelong friendship with Arthur Ford the medium, he was well acquainted with the reality of life after death and some of the conditions in which he would find himself after death. (Readers of this book will have the same advantage!) Third, Melvin himself decided he wanted to move on upward to meet his friends. The Swanns and the Sutleys had been close friends and coworkers for many years in Philadelphia.

Thus, in this very personal experience with Melvin, the first of our research team to make the transition, we see confirmation of the answer to question 12—that like attracts like; that is, we will find ourselves with friends and former associates. We also confirm the answer to question 6, that living a life as was portrayed on the stairway in figure 17–1 is the fastest, most certain, and most pleasant way to have a wonderful life after one dies.

20. Will I retain all of my five senses when I leave my physical body? Will I acquire any new senses?

You will no longer have any need for and in fact will lose the senses of taste and touch. Your senses of seeing, hearing, and smelling will be extended far beyond your present capabilities.

Beginning on the middle astral levels, you will know a person's thoughts by merely looking at him. You will know if what he is saying really agrees with his feelings. He cannot pretend to be anything but what he really is. There is no place for phonies in the worlds of spirit. In general, your sensitivity to your surroundings will be greatly enhanced. You will feel far more alive than when you were in your earth body.

21. To what extent, if any, does a person's formal education determine his new level of existence?

Very little indeed, as you will understand by examining figure 17-2 carefully. Persons who are considered to be the most learned and with many university degrees may find themselves on the lowest portions of the lowest astral planes—if they have grossly misused their knowledge. Back at square one, to use a current expression.

Persons who have had little or no formal education in this lifetime may find that they have arrived on the highest astral in the Biblical land of milk and honey, if throughout earth life they have traveled the proven path for individual soul development diagrammed in figure 17–1.

22. What about food in the afterlife? Do people have to prepare and eat food?

No. Not having a physical body, you will have no need for food.

The higher, finer, vibratory bodies in the worlds of spirit can draw all needed energies directly from cosmos.

23. Is there marriage in the next life?

Yes and no.

Bear in mind that marriage is a device that evolved over the centuries as nature's efficient method of providing the necessary care for the well-being and growth of children until they could fend for themselves. Since there is no generation of new children on the planes of spirit, there is no compelling need for the institution of marriage as such.

On the other hand, if your present marriage is a completely happy one and you would find your greatest happiness in association with your mate when he or she arrives, then it is fitting that the relationship continue. If the present relationship is unhappy, then it will automatically cease. All will find themselves in surroundings and with people with whom they are attuned.

24. Is sexual intercourse possible between males and females when they no longer have physical bodies?

No. Intercourse between the male and female of most species of all life forms—humans, all animals, birds, plant life—was provided by the Creator for the purpose of the continuation of the species; that is, for the production of offspring. In the worlds of spirit there are no offspring among the human dwellers therein. Hence there is no functional need for sexual intercourse. A medical doctor friend, a good psychic diagnostician with much experience in the field of psychiatry, provides an additional insight. "In the lower astral, there is a lot of so-called funny business going on. This includes orgies. It is not uncommon for physically incarnate people to attend these during the hours when they are asleep. This accounts for a lot of dissipation of energy during sleeping and waking hours."

However, as was pointed out earlier, a new arrival on the astral plane is still filled with all the thoughts and bodily desires intact. A person who on the earth plane was filled with lust usually finds himself on the lowest portion of the lower astral. He is still steeped in his attachment to earth and may

Suburban News

A publication of

North Jersey Community Newspapers

41 Oak St., Ridgewood NJ 07450-3805

CARRIER ROUTE PRESORT
PERIODICAL POSTAGE
PAID AT PARAMUS, NJ 07652
& OTHER ADDITIONAL
MAILING OFFICES

‖‖CAR-RT WSS**C-004
82

KRAUS
22 RYERSON ST
OAKLAND NJ 07436-2645

ADDRESS CARD

If we haven't heard from you...Please respond

Do you want to continue receiving **Suburban News**

Seven town-specific newspapers

It's Free!

Of course, we want to continue sending you the **Suburban News** each week. We hope that the local news and ads provide you with a newspaper that has become an integral part of your life. Please help us to continue mailing the Suburban News by taking the time to fill out this card, placing it in any envelope, and mailing it to:

Circulation Department, Suburban News
12-38 River Road, Fair Lawn, NJ 07410

Name _____ | Signature: _____

Address _____

Town _____ | Date: _____

not realize that he is dead. He is thus what we term earthbound. He may, in this condition, get a vicarious thrill out of wandering into a bedroom as an undetected witness to sexual intercourse. Eventually, when he evolves and moves up to higher levels, such fascination gradually disappears.

I use the word "gradually" advisedly. I was somewhat amused to learn that boys will be boys even on the middle astral planes. It came as a surprise to hear an entity (a former university professor) tell us quite frankly that in his present plane of existence he missed having contact with the beautiful form of the female physical body.

However, there is another—and extremely important—aspect of sex that we should mention. Any reasonably mature adult knows that there is far more to the matter of sex than the physical-pelvic aspect. The greater our comprehension of the cosmos and all we have encountered therein, the more obvious it becomes that a duality of forces appears to underlie everything. Some of the more obvious manifestations are day-night, love-hate, male-female, yin-yang, sweet-sour, cold-warm, positive-negative electrical charges, etc.

Each individual human being has within himself a mixture of male and female characteristics—physically, mentally, and emotionally. A person with a female physical body may have the mental and emotional characteristics we usually associate with a male, and vice versa. The important point to note is that we are each, to a degree, both male and female.

We carry this basic duality with us when we die and proceed to move on to one of the worlds of spirit. Many of those persons on the mental and causal planes with whom we have come in contact in our research have referred to having lived some of their earth lives in male physical bodies and some in female physical bodies.

From our research it appears that the melding of the male-female polarity becomes complete only when we accept the final rebirth and move to the celestial planes.

25. Twenty years ago, my daughter died at the age of six months. Did her soul or spirit remain that of a baby?

No. She was received on the middle or higher astral plane and given the most tender and loving care. She was given every opportunity for continued growth and development. She will reach adulthood. If you wish to meet this daughter after you have made the transition to your next level of life, you can do so—that is, provided you are not now living a life that will result in your arrival on the lower astral. In that case, there might be considerable delay before you could meet your daughter, because she almost certainly will not be found on that level.

If she has not been alerted to be on hand when you make the transition, all you have to do is to send out mentally a call for her with all the love and longing you can muster. She will come.

Children in the afterlife are cared for very much as they are here. There are those who find their greatest delight in mothering the motherless and in teaching the young. Under such unselfish care, the children reach mental and bodily maturity much as if they had remained in this world. In most cases, though, they will still return for additional learning experiences on the earth plane of existence.

The etheric process of development is interesting; children need mother love no less in spirit than in earth life. Little do most people know how close the afterlife is, how close its inhabitants come to us, the influence they exert on us, or the result of our thought vibrations upon them. Then again, as the children grow, they keep in touch with us, and when we ourselves go into the afterlife, they know and greet us as we enter "the life that has no night."

There are, in the next life, institutions of learning just as we have here. What is more, the inhabitants do not cease to study and increase their store of knowledge when they have reached a certain age. I can assure you that your daughter will continue to grow in body, mind, and spirit. [Just as our daughter, Nancy Carol, did. She made the transition at age two weeks.

When Jeannette Meek, her mother, made the transition, the two came in touch with each other promptly.]

26. Can the passage of a loved one through purgatory (the lower astral) be speeded by payments of money to a priest?

No. This centuries-old practice does nothing but add to the coffers of the church, and perhaps give a small, psychological consolation to the one who pays the money.

We are all bound by the absolutely impartial and inescapable law of cause and effect. In each of the first three gospels, Jesus is reported as saying, "For with whatever measure ye mete, it shall be measured unto you again." In Galatians 6:7, Paul says, "Be not deceived, God is not mocked: For whatever a man soweth, that shall he also reap."

If during your life you caused pain, hardship, and unhappiness to others; if you allowed yourself to become a drug addict or alcoholic without recovery; or if you were a murderer or suicide, you will reap precisely as you have sown. You will find yourself in the lower astral levels. This most undesirable place has been described in religious lore by the words purgatory, hades, and hell. A person who finds himself in this condition solely because of his own unwillingness to grow mentally and spiritually is totally on his own. No priest can post bail for such a person. Study figures 17–1, 17–2, and 19–1 for a deeper understanding.

Fortunately, the lower astral is completely bypassed by those whose lives included few if any of the above-mentioned activities.

27. In some religious groups it is customary to pray for the souls of the dead. Does this practice serve any useful purpose?

An emphatic yes! The newly deceased person is very much alive. As a pilgrim arriving in a new land, there are many strange and even bewildering experiences on every hand. (How can it be otherwise, when our religious lore has been so deficient in this area?)

It is a great comfort for this pilgrim to hear your spoken or unspoken prayer on his or her behalf. Tender thoughts of love, good wishes, encouragement, heartfelt thanks for shared experiences—these are all easily received by the deceased if he has arrived on the middle astral plane. Even if he is asleep or wandering on the lower astral plane, such prayers are useful, although their effectiveness may be somewhat delayed until the departed has experienced the trials and tribulations which are the fruits of his life's actions.

28. How is time measured on the planes that make up the sprit worlds?

It isn't measured. There is no serial time as we know it. Locked as we are into our present space-time system, it is almost impossible for us to comprehend living in a timeless world. Since our earliest childhood we have each been locked into a life that is rigidly bound into a system of seconds, minutes, hours, days, weeks, months, years, centuries, and eons.

There are no trains to catch at an appointed time. There is no first-of-the-month time payment to be met. There is no growing old or getting wrinkled and senile with passing years.

29. What about political or governmental systems on the astral planes? Is there any equivalent of money?

There is nothing to resemble countries, states, or nations. The principal divisions result from like souls being grouped with like souls. There are no presidents, dictators, kings, or rulers.

Nor is there a need for money or a unit of exchange. Supply is available for all wants to all individual souls.

The generating force is thought, difficult as this may be to comprehend. You can think and have beauty and happiness. You can think base desires and they will be fulfilled—which shows how a benevolent Creator can demonstrate to you the foolishness and triviality of those desires. It is very like the situation in which one finds himself today in life on the earth plane. You may have all the money you want, but you still are not happy. It is pretty clear that happiness on any plane does not depend on money.

Sooner or later each will wake up to this fact and seek the only things that genuinely satisfy—continuing mental, emotional, and spiritual growth.

30. Some mediumistic persons claim they get guidance from departed spirits—counselors, protectors, guides, angels, and so on. Is there any truth to such statements?

Yes, there most certainly is. Any advancement humanity has made in the past four thousand years is due in part to such guidance, often explained as intuition. Indeed, most revelations received by sages, mystics, prophets, and spiritual leaders have come from such sources, as illustrated by paths D, F, and G in figure 17–2.

However, this is an area requiring much additional research in the decades ahead. The human mind is fantastically complex, with the ability to spin dreams that stagger the imagination. Hence it is very difficult to make certain that a particular idea or thought is coming from a friendly and helpful intelligence in the worlds of spirit.

The daily practice of deep relaxation and a prayerful attitude over a long period of years seem to be the only proven way of hearing that still, small voice within—a voice which may, in fact, be from your personal helper in the world of spirit. But, I repeat, this is a most hazardous business. The pages of history are filled with acts which stemmed from self-delusion with respect to heavenly guidance.

31. Can I put much trust in what I am told by a Spiritualist medium?

Yes, no, and then again, maybe.

The very best mediums today, referred to as channels, almost never give sittings to any but their closest personal friends or to serious researchers. My twenty years of searching over much of the world has disclosed only a mere handful of such persons.

Communications from spirits closest to the earth plane—the easiest to contact—are, for the most part, useless as well as inaccurate. This covers ninety-five percent of all survival information that comes through a medium

on the platform of a Spiritualist church. The problem with such mediumistic communications is that the most readily contacted persons are those
who are on the nearest astral planes. These are often recent arrivals and are
no more knowledgeable than before they left their physical bodies. This,
combined with the noise—or the sheer difficulty of communication—gives
rise to misconceptions.

Communications from more elevated spirits also suffer greatly in transmission. A crude analogy is a game in which several people sit on chairs
spaced closely together in a row or circle. A sentence is whispered into the
ear of one person who quickly whispers it into the ear of the next person,
and so on until the last person. When the message in final form is then
repeated to the group, everyone has a good laugh at the gross distortion
that has taken place in the transmission.

No specific rules of guidance can be given. In general, however, the
communications that come through a medium who makes a business of his
or her mediumship, charges for sittings, and handles one client after another,
day after day, hour after hour, should not be taken too seriously.

There are exceptions, of course. In the past fifty years, few of the really
great mediums had other means of financial support than the modest fees
received from their sitters.

Robert R. Leichtman, M.D., in a private communication discussing
this point, says:

There are those who assume anyone who dares to charge for a reading
or sitting with a medium is instantly declaring himself to be a fraud.
True, I see legions of half-baked, half-witted mediums and psychics
running amok at meetings, hustling readings, and making a lot of money.
Nevertheless, a good medium is worth something. Good advice is worth
something. People have no problem paying their minister for his services. The pseudo-spiritual and sanctimonious often protest that "what
comes from spirit should be as freely given as it was freely accepted."
That sounds good, but it is a bit impractical, as one does have to pay

grocery bills and rent despite what might be great psychic talent. The time it takes to develop the talent takes time from other activities also, and this should be compensated.

A bereaved person should strictly avoid trying to contact the loved one through a medium. At best the medium will be tapping the sitter's mind for a description of the deceased. When the medium says, "I see standing beside you…" and proceeds to describe fairly accurately the departed loved one, the medium is usually not in touch with the departed. Moreover, some of the more mischievous of the earth-bound spirits—the only level that most such mediums can reach—delight in masquerading as the departed person and can be quite adept at putting on a performance that convinces the sitter that he or she is in touch with the loved one.

It is infinitely more useful for the bereaved to sit quietly every few days and send prayerful and loving thoughts to the loved one. Again, study figure 17–2. Visualize where the loved one is. Speak out loud, as though the loved one is present. Often, in fact, he is! Wish him well in his new surroundings. Of course, tell him that you miss him but that you are no longer grieving, because you know that he has returned home, that he is among loved ones who are looking after his every need. State that you are so thankful for his love and companionship, and that you are content that you will again meet and continue your relationship—if that then suits your mutual purposes. All of this is a far more effective way to spend time than running from medium to medium—and it saves money!

32. Twice you have mentioned the many pitfalls that you and your fellow researchers were obliged to avoid in communicating through even the very best of channels. What about the persons in spirit who try to communicate with you? Is is easy for them to communicate?

Yes and no. It is relatively easy for those on the lower astral or even the lowest part of the middle astral planes to communicate. But they are of little help in providing useful knowledge for mankind.

It is extremely difficult for those on the mental and causal planes to communicate, even through the best of mediums. The difficulties experienced by spirits in trying to communicate are outlined in great detail in the book *Gilda Communicates* by Ruth White and Mary Swainson, in the chapter "Technical Difficulties."

For a short explanation of these difficulties, consider the comments of Leslie Flint, the great English medium. Flint's mediumship is of a very rare kind. His helpers in the spirit world use ectoplasm from his body to create an etheric mass a few feet from his head. The spirit communicator "talks into" this substitute voice box and the spirit's voice becomes audible to all persons in the room. In the course of fifty years, many hundreds of spirit beings have communicated through this system. In his book *Voices in the Dark*, Flint reports an important sitting as follows:

A spirit with a marked French accent introduced himself as Richet and, in the course of conversation with him, we learned that he was the late Professor Charles Richet, the eminent French physiologist who in 1905 was President of the Society for Psychical Research in London and who won the Nobel Prize in 1913.

He told us that not only must the communicating entity lower his own frequency to the lower one of earth, but simultaneously he must remember what his voice sounded like in his lifetime and recapture memories of happenings which will give proof of his identity to the person with whom he wishes to communicate. When the professor was asked by a sitter whether he could see or hear people at a seance, he answered that it depended on the amount of concentration he put into the effort to do so. If he focused his mind sufficiently, he could both hear and see people on earth; but he found it simpler to apprehend their thoughts before they were uttered as words.

He grew quite testy when someone suggested that sometimes the voices of communicators from the spirit world did not sound exactly the same as their voices during their life, and he said it was hardly likely they would sound the same, seeing they were not using the same vocal cords they had in life. He added that we must take into account, also, that the communicating spirit was trying to concentrate on three different things at the same time while communicating. Most of what Richet said made sense to me. I had often heard communicators remark on the difficulty of "speaking through this box thing which wobbles about all the time," or say plaintively how confusing it was to remember some event which would prove beyond doubt who they were while concentrating so hard on other things. As the disincarnate Professor Richet remarked rather grumpily, "The miracle is that we can communicate at all."

Yes, indeed, it is a miracle that we and they can communicate at all. But in spite of all the troubles at both ends of the line, we are beginning to bridge the gap between our physical world and the worlds of spirit with increasingly sophisticated electronic devices.

33. Mediums and other psychic persons speak about raising the vibrations when trying to contact those who have died. Is this just nonsense?

No. Recent advances in physics and related fields of science show that matter—indeed, apparently, everything so far encountered in the cosmos—is composed of energy, which is vibratory in nature. Consider the following analogy: If we put a pan containing ice on the stove and apply heat, the atomic particles increase their vibratory action. Thus the vibratory rate of the newly formed water is higher than that of the solid ice. Applying more heat to the water raises its vibratory rate still more. Then the application of still more heat can cause the water particles to fly into space. The resulting steam represents energy at an even greater level of atomic vibration.

Conditions relating to thought, both in this and in the astral world, represent energy levels and vibratory rates far beyond that of steam. We have every reason to believe that this admittedly crude analogy of changing vibratory levels of ice-water-steam applies to thoughts in the physical astral, mental and spiritual, or celestial levels. Each succeedingly higher level of thought in the worlds of spirit represents even higher rates of vibration.

Look at this the other way around. People living on the mental and causal level cannot come directly through the mind of a poorly developed medium. Their rate of vibration is so high that they might damage the medium's brain if they attempted direct contact. Communications from these higher levels have to be relayed down in steps. Look again at figure 17–2 and note particularly items D and F. Often the relay-stations or transformers that serve to step down the vibratory level cause a loss in content, a loss in quality—and may even represent a gross distortion of what the higher level being is trying to pass down.

34. Can a person ever visit the astral planes while still residing in the physical body?

A very definite yes, and this offers one of the most exciting prospects for humanity's development in the century ahead.

Usually when we go into deep sleep during the early portion of each night's rest, the astral body leaves the physical body but remains connected to it via the so-called silver cord. As it is of course already existing in the astral world, it has no trouble traveling at that level. What it can or may do in such travel is too long and involved a topic for us to discuss here. I can say, however, that it is able to gain knowledge that will be of help to the conscious mind upon its return. This is one reason why many people learn the habit of saying, "Well, let me sleep on that matter."

Senile persons and persons nearing death often find that their astral bodies are starting to spend time away from their physical bodies, even in the daytime, when they are judged to be awake. This, of course, is the basis of so much of the research reported by Kübler-Ross, Moody, Osis, Crookall and others. [This situation occurred with Jeannette Meek during the closing weeks of her illness.]

What is still more exciting is that through meditation techniques it is possible to sit down in a quiet and secure spot, relax, and then attune to the higher astral planes and let the astral body travel. Remember that the levels of mind and soul are contained in the astral body so that they too are out of the body. This allows direct mental contact with intelligences on the astral plane. Not only can such contact greatly increase the knowledge available to the meditator, but it can also bring increased wisdom that can be gleaned from the much older and wiser souls.

35. Often small children insist that they see and hear other children or playmates who are invisible to adults. When they get older they seem to grow out of this. Are their playmates figments of their imaginations?

Most certainly not! We have recently learned that up until the age of six or seven, the eyes of many children can see light at wavelengths considerably shorter than those detected by the eyes of adults. But they also have a high sensitivity to energies outside our own electromagnetic spectrum. Sensitivity to this latter type of energy in adults is possessed only by those relatively rare individuals who are known as clairaudients and clairvoyants. This ability of small children enables them to see and tune into what we call the astral or etheric world—perhaps even into the middle astral planes.

A recent study has found that a large number of children today have imaginary playmates or companions such as an invisible older friend. What's more, the same study has found that apparently having a make-believe friend is apparently good for a child.

A recent *Psychology Today* article says that up to sixty-five percent of the kids in a study group reported having imaginary friends. The article points out that only a generation ago, children with imagined playmates were thought to be hallucinating and dangerously removed from reality.

Researchers have since found that children who have make-believe companions are different from those who do not—they are said to be less aggressive and more cooperative, they smile more, they show a greater ability to concentrate, they are seldom bored, and their language is richer and more advanced.

36. Why is the word "causal" combined with the word "mental" in identifying the next-to-the-highest plane shown in figures 2–2 and 17–2?

Many persons know little or nothing about the role that thoughts play in creating our material world. Hence, let me give some specific examples to show how thought actually causes things to happen in our everyday world—and in the worlds of spirit.

Consider this book. Every facet of it is the result of many individual thoughts by hundreds of people. The words you read are the product of my thoughts. The paper was made on machinery perfected over decades by hundreds of individual thinkers. An operator used her thinking process to help lay out these pages and operate the word processor and laser printer. Then there were the contributions made by the printer, the bookbinder, the transportation company, the bookseller, etc.

Let's consider our own bodies. The knowledge acquired in the last thirty years regarding the subject of psychosomatic illness shows clearly that our thoughts can and do affect the several trillion cells in our own bodies and bring about either health or illness.

In part I, I presented the concept that your mind is the programmer of your brain (the computer). Your brain is of no functional value unless your lower self—your very wise unconscious mind—programs the body on all details of its routine daily functioning. Unless your conscious mind thinks thoughts, you cannot turn from one page to the next, nor can you weigh and evaluate these thoughts that my fingers are pecking out and putting on paper.

In my book *Healers and the Healing Process*, I told how Olga and Ambrose Worrall, seated in Baltimore, Maryland, focused their thoughts on a laboratory six hundred miles away in Atlanta, Georgia. They undertook to use their minds to accelerate the growth rate of individual shoots of rye grass planted in a pot in the laboratory. They did increase the growth rate by more than five hundred percent. Later, Mrs. Worrall, still seated in Baltimore, focused her thoughts and healing energies on an atomic cloud chamber in the Atlanta laboratory. She displaced matter in the cloud chamber sufficiently so that it was possible to record the resulting disturbance on photographic film.

In subsequent research, Mrs. Worrall succeeded in changing the molecular bonding between hydrogen and oxygen in water—one of the most stable substances in our physical world—and most sensitive to subtle radiations. (Recall that your body and brain are largely composed of water.)

With these few examples of our growing understanding of how our thoughts can cause effects in the world around us, it will not be such a great step to explain why the term causal is coupled with the term mental in describing the levels nearest to the level of the Godhead. Most of what we have in this three-dimensional world, including most of our inventions, first existed in the mental and causal worlds.

Please refer again to figure 17–2. Note path A. This indicates how a soul or spirit in the lowest astral plane can obsess a person living on the earth plane—that is, cause a person to be possessed. Paths D and F indicate how friendly and helpful souls or spirits on the middle and highest astral planes can serve us as guides, protectors, and teachers. If you can accommodate these ideas, then it should not be too great a step to contemplate that extremely wise intelligences on the plane nearest our Creator have many good ideas far in advance of anything we yet have on the earth plane. This is the true course, the pathway of humanity's highest creative work—for artists, sculptors, writers, medical discoveries, inventions, and so on. It is represented by path F.

Thus we now have a rapidly growing basis for understanding the power that thought has in the whole scheme of creation. We can understand as never before the causal nature of thought.

37. How do you personally feel about reincarnation?

I grew up in a strictly orthodox Midwestern Christian Protestant denomination. As the decades of my study, searching, and world travels passed, I continued to reject the subject of reincarnation. Not until I was well past the age of sixty had I assembled sufficient knowledge to change my views. Not until I had logged hundreds of hours of contact, via mediums, with beings in the worlds of spirit did I find the evidence overwhelming and convincing. Only then did my conscious mind accept the evidence that is a reality.

With this background, I understand the feelings of those who have closed minds on the subject. As stated at the start of this book, I have no desire to preach any dogma, gospel, religion, creed, or "ism."

In the next four questions and their answers, I deal with the subject of reincarnation. While some people in our Western culture will consider these comments with an open mind, many readers will not. In fact, the latter may even label the whole subject "stuff and nonsense, unbelievable, obnoxious, and distasteful."

If you are one of the latter, simply skip over the questions and their answers and move on to question 42, so as to concentrate on the overall theme of this book.

38. Perhaps you should clarify what is meant by the term reincarnation.

Yes, that is very important. There are many misconceptions about the term. *Webster's New Third International Dictionary* defines:

Incarnate—invested with flesh or bodily form

Disincarnate—having no physical body

Reincarnate—rebirth in new bodies or new forms of life, especially a rebirth of the soul in a new body.

I use the term strictly as "rebirth of the soul in a new body"—a new human body. The Eastern concept of metempsychosis or the transmigration of souls maintains that human souls can go into animal bodies. However, there is no evidence I am aware of to support this belief.

39. I am mystified as to how reincarnation actually works. Can you give me some specific guidance on this bewildering matter?

I can certainly try. But let me caution you that what follows is a highly simplified presentation of an extremely complicated subject, which we are only beginning to understand.

In recent years, as the world's raw materials have become scarcer and higher in price, there has been a trend toward recycling. Whereas in the past we shipped vast quantities of materials to the dump or incinerator, today we have started to reclaim or recycle materials. Now we carefully gather up empty aluminum cans and sell them back to the mill. At the recycling plant they are melted or molded into ingots. The ingots can then be used to extrude shapes for storm windows, automobile parts, or more cans. Similar recycling plants are set up for reuse of automobiles, glass containers, newspapers, shipping cartons, and many other useful and increasingly valuable materials.

Has it not occurred to you that if death is the end for each of us, our Creator's plan is a very wasteful one? What in all the world is more precious than a human soul? Stop for a moment and think about yourself. Do you have any material item more valuable than your own self—your soul? Does it make any sense to think that an all-wise Creator is going to send your precious soul to the dump, the graveyard of your dreams, the incinerator? Has not science in this century showed us that energy cannot be destroyed—that it can only be changed from one state or vibration to another state or vibration?

What could be more logical than the recycling of your soul?

Therefore, if you will permit a bit of fanciful humor or a late twentieth-century parable, let us consider the following diagram, "The Original Recycling Plant."

Let's start our discussion at the bottom left of the diagram. Here I stand. At age eighty-one, I have traversed much of this lifetime. I am headed for the elevator. Sometime in the years ahead, I will cast off this worn old body. I will be ready for a free ride to some higher plane of being.

I see three elevator doors, all closed. Which one of these will open and offer a ride? Well, as I said earlier, I have learned that this is a world of cause and effect. I have learned that nobody can cheat or beat the rules of the game. Hence the door that opens will be determined by the life that I have led.

If I have failed to learn the rules that have been spelled out over the centuries by the enlightened souls who have done their best to illuminate the path to a happy future life, I have no one to blame but myself. In the school of life I must then be judged a failure. I get an F on my report card for this life. The door marked F opens and I soon find myself in some very uninviting surroundings when I am kicked off at the second floor.

One who did somewhat better in learning his lessons and putting them in practice will be welcomed for a ride on elevator B to the third floor. On the other hand, for the person who has been very diligent in learning and putting into practice the admonitions illustrated in figure 17–1, door A opens and he or she takes the express to the fourth floor. [This is what happened to my co-author, Jeannette!]

Let's assume that I get only as far as the second floor. I will have three questions:

- Stay where I now find myself—for a very long time, even centuries by earth time.
- Start looking for some beings whose light shines through the gloom and who offer to lead me upward to the third floor where I can get some more schooling.
- Because of my gross preoccupation with myself and burning desire to get back to my old haunts, I stumble into the down elevator.

If the latter happens, I find myself again squeezed into a small physical body for still another life on the surface of planet earth. The recycling plant has done its job! Or to put it more crudely, by using the terminology of the computer programmer—"garbage in, garbage out." I am merely back at square one and have to start all over again. In fact, if my life has been particularly hurtful to others, I may find I have some additional handicaps

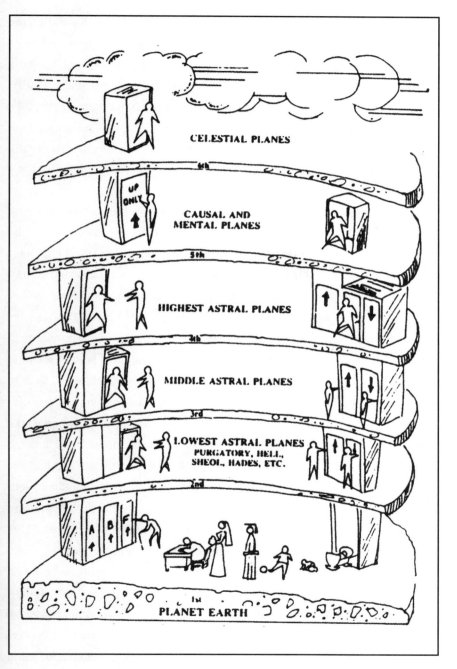

Fig. 17–3.—The Original Recycling Plant

to carry in this new life. For centuries the Oriental religions have used the term "bad karma" to cover this accumulation of unlearned lessons.

If a person finds himself on the third floor, the first order of business is to relax and enjoy life. In principle, it is possible to apply oneself sufficiently to earn a ride up to the fourth floor. On the other hand, if the individual prefers to come again to the challenge of living and learning on the surface of this fascinating and often frustrating planet, he may eventually take the down elevator back to the first floor. There is no pushing for a decision. It is always up to the individual.

When a person finds himself or herself on the fourth floor (having arrived by express from ground level, or the local from the third floor), he or she is really in for a delightful period of post-mortem life. [This happened to Jeannette.] One of my humor-loving friends says that in any description of the summerland we should abandon the old phrases of "pearly gates" and "streets paved with gold." We should talk in terms of wall-to-wall carpeting, air conditioning, and celestial stereo! This is not as facetious as it sounds. We learned the crucial role our thoughts play in forming our reality in this nitty-gritty everyday world. We will find that in heaven or hell our thoughts will play an even greater role in creating our reality.

Here, as always, the law of cause and effect is operating. If a person's mental or spiritual growth continues to the point of graduating, he will undergo what has been referred to as the second death. This involves shedding the astral body that has served as a containment vehicle; then the mind and soul can progress to the higher level of vibrations of which the next planes are composed. The person is thus born on the mental and causal planes. [This happened to Jeannette after nine months on the higher astral planes.]

If because of great altruism and compassion for his fellow beings a person wishes to return from the mental and causal level for still another earth walk, this is the last level from which a return can be undertaken.

Much of the material in this book has come from our friends now living on the mental and causal planes. Most of these left the earth plane within the last thirty-five years. There is much reluctance for any of these intelligences to come back to the chaotic world of today. Some say frankly that they will wait and take a look at things in the twenty-first century. Who are we to suggest otherwise? They need be in no hurry.

If they continue to work and study and grow mentally and spiritually, they eventually have the possibility of taking the local elevator that makes the short run to one higher level—the celestial planes. Again, due to the change in the vibratory levels of matter, this involves shedding what has loosely been called the mental body and accepting what is known as the final rebirth.

Since, as I've pointed out elsewhere, modern man can hardly conceive of the level of existence of the celestial planes, we can end our effort to explain the reincarnation process here.

40. Those who believe in reincarnation talk a lot about karma. What is karma? Is karma good or bad?

If my actions are beneficial and help me and my associates or family to grow mentally and spiritually, the effects will be good. This is called good karma. If the actions hurt my mental and spiritual growth or that of others, they are called bad karma. A reader well versed in the Eastern religions and/or theosophy may think that this is an excessively simplfied discussion of good and bad karma. It is intended as such. There is reason to believe that much of the traditional concept of karma is as distorted and nonproductive as are many portions of the dogmas and creeds of various religions. Discussions with present occupants of the mental and causal planes indicate that until man evolves sufficiently to understand the true nature of karma and the whole reincarnation process, he will do well to stick to basics.

To be honest, I must acknowledge that the concept of karma is not universally accepted. There are those who think that no matter how greedy, lazy, dissolute, jealous, and hateful a person may be in this life, all such actions are forgiven, and a life of eternal bliss awaits the saint and the sinner alike. As the evidence shows, however, such thinking is unfounded.

41. In spite of what some people say about the possibility of reincarnation becoming obsolete in the new age, I might want to look more deeply into what people around the world have thought about reincarnation. Where can I find the best source of information?

I consider the best single book to be *The Phoenix Fire Mystery* by Joseph Head and S. L. Cranston, Julian Press, 1977. If I had had this book thirty years ago, it would have greatly speeded up my own research. It is, by far, the finest summary I have found of the centuries of East-West dialogue on death and rebirth from the worlds of religion, science, psychology, parapsychology, philosophy, art and literature, and from great thinkers of the past and present.

It is gratifying to know that what I have presented in my writings on the subject of reincarnation is in no way contradicted by this monumental study by Head and Cranston.

42. I have had intelligent pets with wonderful personalities. What happened to them when they died?

A long-cherished pet is just as certain to survive the death of its physical body as you are. Cats and dogs have provided a substantial amount of evidence on this point over the years. There are even well-documented cases of the survival of pet monkeys and favorite horses. If the survival of well-loved pets were not a fact, heaven or the afterlife would be a less happy place for animal lovers all over the world.

Unlike man, the lower animals do not ordinarily possess individual souls. Each species has what is known as a group soul. All wild animals and animals raised by man for food return to their respective group soul upon the death of their physical body. However, it seems that a domesticated dog or cat that becomes a pet takes on a certain individuality from its very personal association with its master. According to Maurice Barbanell in his book, *This is Spiritualism* (Spiritualist Press, London, 1959), and others, it seems to develop a humanness that it did not formerly possess, as a part of the friendship. It may be a part of man's contribution to the evolutionary scheme to confer this attribute on those animals who come within his care.

It could be this quality that determines the survival of a beloved pet. Beyond the grave, the domesticated animal will not continue the process of perfecting its individuality, but will return ultimately to the group soul of its species. But for all animal lovers, yes, when you come to your next life, you will find your favorite pet waiting. [Our daughter, living with her mother, Jeannette D. Meek, on the highest astral plane, in 1990, told us the pleasure she was having with her dog, Snowball Allen, a friend's pet which had recently departed its physical body.]

43. Immortality and eternal life certainly appeal to me. How can I comprehend such a mid-stretching concept?

Locked into our little individual lives as we are, it seems almost presumptuous to think we are made of the same stuff as God our Creator. But this is the truth of the matter. We have no trouble thinking that God will be alive for ages to come. Therefore, if we think of ourselves as some small part of Him, we can visualize more clearly that we already have eternal life. Stop thinking of eternity as something in the far-distant future. You live in eternity now. Eternity is this instant, the next instant and so on. You already live in eternity. After all, you cannot die!

44. One final question: Of all the messages you have received from all the persons you have contacted in the worlds of spirit, can you single out one that is the most helpful to those of us trying to understand these issues?

Yes. Wilfred Brandon dictated four books through the mind and hand of Edith Ellis of New York City during the period of 1935 to 1956. In 1935, Brandon gave his credentials in *Open the Door* as follows:

I was killed in 1132 in France, again in 1373 in England, and once more I fell by the sword in 1647. I was too weary to incarnate again until 1762, when, like many other adventurous spirits, I wished to try life in America, a life of free democracy. The New World was for me only a soldier's grave. No use of my heart or mind was made on earth for six centuries. Whatever I have made of myself as a thinker was accomplished here in the worlds of spirit. I hope to incarnate once more, but only when the Age of Reason arrives. How far distant that time seems now!

Here is the Brandon statement that I single out as a fitting and helpful conclusion for part V:

There is no death. That is the key to what you have to learn in the years to come on earth. You are all preparing to end your lives with bodily death. You have made no preparation for going on with existence. Most people, if they have a belief in immortality, have such a fantastic idea of what it will be like that they are not making plans for anything but an eternity of idleness and some singing, for which they perhaps haven't the least talent.

What a picture!

Here, we are far more interested in getting on with life than you are. We see our wasted incarnations and wish we might have been sure of life after death. We could have fitted ourselves to meet it had we known what we know now.

Certainly Wilfred Brandon's experiences in lifetime after lifetime for 850 years support the key message of this book—*the continuity of life*.

Chapter Eighteen
Unlimited Horizons

The implications of the material presented in the preceding seventeen chapters are enormous, profound and sweeping. Consider first the implications for mankind as a whole:

• For the first time in mankind's history, communication with other planes of existence via electronic instrumentation has provided inescapeable evidence that death is merely a new birth into continuing life.

• It is now certain that individual consciousness—often referred to as personality—continues to exist and to function in a disease-free and pain-free environment.

• The needless and destructive fear of death can be removed, as well as the deep concern over the passing of a loved one.

• The taboo that our whole culture has imposed on the whole subject of death can be removed.

• The knowledge that the mind and soul can transcend death of the physical body will help Man begin to understand that it is his own thoughts and emotions that largely determine whether he will experience sickness or will enjoy vibrant physical and mental health in this life.

• Each individual can begin to realize that he or she is a permanent inhabitant of an apparently limitless cosmos, and not just a soulless, maze-running rat or corn-pecking pigeon, as proclaimed by present-day behaviorist psychologists.

• In the decades or centuries ahead, when instrumental systems evolve to the point where they can be used to communicate with the mental and causal planes—and mental telepathy becomes the norm— mortal Man will have access to the accumulated wisdom of the ages on any subject.

• This book has developed solid confirmation in support of the key spiritual teachings assembled in what Christians call the Sermon on the Mount and in the basic moral teachings of Judaism, Hinduism, and Buddhism.

• We can begin to jettison some of the accumulated nonproductive religious dogma that has ruined countless lives over the centuries to the extent that it imposed burdens of fear and guilt.

• Finally, the material assembled in this book suggests the possibility of constructing a bridge by which science and spirituality can meet on common ground, with the resulting changes in establishment science and organized religion benefiting all persons on the planet.

Yes, the implications are indeed staggering. They necessitate, for example, tremendous changes in our present theories and practices for treating both physical and mental illnesses. They do the same for our existing political and social structures, and for all religious creeds.

There will never be a better world until there are better people in it. Since society is composed solely of individuals, major changes in

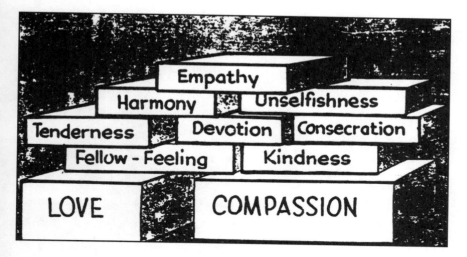

Fig. 18–1.—Time-Proven Foundation Stones

individuals will be reflected in civilization as a whole. Therefore, the important thing at this point is to consider a better means for achieving major changes individually.

Since we have already shown that research into life after death has confirmed the core truths of the great spiritual traditions, it behooves us to pay attention to what those traditions have to say about "better." In my judgment, two points stand out.

First, all of them have some form of the Golden Rule. What Christians learn as "Do unto others as you would have others do unto you," members of other faiths also learn, although the language differs slightly. Second, whether it be Judaism, Buddhism, Taoism, Confucianism, Jainism, Zoroastrianism, Islam, Hinduism, or Sikhism, the same idea about how to relate to others is at the heart of each ethical system or program for self-improvement.

These emotional patterns are the time-proven foundation for a satisfying life here and hereafter.

A simple, painless, practical, pleasant, and proven technique has been devised by which each person can build this spectrum of emotions into daily thoughts and actions. Each night, just before falling asleep, and each morning immediately upon awakening, slowly, thoughtfully, silently, prayerfully and with eyes closed, repeat this sequence of thoughts: "May the wisdom, love, and compassion of the Christ-consciousness so permeate my being, that there is less and less of selfish ego, and more and more of the love for and service to all mankind—to the end that God's infinite spirit shall manifest in me and in all and through all persons on this planet!"

We have shown throughout this book that your astral body—your butterfly body, if you please—can and does travel while your physical body is asleep. It is possible, in a meditative state, to learn to visit the various planes or levels of the diagram we have called "The Interpenetrating Levels of Life and Consciousness" (fig. 2–2). You don't have to wait for the death of your physical body. Ordinary psychics regularly visit the lower levels. Extraordinary psychics such as those with whom I have been working visit the higher levels. The truly enlightened, however, have become familiar with all levels, from the lowest to the highest, and have realized that those levels are present with us here and now.

This enlightened condition is rare, of course, and has been limited to a mere handful of sages, seers, mystics, prophets, and holy men—people who reached levels of cosmic consciousness while still in the flesh. What they tell us is that their condition is possible for us, too—you and me—if we are genuinely set in our hearts and minds on having God, not ego, as our center of self.

Moreover, they have often condensed their experience into systems designed to help people in their quest for God. These spiritual systems provide efficiency and security for the unwary beginner. Their essence is not a moralizing lecture on good behavior, but rather a method by which one can personally experience a deepening of wisdom, a growth in character, and a realization of higher values in life. All of these systems have some form of prayer and meditation as a major part of the discipline involved.

Prayer and meditation have the effect of dissolving the ego—the petty little personal self that wants to remain in control and get the glory. As as ego goes, the light and love of God shine forth more and more clearly, so that the personal becomes transpersonal. There is an outreaching, a self-lessness, an all-embracing attunement with the human race and all creation. The other side becomes more and more integrated into our awareness in everyday waking life, not occasional transcendental states. The various levels then become perfectly obvious aspects of the single reality, which is none other than here and now. You can learn to tap daily the wisdom of the astral and higher planes without waiting until you shed your present physical body.

It is no accident that society's models of the fully developed human being, the worthy examples, have included many saints and holy people. They have been revered for many reasons: their compassion, devotion, inspiring words of wisdom, service to the world, lack of fear about death, and tranquility and peace of mind and heart in the face of circumstances that for most others would be extremely stressful, if not overwhelming.

What has been their secret? Each of them, in his own way, arising from his particular tradition, has discovered the truth of the sayings, "Let go and let God" and "Thy will be done." A sense of the infinite replaces the usual narrow self-centeredness. The personal becomes transpersonal.

Their secret—and the message of this book—was captured in only four lines by R.W. Raymond:

Life is eternal;
and love is immortal;
and death is only a horizon;
and a horizon is nothing save the limit of our sight.

Yes, of course, there is a funeral at the end of the road—be you a mighty ruler, an office or factory worker, banker, scientist, international financier, priest, rabbi, janitor, homemaker, billionaire industrial tycoon, or pope.

Every one of the billions of souls occupying a physical body travels a similar road. But now you understand the seeming magic by which your soul and mind, memory banks, and personality will still be very much alive. You can now understand that you cannot cop out by the drug or suicide route. There is just no way that you can terminate the wonderful, total being that is you. This is the magic of living forever: you cannot die! And though you will be living forever, the quality of life—here and hereafter—depends on you.

A most outstanding autobiography, *The Magian Gospel* by Brother Yeshua (channeled by Charles C. Wise, 1978) concludes with this inspired insight:

> It is good to know that life goes on. Such knowledge permits life to be lived without fear. Of course, no one enjoys the pain that often accompanies the passage through the portal of death, but that is fleeting. Live not in the limitations of time, but in the intimations of immortality. Go onward and inward. Seek understanding and the Light. And, above all, be joyful.

You can now be certain that after your funeral your own precious mind, memory banks, personality, and soul will be vibrantly alive and ready to continue a journey that has unlimited horizons.

Man in the closing years of the twentieth century has at last rent the veil between heaven and earth. With the help of the material in this book and Jeannette's shining example, you have peered through to the "other side" and have acquired the priceless knowledge that—

YOU HAVE UNLIMITED HORIZONS

Chapter Nineteen
The Price Tag of
a Happy Forever

In day-to-day life in the physical world, we have to pay as we go. Food, shelter, clothing, education, pleasure, travel, and so on have to be paid for with money. But what about the next world—the world we will live in when we part with our physical body? Is everything free? Do we actually have to pay a price of some kind in order to have a happy forever?

Yes, we do have to pay a price if we want to live in a fine mansion on the middle of the highest astral planes. We cannot use our life's accumulation of dollars, francs, crowns, marks, cruzeiros, rubles, pesos, rands, yen, lira, etc.—even if we have millions or billions of them! And neither are plastic credit cards or IOUs of any value. It's a whole new scheme of things.

Someday when you have shed your physical body and walk through the door labeled "New Beginnings," you are due for a shock: Material wealth is of absolutely no value! You will find yourself in a totally non-physical world, a new nonphysical spirit world.

The coins of this realm are the nonphysical thoughts and actions which dominated your just-concluded session in life's schoolroom here on planet earth. Based on a review of your recent life experience, you will, in effect, be issued a new spirit credit card. The credit available to your account will be determined by the extent to which you did or did not live your recent physical life in accordance with the thoughts and actions diagrammed in figures 18–1 and 19–1.

No, the authors did not draw up this list of positive virtues. They filtered down to mankind over the passing centuries via guidance from the most enlightened souls in the spirit worlds.

However, if the reader is a medical doctor, a scientist, a psychiatrist, a psychologist, an engineer, an educator, a parapsychologist, or a possessor of any other advanced academic degree, he or she may think figures 18–1 and 19–1 are far too simplistic or nonscientific. Such readers may find the following terminology more comfortable with their present late-twentieth century mind-set.

The time-proven pathway to your Happy Forever is to:

- Realize that God is the invisible energy force or intelligence that animates every cell of every living object in the universe, including this planet on which we travel through space.

- Realize that for convenience, up to this time, mankind has been limited to calling this energy force by the terms "love" and "light."

- Realize that the passing centuries and all civilizations have demonstrated the need for loving oneself and for loving one's neighbors.

- Realize that all mankind's worsening economic, political, social, environmental, banking, nuclear waste, and military problems result from the mental and emotional energy form we know of as greed—the very opposite of the mental and emotional energy form we call love and light.

But carefully note—a person's academic degrees, no matter how many, are of no value when buying a ticket to a Happy Forever!

Fig. 19–1.—The Proven Path to a Happy Forever

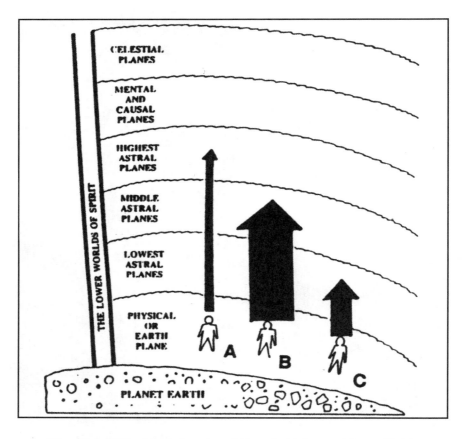

Fig. 19-2.—The Next Stop for all People Living on Planet Earth

After pondering your own life in relation to figures 18–1 and 19–1, you may still want to ask, "On what level in the spirit world am I likely to find myself?"

Not knowing you, I cannot answer your question. However, you can look at figure 19–2 and then re-examine yourself. Categories A, B, and C in the diagram are as follows:

A. Individuals who have made more than average progress in this and/or past lives and whose souls have evolved to the point that they just naturally are living their present lives in harmony with the characteristics depicted in figure 19–1 will arrive on the highest astral planes.

B. The average, kind-hearted, considerate, well-meaning, hard-working adults, and all infants and children, will arrive on the middle astral planes.

C. Greedy, cruel, selfish, materialistic, highly egotistic and unloving persons, including, for example, swindlers, rapists, unrecovered drug addicts, sex perverts, suicides, murderers, hardened criminals, and political despots will find themselves on the lowest astral planes. This classification includes those persons who failed to benefit from the spiritual learning opportunities provided in their just-concluded physical incarnation on planet earth.

The width of the individual arrow is roughly proportionate to the number of people in each category.

With the helpful understanding provided in figures 19–1 and 19–2, it would be well to decide on which of the three planes you want to function—and to start now to make some payments toward the purchase of your gate pass or ticket.

You can be sure the seat will be reserved for you. However, you have to decide *now* how much you are willing to pay for your ticket.

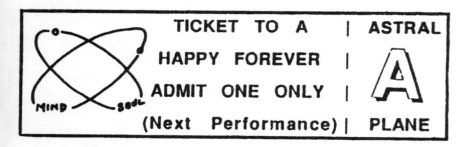

Fig. 19-3.—Your Gate Pass or Ticket

If you think you will wait
Until you get to the gate,
Sorry, that's too late!

Do you want a reservation in section A, B, or C?
Your actions will determine which it shall be, but Jeannette and I are happy in the knowledge that it is within the power of each of you to—
Live a Happy Forever!

The afterword on the opposite page is certainly not for self-glorification. It is offered as evidence that the basic concepts of life, as presented in this book, are time-proven and can be trusted.

Afterword
Happily Forever After

The fairy stories read to and by children in the last century and in the early portion of the twentieth century often ended with the assurance that the leading characters lived happily ever after.

The authors of this book had the great pleasure in playing roles in a fairy-tale-like romance that lasted for fifty-five years of physical life. During the last two decades of that period, their research and that of their professional colleagues in some twenty countries documented that death of the physical body is never a barrier to ongoing life.

In closing this book, they share with the reader the closing lines of an unexpected and uniquely personal message channeled via Mrs. Lucille McNames of Cedaredge, Colorado, on December 17, 1990. (Mrs. McNames is one of perhaps the dozen finest channels we discovered in twenty years of worldwide research for such talent.)

While most of her messages have come via the typewriter, an intelligence which described itself as the "Nameless Source" took control of her eighty-two-year-old hand and carefully, but forcefully, printed out its message in capital letters, letter by letter. The message, completely unsolicited, concludes—

...THIS ENTITY [GWM] HAS BENEFICIALLY FULFILLED HIS MISSION. ONE OF HIS REWARDS SHALL BE THE MERGING

OF TWIN SOULS BETWEEN SELF AND HIS BELOVED MATE.
FOREVER SHALL THEY BE SIDE BY SIDE, FOR THEY HAVE
EXPERIENCED LOVE BEYOND THE HUMAN CONCEPT OF
LOVE.

Jeannette and I hope the documentation we have assembled within the covers of this book now puts you, the reader, in a position to enjoy *your* "Graduation Exercise," be quickly at home in *your* "butterfly body," and embark on

UNLIMITED HORIZONS

and live

HAPPILY FOREVER AFTER.

Appendix A
Who Says So?

A t no prior moment in eight thousand years of recorded history, would it have been possible to assemble the insights into the basic nature of man on which this book is based. Only the year-after-year pioneering work by hundreds of courageous and capable researchers worldwide provided a database for rending the veil between man's everyday life in the physical and the equally real but normally invisible and interpenetrating worlds of spirit.

Database A

Many of the courageous persons listed here are scorned by their contemporaries. Some lost their positions. Some ended their lives in poverty. Some were imprisoned. A few were brought to untimely death. Very few have received the recognition they deserve.

This list is far from complete. However, it should be sufficient to cause any skeptically inclined reader to know that in greater and lesser ways, each of these persons deserves credit for relevant research as the database underlying this book.

Abrams, Albert; Anderson, Gilbert; Babcock, Erl; Bach, Margaret; Bandy, John & Roberta; Bayless, Raymond; Berger, Robert; Besant, Annie; Brown, William and Maria; Burr, Harold; Buschbeck, Hanna; Carey, Ken; Cayce, Edgar; Cerney, Will; Constable, Trevor; Cooke, Grace & Ivan;

Crookall, Robert; Crooke, Maurice; Crooks, William; de la Warr, George; Doyle, Arthur Conan; Drowns, Ruth; Edwards, Harry; Eisenbud, Jule; Essene, Virginia; Estep, Sarah; Flint, Leslie; Friedman, Simon; Fukari, T.; Geller, Uri; Gough, Bill; Gross, Jerry; Hall, Manley; Hamilton, Glen; Harris, Bertha; Heckmann, Hans; Hieronymus, Galen & Sara; Houck, Jack; Hudson, Thomas J.; Jevons, David & Ann; Jones, Paul; Juergenson, Friedrich; Karagulla, Shafica; Koenig, Hans; Kübler-Ross, Elisabeth; Laidlaw, Robert; Lakhovsky, M.; Leadbeater, C. W.; Leichtman, Robert; LeShan, L; Love, T. & J.; Luckwell, Judy; Mandel, Henry & Mary; Manning, Matthew; McNames, Lucille; Moody, Raymond; Mueller, George; Munters, Carl; Nagorka, Henry & Diane; Northrup, E.; O'Neil, William; Ott, John; Pegado, Agenor; Penfield, Wilfred; Peterson, Jean; Price, Leslie; Raudive, Constantin; Reich, Wilhelm; Reif, Royal; Ring, Kenneth; Rossner, Marilyn & John; Rudolf, Theodor; Russell, Walter; Scott, Lillian; Scott, Mary; Seidel, Franz; Shacklett, Bob; Sheldrake, Robert; Sherman, Harold & Martha; Shultz, Don & Shirley; Singer, George; Smart, Ted; Swainson, Mary; Tesla, Nikola; the Kirlians; Thompson, Howard; Tiller, William; Valentin, Ann; von Szalay, Attila; Ward, Robert; Welch, William; Wenzel, Martin; White, Ruth; White, Stewart; Worrall, Olga & Ambrose.

Database B
During the decades of the 1970s and 1980s, the authors supplemented their own knowledge by assembling a very informal International Advisory Panel of pioneering thinkers in many disciplines. In order to collaborate as fully as possible, the authors supplemented the heavy two-way flow of worldwide correspondence by frequent personal contact via five trips around the world and more than twenty foreign trips, which took them within 590 miles of the North Pole and within 730 miles of the South Pole.

Dr. Hernani Andrade, scientist and parapsychologist — Brazil
Itzak Bentov, Israeli scientist — United States

Maj. Gerhard Buchinger, psychic,
  UN Peacekeeping Force — Golan Heights
Joaquin Cunanan, psychic and spiritual healing — Philippines
Arthur Garside, business executive and psychic — South Africa
J. & M. Harsch-Fischbach, instrumental researchers — Luxembourg
H. T. E. Hertzberg, anthropologist — United States
H. L. Hingorani, Life Beyond Death Foundation — India
Nils Jacobson, M.D., psychiatrist — Sweden
Dr. Robert Jeffries, Edgar Cayce expert
  and parapsychologist — United States
Dr. D. M. A. Leggett, Surrey University — England
Alexander MacRae, electronic specialist — Scotland
Marcus McCausland, holistic health researcher — Greece
Prof. Dennis Milner, metallurgist and parapsychologist — England
Dr. Hiroshi Motoyama, scientist and Shinto priest — Japan
Hans Naegeli-Osjord, M.D., psychiatrist — Switzerland
F. O. Petersen, psychic researcher — New Zealand
Dr. Andrija Puharich, M.D., pioneer parapsychologist — United States
Jeanne Rindge, founder, Human Dimensions Institute — United States
Prof. Pedro Romaniuk, parapsychologist — Argentina
Dr. Alex Schneider, physicist, President, Swiss
  Parapsychology Association — Switzerland
Dr. Werner Schreiber, physicist and parapsychologist — Germany
Prof. Ernst Senkowski, physicist and parapsychologist — Germany
Dr. Sigrun Seutemann, homeopathic medicine — Germany
C. Norman Shealy, M.D., neurosurgeon — United States
Sir Kelvin Spencer, scientist — England
Count Mancini Spinucci, parapsychologist — Italy
Dr. Alfred Stetler, inorganic and nuclear chemist — Germany
Prof. Walter and Mary Jo Uphoff, parapsychologists,
  Founders of Spiritual Frontiers Fellowship — United States
Lyall Watson, Ph.D., biologist and author — England

Database C

The pioneering individuals listed in both A and B all had one thing in common—their contributions to mankind's knowledge were made while each
was still in his or her physical body.

However, the following individuals provided material used in this book
after they died and were buried or cremated. Their contributions most clearly
serve to help document the primary message of this book—the continuity
of human life.

Relatives, close friends, fellow researchers, and others:

Co-Author	"Died"	Country
Jeannette Duncan Meek	1990	United States
Nancy Carol Meek	1938	United States
Dr. George W. Mueller	1967	United States
Ann Blakeley	1989	United States
Angeline Fulton Duncan	1957	United States
Phyllis Garside	1960	South Africa
Dr. Wm. F .G. Swann	1962	United States
Dr. Konstantin Raudive	1974	Latvia
Melvin Sutley	1977	United States
Dr. Jessie H. Holmes	1942	United States
Eleanor Roosevelt	1962	United States
George Washington	1799	United States
Abraham Lincoln	1865	United States

Plus relevant channeled material in the following books:

Valentin, Ann, and Virginia Essene, channelers. *Cosmic Revelations*. Santa
   Clara, Calif: S.E.E. Publishing, 1987.

Valentin, Ann, and Virginia Essene, channelers. *New Teachings for an Awakening Humanity*. Santa Clara, Calif.: S.E.E. Publishing, 1986.

Pelley, William Dudley. *The Golden Scripts*. Noblesville, Ind.: Fellowship Press, 1961.

Sananda. *Oneness Remembered: UltraConsciousness*. Castle Rock, Colo.: Meridian Light Publishing, 1990.

Appendix B
Historical Overview
on the Development of
Instrumental Contact with the "Dead"

by Prof. Walter Uphoff, Mary Jo Uphoff,
Dr. Ernst Senkowski, and George W. Meek

1. Early Efforts to Contact the Dead

1928   Thomas Edison works on equipment he hopes will permit communication with the dead, using a chemical apparatus with potassium permanganate.

1936   Attila von Szalay starts to experiment with a Packard-Bell record-cutter and player, trying to capture paranormal voices on phonograph records. He gets some voices but the quality is poor.

1947   Von Szalay buys a Sears Roebuck wire recorder and gets somewhat better-quality voices, but the wire is too thin and often gets so tangled that this method is also abandoned.

Early '50s   Von Szalay starts experimenting with magnetic tape recorder and gets voices, some of which are quite clear.

2. The Electronic Voice Phenomenon (the tape recorder and microphone stage)

1956   Raymond Bayless joins von Szalay in experiments and writes an article for the *Journal of the American Society for Psychical Research* (written in 1958, published in 1959).

1959   Friedrich Juergenson, a Swedish artist and film producer, goes into the woods to record bird songs. On playback, he discovers paranormal voices. After four years of experimental recording, he calls an international press conference (1963).

1964   Juergenson's first book on this subject appears in Stockholm as *Roesterna fraen Rymden (Voices from the Universe)*.

1964   Von Szalay gets voices of his deceased relatives on tape for the first time.

1965   Dr. Konstantin Raudive, a Latvian psychologist and philosopher, visits Juergenson, concludes the phenomenon is genuine, and starts his own experiments in Bad Krozingen, Germany.

1967   Thomas A. Edison speaks through the German clairvoyant, Sigrun Seutemann, in trance, about his earlier efforts in 1928 to develop equipment for recording "voices from the beyond." Edison also makes suggestions as to how to modify TV sets and tune them to 740 megahertz to get paranormal effects. (Session recorded on tape by Paul Affolter, Liestal, Switzerland.)

    Franz Seidel, Vienna, develops the "psychophone."

    Theodor Rudolf develops a goniometer for Raudive's experiments.

1968   Father Leo Schmid, Oeschgen, Switzerland, is assigned a small parish to give him time to experiment with taping voices. His book, *Wenn die Toten Reden (When the Dead Speak)*, was published in 1976 shortly after his death.

Raudive publishes his book, *Unhoerbares wird Hoerbar (The Inaudible becomes Audible)*, based on seventy-two thousand voices he has recorded.

1971   Colin Smythe, Ltd., England, published expanded translation of Raudive's book, *Breakthrough: An Amazing Experiment in Electronic Communication with the Dead.*

Marcello Bacci and co-workers in Grosseto, Italy, make weekly instrumental contact with spirit communicators, which is said to continue in 1991.

1972   Peter Bander, England, writes book on the voices, *Carry on Talking.*

During the 1970s and 1980s, two membership organizations in Europe and one in the United States are formed to experiment with and study the implications of EVP: the VTF (Verein für Tonbandstimmenforschung) and FGT (Forschungsgemeinschaft für Tonbanstimmen) in Germany and the AA-EVP (American Association for Electronic Voice Phenomena) in the United States, founded by Sarah Estep.

1973   Joseph and Michael Lamoreax record paranormal voices after reading Raudive book, *Breakthrough.*

1975   William Addams Welch, a Hollywood scriptwriter and playwright, authors *Talks with the Dead.*

Note: Space does not permit details of work by many other researchers, some of whom are Paul and Edith Affolter; David Lothamer; A. J. Loriaux; Harry and Gerri Loudenslager; Ray Patterson; Andrija Puharich, M.D.; Mary Sharpe; Cyril Tucker; Paul Bannister; Raymond Cass; H. V. Bearman; Carlo Corbetta; Virginia Ursi; Bill Weisensale; David Ellis; Richard,

Fred, and Joseph Veilleux; Davis Peck; Gilbert Bonner; Richard Sheargold; Alex Schneider; Robert Crookall; Hans Heckmann; and Burkhard
Heim.

3. The SPIRICOM Research

1971   Paul Jones, G.W. Meek, and Hans Heckmann, Americans, open
            laboratory. First research to create a two-way voice commu-
            nication system far more sophisticated than in the EVP
            approach.

1978   William J. O'Neil, using a modified side-band radio, has brief
            but evidential contact with an American medical doctor said
            to have died five years earlier.

1982   GWM makes a trip around the world to distribute taped record-
            ings of sixteen excerpts of communication between William
            J. O'Neil and an American scientist who died fourteen years
            earlier. He also distributes one-hundred-page technical report
            giving wiring diagrams, photos, technical data, and guidelines
            for research by others. Upon return, he holds a press confer-
            ence in Washington, D.C., and distributes (free) the tape cas-
            settes and technical manuals to the representatives of the press,
            radio, and TV.

4. Sophisticated Instrumental Systems (Voice Only)

1982–88   Hans-Otto Koenig, Germany, develops sophisticated electronic
            equipment using extremely low-beat-frequency oscillators,
            ultraviolet and infrared lights, and so on.

1985–88   Jules and Maggy Harsch-Fischbach, Luxembourg, with spirit
            help, develop and operate two electronic systems superior to
            any of the EVP equipment up to this time. The communications

become significantly more dependable and repeatable than the systems developed earlier.

5. Photographs of Deceased Persons on TV Picture Tube

1980s   Researchers in several countries have pictures of the dead appear sporadically on their TVs. There is no control over the appearance of the images.

1985   Klaus Schreiber, Germany, with technical assistance from Martin Wenzel, begins to get images of dead persons on TV picture tubes, using opto-electronic feedback systems. There is positive identification in many cases by accompanying audio communications, including audio-video contact with Schreiber's two deceased wives. This work is the subject of a documentary TV film and a book by Rainer Holbe of Radio Luxembourg.

1987   Jules and Maggy Harsch-Fischbach, with assistance from an earthside colleague and from the spirit world, get TV picture sequences of good quality.

6. Use of a Computer System for Two-Way Communication

1980–81   Manfred Boden, Germany, obtains unsolicited computer printout from spirit communicators.

1984–85   Kenneth Webster, England, receives (via several different computers) 250 communications from persons who lived in the fourteenth to sixteenth centuries. Most printouts are in English text consistent with speech at that point in history. Personal details fully supported by library research.

1987–90   Jules and Maggy Harsch-Fischbach establish sustained computer contact with superb guidance and assistance from otherworld collaborators. The allows submission of technical questions with high-speed computer printout of the carefully considered replies.

7. Use of the Telephone System for Two-Way Communication

1960s–
1970s

Scott Rogo and Raymond Bayless, Americans, conduct extensive literature research and publish a book, *Phone Calls from the Dead* (1979). They report many well-documented cases of the newly dead endeavoring to communicate with their bereaved survivors on "unfinished business."

1981–83

Manfred Boden has unsolicited contact with communicators of nonhuman evolution. (Gets massive phone bills for unsolicited calls!)

1990

Jules and Maggy Harsch-Fischbach, with superb guidance and cooperation from the higher planes, use a standard telephone-answering device to receive unsolicited incoming telephone calls from a scientist collaborator in the spirit world. The voice is clear, easily understood, and substantially free of static. This activity continues.

Appendix C
Additional Information on the Nature
of Time in the Worlds of Spirit

The answer given to question 28 in chapter 17—*How is time measured on the planes that make up the worlds of spirit?*—was very elementary. The true situation is so far beyond the comprehension of lay readers that we sidestepped some of the complexities. For the technical or scientific reader, the following may be of interest.

Several times a year for several years in the 1970s, the electronic specialists connected with METAscience Foundation utilized the services of two of the most capable mediums who had been discovered by searches in this country and abroad. Through them we discussed our research efforts with a team of former scientists and inventors now residing on the mental and causal planes. The team in the worlds of spirit was organized and directed by Dr. W .F. G. Swann, who in the 1960s was reported in *Who's Who in Science* as follows:

Swann, William Francis Gray, physicist; b. Ironbridge, Shropshire, England, Aug. 29, 1884; 1900–03, Royal Coll. of Science (London), Univ. Coll., King Coll., City and Guilds of London Inst., 1903–07; B.Sc., London, 1905, D.Sc., 1910; assoc. Royal Coll. of Science, 1906; hon. M.A., Yale, 1924; hon. D.SC., Swarthmore Coll., 1929; hon. F.T.C.L., London 1936; Litt.D. (hon.), Temple U., 1954. Chief Phys.

div. Dept. Terrestrial Magnetism, Carnegie Inst., Washington, 1913–18; mem. faculties U. Minn., U. Chgo., Yale, 1918–27. Bartol Research Foundation of Franklin Inst., 1927–59, dir. emeritus, 1959–62, sr. staff advisor Franklin Inst. Labs for Research and Development, 1945–62. Fellow Imperial College of Science and Technology (London, Eng). Author: *The Architecture of the Universe,* 1934; *Physics,* 1941. Contr. to study cosmic rays, atomic structure, relativity and atmospheric electricity. Died 1962.

Of course, in keeping with the Biblical admonition to test the spirits to see that they are who they say they are, we established in 1972 that our communicator was in fact the man referred to in the above biographical sketch. This was made easier in the case of Dr. Swann because one of our team members, Melvin Sutley, had been a very close personal friend of Dr. Swann. The Swanns and the Sutleys both lived in Philadelphia and had the closest of friendships. Melvin, who died in 1977, was the first of our research team members to make the transition.

After reading the above biographical sketch, the reader might say, "This certainly shows the intellectual level Dr. Swann reached during his recent stay on the earth plane. I wonder on what level of figure 2–2 he is now functioning?"

We contacted Dr. Swann many times over a period of five years and had many hours of discussion. He told us that since his death in 1962, he spent only a short time on the mental-causal level. He told us that he is almost formless and is largely pure mind. He is the organizer and leader of a large team of scientists, philosophers, mathematicians, and inventors, most of whom passed over within the last fifty years. Dr. Swann has already made the decision that upon completion of the project on which his team is now working, he will accept the final rebirth, shed his mental body, and move into the causal levels above.

In preparation for a session in July 1979, my associates and I had carefully composed six questions for submission to Dr. Swann and his associates—

questions that had an important bearing on decisions we were facing on the design and operation of some very sophisticated electronic equipment. Here is a portion of the transcript of our session through the medium.

MEEK: All right, question number five: Can your energy be made to interact with a stream of electrons in a vacuum tube such as a cathode ray tube or in a traveling-wave antenna?

SWANN: If so, it would have a scattering effect. A wave-guide as we understand it would possibly be the better equipment to work with than the cathode ray idea. We do not know if it would interact with that, but we believe it would.

MEEK: And the the sixth and last question, of a somewhat different nature. First, by way of explanation, we speak of the vibratory nature of all creation. To identify vibratory rate, you and we speak of higher and lower frequencies. Yet you and other communicators have told us that there is no time in your dimension. Therefore, this question: How can we discuss frequency and frequency stability without a time base? The word frequency denotes cycles per unit of time. Yet you say you have no time in your dimension. How is it possible to discuss vibratory rates and frequencies independent of time?

SWANN [chuckling]: We feel that there is a great deal of misunderstanding in this area. Our lack of time relates to days, hours, minutes, and seconds such as we knew on the physical plane. Our area of dimension is a type of frequency in itself. The vibrating energies here are those which comprise that which we are. They even now comprise a portion of your own being, but you will experience them more fully after you lay aside the physical body and lose the connection with your present etheric body and astral form and frequency. So that is the nature of dimension of being—that which is at a higher frequency.

On the physical plane, atoms are in motion and are vibrating at such a higher rate that although there are great spaces between them, the surface actually appears to be solid. Here the spiritual atoms far outnumber your physical atoms and are vibrating and interacting with each other at a far greater rate than on the physical plane or on the astral plane. They are also somewhat different in composition. It is what many others have called "finer matter," because all energy is matter in some form or another.

This energy which comes into your area from other sources functions according to the numerical atomic numbers governing such energies. They are different from those on the physical plane inasmuch as they are not measured by time. They are not measured by so many vibrations per second. They are composed of an extremely fine substance which does not follow the laws of the physical plane. In making the transition from the physical plane, a person must go through an intermediary zone which is known to many on the physical plane as the astral world or the "summerland" and comprises a number of areas where vibration changes, or the nature of energy changes.

At last on the upper astral planes, the being dies or lays aside the astral body, much as he laid aside the physical body and proceeded in a body of finer matter into the area where we now live. [Jeannette made this gradation eight months after she arrived on the highest astral plane.] The energies which come into this area are from a much greater being, one who has evolved far beyond the imagination of most beings upon the physical plane where you now reside. This energy is a pure light and as it comes into our area, it becomes differentiated. This is the energy that we use. It is not possible to find words to describe it.

We have said "frequency" several times because it seems to fit that which we work with, but it is not frequency measured in days, hours, minutes, or seconds. There is very little with which to describe this energy. Let us say that it is very fast. It comes in spurts. So far as our measurements are concerned, it could be slowed down if we could get it to be constant. We could possibly hope to compress it into a more solid beam that would provide exactly what we are looking for: a carrier of voices.

We would desire to use this because of our plans to place these instruments in many dimensions, in each of many dimensions in the world of spirit. We thought that since this energy comes into many of the higher dimensions, it would be more native than anything else that we could plan to use.

Perhaps I have not made it clear that to us frequency is that which we can see, which we can feel, or which affects us in any way. It has no magnetic qualities. It is pure energy although tinged with the rate of atomic energy existing on our plane. One cannot now measure it in any way. You express a vibration in gigahertz and we say, "Yes, it is akin to that."

We have not true measurement here. We have a name for it, but we have no true measurement that you would understand. (And I can already imagine your associate Paul saying, "Try us!") It is only a term, just as your term "gigahertz" was coined to name something which previously had no name. So that is what we have done here—coined a term for what we are working with.

MEEK: All right, we will be glad to share this tape with Paul, Hans, and Will. This is the extent of our questions. If there is anything else tonight, Dr. Swann, that you or one of your teammates wish to share with us...

SWANN: Yes, we have two new arrivals in our midst, Melvin and Margaret. [The continuation of this transcript involving the Sutleys was presented in the answer to question 19 in chapter 17.]

From these comments by a scientist with the qualifications of Dr. Swann, it is obvious that we earthbound mortals, locked as we are into our little, three-dimensional, sequential-time system, cannot explain the workings of the cosmos within the framework of what we now know of the electro-magnetic system.

Appendix D
Notes on Reincarnation

by Robert R. Leichtman, M.D.

Robert R. Leichtman, M.D., supplied some thoughts on reincarnation after reading an early draft of our book, After We Die, What Then? *Dr. Leichtman is a psychic of outstanding ability and the author of* From Heaven to Earth, *a twenty-four-book series of mediumistic interviews.*

Y ou make several statements about reincarnation that sound a bit too permissive to me. I have never found that the personality (which is what survives physical death initially) can make simple choices such as "to go on the causal planes or reincarnate." If that were the case, I doubt that more than a very tiny percentage would ever return to the earth plane. While free will and the development of wisdom to choose are objects of incarnation, this free-will choice rarely would extend to deciding whether or not to reincarnate. The soul, in the average person, is impelled to reincarnate again and again because there are magnetic ties which keep pulling it back to earth again until it is complete. There are various laws of karma (or call it universal law, if you like) which demand this. It is unfortunate that the surviving astral personality and even the surviving mental essence of the personality would like to believe differently, but this is usually not the case. The soul is concerned with the evolution of consciousness and the work of service. Many can stay a long time on the inner levels

281

working toward that, but there is often unfinished business in the life of that soul—business that can only be worked out here in the earth plane. There is a certain magnetic appeal that this unfinished business applies to call people back into incarnation.

I have seen the tomes that are written by people who get overheated with the notion that God is a loving Father who would not permit his children to suffer, so "of course He would not make us come back here!" Unfortunately, some lessons are a bit painful but are necessary anyway. Every good parent feels some anguish at times when his own children fight to stay home from school or fight to stay away from the dentist or rebel against getting cleaned up and doing their chores, but the long-term progress of their children toward maturity demands that parents discipline their children to ensure their progress and to avoid creating a monstrous and childish mess which demands indulgences and has temper tantrums during the adult years. When the life of the personality gets too strong, it often tries to speak for the spirit within and begins to make up a self-serving concept of God that is something resembling a Santa Claus who showers a lot of gifts on "nice" people but not quite so many on "bad" people.

While it is true that a lot of difficulty and immaturity does get worked out after passing over, and many new talents and insights are gained, this is similar to the lawyer who learns a lot of theory in law school but still hasn't had any real-life, personal practice in the field. Insights, compassion, talent, and harmony—whether gained in heaven or in an earthly school—must be grounded, eventually, in the physical plane. That is the way new light enters the physical plane and collective humanity is enriched. Escape to heaven, however desirable, is not always possible, except for short bursts between lives. Not liking that idea has nothing to do with its reality.

Appendix E
Twelve Types of Evidence for the Continuity of Human Life

For readers wishing to make further personal studies on the continuity of human life, we point out that there are masses of material in these twelve areas:

1. Historical and Religious Writings. Since the beginning of recorded history, in all parts of the world, and in most of mankind's religions, there has been a common thread that indicates survival.

2. Deathbed, Near-Death, and Out-of-Body Experiences. Careful research has clearly established that people in various cultures and with totally different religious backgrounds see loved ones and/or helpers coming to help them make the transition from their dying physical body into their new state of existence. Research has also clearly documented that the real you can leave the body and travel, and that this same spirit body (referred to by Apostle Paul two thousand years ago) carries you into your next state of existence.

3. Apparitions, Hauntings, and Ghosts. Encounters with ghosts over four thousand years in all parts of the world indicate that something survives death of the physical body.

4. Obsessing Spirits. Obsessing spirits (the "demons" of the Bible) are still a reality today. They may be elementals, thought-forms, or spirits or souls of people who have departed their physical bodies and who, due to their baser habits of thought and behavior, are very much confused and in darkness. Still being attracted to the earth plane from which they have only recently departed, they attach themselves to the magnetic auras of living persons. They actually affect the thoughts, emotions, and actions of the obsessed person.

5. Spirit Doctors. Very careful research by medical doctors, psychiatrists, psychical researchers, and others suggests that healers in various parts of the world do, in fact, get help from dedicated medical doctors who themselves now live in the worlds of spirit. These doctors desire to continue their ministrations to ailing humanity. From their present vantage point, they know far more about the causes of and cures for physical and mental illness than they ever did when occupying their physical bodies.

6. Spirit Photographs. Dozens of photographers in many countries, using many kinds of cameras and film, with many types of lighting conditions (including total darkness) have obtained photographs of persons known to have died and whose bodies were buried or cremated. While this phenomenon is easy to duplicate by fraudulent means, there are fully documented cases of the genuine thing.

7. Materialization. From Biblical times down to the present, competent witnesses have observed, touched, examined, and even weighed bodies of persons and animals known to have died and to have been buried or cremated. Our present-day studies of the phenomenon and the rapid expansion in our knowledge regarding the physical universe and the interpenetrating nonphysical universes at last make it possible to begin to understand the natural laws behind this miracle.

8. Reincarnation. The beliefs of more than half of the world's billions of people, together with scientific research, suggest that the individual soul survives the death of the physical body and may, under certain circumstances, inhabit a new human physical body.

9. Space-Time Relationships. The mind, personality, and soul already exist in a separate and interpenetrating space-time system. This same interpenetrating, space-time system is where we continue to live when we cast off our physical body.

10. Conservation of Matter and Energy. We have seen that science now accepts as one of its basic tenets that matter-energy can be neither created nor destroyed. The higher, finer matter that is our spiritual body continues to exist after the grosser physical body decays and returns to nature as a gas, water vapor, and particulate matter (dust).

11. Communications from Mediums and Telepathic Channels. From the earliest Bible days down to the present moment, there have been and are persons who have the ability to live in two worlds at the same time, and thereby bring communications from persons who have passed into the world of spirit. (Jeannette's nurse Loree is an example.)

12. Electronic and Light Systems. This research has been under way for forty years. In the late 1980s, this work was greatly stimulated by the breakthrough of O'Neil and Meek (described in chapter 4). This activity encouraged research in many countries, including Russia. Limited-scale communication via radio, TV images, computer, and telephone-answering machine is being researched as we enter the 1990s. (See appendix B and the bibliography.)

The vast accumulation of experiences summarized in these twelve areas provides monumental evidence that your mind, memory banks, personality, and soul will still be very much alive and active when your day arrives to lay aside your current physical body.

The bibliography provides extensive evidence for the continuity of human life, assembled under fifteen categories.

Appendix F
How to Die

by Mabel Rowland

We spend all our earth years in temporary occupancy of this current phys-
ical body. Quite naturally, all of us are concentrating our thoughts and
actions on the business of living. But what about the important business of
dying?

As we move through our sixties, seventies, and eighties, what guidance
is available to ease us through the gates of death? Suddenly, we find we
are really going through the birth process—rebirth into an exciting new
world. What steps are involved? Who is there to help us?

For those who want a short but good overview of the subject, we reprint
herewith the substance of an address presented in various cities in the
United States by Mabel Rowland more than fifty years ago. It was issued
a small booklet in 1942 and sold widely in the following decades. It is now
out of print. Since our own twenty years of full-time, worldwide research
in this area fully confirms all details of the Rowland material, we use this
occasion to help all readers in this and the coming decades.

Regardless of who we are and how we feel about it, each one of us
must one day leave the body. But there is absolutely no reason to
fear this change, for life is continuous and, what is still more comforting, consciousness and individuality are continuous.

What happens is that the soul leaves the body we now dwell in and starts anew in its next phase of existence, vibrating at a different rate. The change is as natural as breathing and we should be as trusting and fearless concerning it as we are about breathing. There is nothing to fear any more than when we lie down to sleep for the night.

As God's creatures, we are privileged to live life and this privilege includes stewardship of the body—a body housing this dynamic, precious and most wonderful thing in the world—life. We must take care of the body, but we are not to presume that we own it. We dwell in it. We do not own it. The Creator put us into these bodies for the duration of our earth lives, and we are to follow the first law of nature and strictly observe self-preservation. We are to fight for our lives to the very last ditch and to protect our bodies to the very best of our ability. Even an insect does as much, instinctively.

Painless as we know dying to be, it is nature's own process and is arrived at upon the Creator's exact moment scheduled for us in the great plan. When will it be for me? Forget it! It is none of your business, but preparing for life after is.

It is only fair to yourself to take in these few facts which I shall give you and remember them—you may not believe them, nor do you need to—but it is necessary for you to read and remember them. That is the intelligent thing to do. Then when you need the information, it will suddenly pop up out of your subconscious mind and be useful.

Now when we have completed this cycle of earth life and it is over—finished—we awaken in the next state of existence, discovering that our thought and feeling reactions are exactly the same as they always were! Remember that. You are you. There is no death. There is only a change of apparel, so to speak. You have shed the body, but your thoughts and feelings do not undergo any change in the passing out. [This was precisely Jeannette's experience!]

However, you become quickly conscious of the fact that things other than yourself are slightly but definitely different, and it is for that very reason that I am making this talk. So please heed this, that you may not be at all panicky, but know exactly what to do.

You probably at some time have dreamed that you are falling. If so, then you know that the dreamer never hits and hurts himself. He wakes up. In the experience of dying, sometimes the individual realizes he is going—or he may merely suspect it—but the truth is, that while people rarely admit it, even to themselves, most of them fear it.

There is no need to. There is no death: it is a misnomer. The truth is that the actual passing out is not only painless, as I told you a few moments ago, but often beautiful—a natural transition, never to be dreaded.

We do not get whisked to a city with golden streets and see angels flying around—no. If there is any such place, which was held out to us as bait to be good in the theologies we were raised on, then we are certainly not ready, in our present state of being, to take up residence there anyway.

The real essence of the person leaves the body—very much as a butterfly leaves its old chrysalis. Many, many persons everywhere have seen this passing out. I have seen it myself. Ask any experienced nurse. She will probably tell you of seeing a vaporous cloud of ectoplasm—that's what it looks like to our human vision. It is the silver cord that holds us to our bodies. Everyone has it and here in our earth life it is never severed, but it stretches when we are asleep to let our souls or entities, the real of us, go from the body and experience dreams. Then it shortens again and comes back to the body. It holds body and soul together. There might be four or five people present at a bedside when a soul passes out and maybe only one or two of them will have their human vision stepped up to the frequency even to see this much.

Some of us have seen a great deal more. There *is* no death.

Now you understand that you are the same individual after you leave the body as before. You may be pleased with conditions, or you may at first be a little disappointed. It just depends on what you expected.

For the first few days, everyone's fate is the same, whether saint or sinner, and after that there are spheres of life where you will belong—and nothing can keep you out of your sphere. You are drawn into it by the law of attraction; that law proves that like attracts like. We will be with people of the same tastes and degree of spiritual interests as ourselves, just as we naturally gravitate to and choose suitable associates here.

Individual reactions are just that—individual reactions. And there are some people who have lived a sheltered earth life to a ripe old age, steeped in theological tradition and with fixed ideas about streets of gold, gates of pearl, harps, and so forth. These good souls are oftentimes their own worst enemies, being stubbornly unwilling to adjust to anything even similar to their earth-life conditions, although the next plane is similar—surprisingly so. Some people, through theological training, actually expect, when they realize they have died, to find the streets made of gold. Certain it is that if they believed that literally while here, they will be of the same opinion still.

Some theologies teach that when we die, the body, soul, and entire entity lie in the grave and sleep until the "judgment day." Well, these dear souls actually believe that literally. And when helpers on the other side of life try to tell them they are the same John or Annie Smith they've always been, but that now their life is going to have a few changes in its working out, they are skeptical and react as they might to a bunko man at the county fair. Some folks of this persuasion insist on sleeping until Gabriel shall blow his horn. They often sleep for years!

Let us consider now a soul just out of the physical body through a natural, leisurely process. It is yourself perhaps. You are greeting your parents. How wonderful they look and they have been gone for years! They were quite old and a little bent when you last saw them in earth life. It used to grieve and tug at you a little to see them aging and failing. But here they are as lovely looking and as smiling and happy as you remember them when they were young and you were very young, just starting to school back in the little home town.

Perhaps you are dreaming—something like this has happened to you before in dreams. No, they were very brief and fleeting flashes, those dreams. This is real and enduring. Still, your parents aren't saying very much—that is like a dream, too. But their gaze is fond and steady and they smile so reassuringly. It is real. And what a nice, cool, light feeling you have! They embrace you. It is real!

Lovingly, they lead you off into their own circle or vibration, where you will rest and talk. Soon you will experience a lovely drowsy, but very safe, feeling, and letting yourself go, will fall into a sleep of anywhere from three days or so to several weeks. Even the most spiritual personalities we have any record of remained and rested the first sixty hours or a few days, in the astral, then sometimes reappeared here on earth, briefly, before ascending into higher realms.

The dead person doesn't feel or act any differently for having died, but adjustments have to be made, just as they have to be made here on earth. For instance, when summer is waning we move in off the sleeping porch, wrap up a bit, and get out our furs and make a hearth fire. That is all there is to it: it is that simple.

When you have slept for your few days or so after dying and wakened to start living in your new environment, you never sleep again. You rest as all do in the spiritual realms, but they do not sleep. The exception is those people I just mentioned, waiting for Gabriel.

Please bear in mind that when the soul leaves the body it doesn't go anywhere. The change geographically is no greater than you would experience in life if you walked from one room to another, from a darkened room into a lighted one, or from a warm room onto a cool balcony. Please realize also that while your body is to be protected and cherished, leaving it, in God's own time, is no more to be feared than sliding out of your overcoat, letting it fall on a chair, and walking away from it. And at first there is no consciousness of this shedding, as it were, of the body of flesh. Our rate of vibration has changed, that is all. And the life we have entered is so very much like the earth life the new arrival is often quite confused, particularly if he has been taught all his life to expect something different.

Should you ever experience the baffling sensation of walking up to your loved ones, embracing them, while they, completely unaware of your presence, walk through you, just do not get panicky. Do the same as you should do in an earth emergency, or any situation which you do not understand. We are told by the Psalmist to "be still" (Psalms 46:10). It matters not what your religious belief is, or whether you have any—that is perfect advice. Just be perfectly still within your own mind and lift your thought to your highest concept—whatever you think of a God. Call to it or Him or breathe His name silently or aloud, just so it is from the heart, which it will be then—it will be you as a little child and immediately—even more quickly than I can tell you this, help comes. Pleasant, friendly aid, and you are never in that spot again.

The helper finds your relatives and loved ones for you. This is necessary when deaths occur accidentally and suddenly. Remember what you are reading, please. Simply raise your consciousness. It is your same old consciousness you know, to your own heavenly father. Just say as much as "Father!" and help will come. The astral realm is organized. I repeat: you need not believe this that you are reading but please remember it. In accidental death and in wartime it all happens so suddenly that the soul may be hurtled out of the body and stand amid a hellish scene of disaster and destruction and see his own body lying there. It isn't a pleasant experience, but it is life. Life is progressive. It blooms and fades and grows again and lifts us from sphere to sphere individually according to each one's consciousness. Stand still and pray. Death is a natural part of life.

If your life here has been devoted to the accumulation of material things or to the making of money, to the extent that you have come to be steeped in it—to enjoy it, say more than anything else—you are building up a hazard for yourself in the next world. Be wise enough not to have as your chief interest a material one like collecting or selling to make money, because

when we leave the body, we go where there is no economic standard—
money is not used. You will be a fish out of water unless you have a hobby
that is something less material, more tangible, and important than buying
and selling.

Things of the earth are just that. Be careful not to grow so fond of them
as to be obsessed by them, for once we actually love things or money, then
we are in danger of being drawn and held by this earth vibration. Briefly,
that would mean we should, as a disembodied soul, hang around others
still in earth life whose tastes and activities are the same as ours used to
be. Our satisfaction would be merely vicarious. There are hoards of these
pitiful earthbound souls haunting clearing houses and money markets and
trade centers of all sorts. Also, we see the souls of the morally weak and
depraved in drinking joints and low places.

While you are still living your physical existence, realize that money is
important to you merely for body-comfort needs. This is temporary, so don't
feed your soul on it. In the next plane you won't see any business as usual
signs. It is then that your artistic attainments may be enjoyed and you will
receive instruction for far more noble service than money grubbing.

So, my advice is to be prepared—to prepare while still living here. Cul-
tivate your soul side. Learn to love and serve your fellow man. If it is not
easy for you to love people, it can be an impersonal kind of love until you
become a more loving creature. Cut down on the criticisms of others and
magnify their desirable qualities. I mean just to yourself, as they start to
irritate you when you think of them. The way they walk or talk or some
little fault—forget that and refuse to see it. The Hindu, when passing another
human soul, mutters *pronom,* meaning, "the god in me salutes the god (part)
of you."

I am not being sentimental. I am giving you the key to the situation of
living, more fully, both here and now and afterward! Let us live with our
thought upon God and with this attitude of mind we shall be living the right
way—and then surely we will die the right way.

Appendix G
A 1949 Prophecy by Dr. George J. Mueller That He Helped to Fulfill Fourteen Years After His Death

While helping O'Neil and Meek develop Spiricom in 1981, Dr. Mueller referred them to pages 66 and 67 of a small booklet he wrote for the U.S. Army in 1949 under the title *Introduction to Electronics*. After months of searching, we located the book in the Army section of the archives of the State Historical Society of Wisconsin, his native state. Little did Dr. Mueller realize when he wrote the following prophetic material in 1949 that, in a most dramatic way, he would provide the "sparks of genius to reconcile the irrational, and so accomplish the impossible." Here is what he wrote:

By 1895, the people of the world felt that their men of science were due for a long-deserved rest. It was the popular belief of the time that everything of importance had already been discovered and that the great inventions had already been contrived. With justifiable pride the scientific achievements of the eighteenth and nineteenth centuries were considered the ultimate in all that could possibly be accomplished in the universe. The predictions of the year were that future generations would have to be content with making minor refinements and rearrangements to the established order of science.

Within the past fifty years, the events which have transpired prove how erroneous were these predictions. Even before the celebration which marked the arrival of the twentieth century, Pierre and Marie Curie had announced a discovery that was to have far-reaching effects and was to change the theories on the structure of matter. The Curies, working in France, had discovered radioactivity and had manufactured a radioactive element, radium, from pitchblende. The subsequent developments of the twentieth century continued to prove how mistaken were the predictions prior to 1900.

Today, men are eagerly searching for the undiscovered in electronic research. Men are at work exploring the known and unknown portions of the frequency spectrum—from sound waves to supersonics, from the lower radio frequencies through the infrared, the visible, and the ultraviolet regions, up into the area of the x-rays and gamma rays, those minute wavelength radiations associated with radioactive elements.

Men are even reaching into the spectrum heights of those fabulous cosmic rays. Out of this work, new techniques and instruments of electronic wizardry will emerge, but only after seemingly impossible problems have been solved. These solutions will require the careful thought and patient work of many people, whose findings will be correlated with other efforts, verified by experiments, and aided now and then by sparks of genius to reconcile the irrational and so accomplish the impossible.

As a conclusion, a salute is given to all men of electronics and a greeting is extended to newcomers in the field. Through their zeal, new magic will be created from electrons in motion and electromagnetic waves in space. Through their initiative and industry, future accomplishments will be achieved to challenge those of Oersted, Faraday, Franklin, Bell, DeForest, and the other masters of earlier years.

Certainly in the years ahead, the name of Dr. George Jeffries Mueller will be ranked with those of "Oersted, Faraday, Franklin, Bell, DeForest, and the other masters of earlier years."

Appendix H
The Historical Relationship Between Jeannette and Loree

Within days of Jeannette's going through the tunnel, a photo of her and a photo of Loree were sent to Lucille McNames, a psychically endowed research colleague in Colorado. As Lucille psychically attuned to the two photographs, she was conscious of nothing but a voice that caused her to type the following:

The entity called Loree is much more than a nurse. She gave up the ghost during the Civil War when she served in the capacity of a nurse to the wounded and dying on the battlefield. She herself moved to the higher planes in her early forties and due to her love of God and kindness to the soldiers, she quickly became an Angel of Light as her reward! Even so, she did not feel she had totally fulfilled her earth mission and decided to return to earth once again to resume her nursing profession.

As you and George Meek have learned, the high self attracts and magnetizes the soul of other high selves, one to the other. Thus in past lifetimes, Loree and Jeannette Meek were kindred souls, not just in one cycle, but in several lifestreams. So it was natural that Loree was magnetized to the soul of Jeannette Meek in Jeannette's recent terminal illness to help the wounded psyche that caused this illness. During Loree's sojourn in higher realms, she had learned how to integrate and heal units of energy in the total body, and this is precisely what she accomplished for her beloved Jeannette.

Now you can see how it was possible for Loree and Jeannette to accomplish such a rare telepathic communication. For now, Loree is an angel in human flesh. They shall meet again.

Also, you can see the importance of Loree's channeling for Jeannette's mother during the period Jeannette was trying to let go of her earth prison. Do you now see that an angel with such wisdom was required so that Jeannette and her mother could merge into divine consciousness?

Bibliography

The libraries of the world contain thousands of books that relate to life after death. The following listing is representative only. For the convenience of the reader who may want to pursue seriously a particular aspect of the subject, this sampling of books has been listed under these headings:

1. Angels
2. Apparitions, Hallucinations, and Ghosts
3. Communications Through Channels
4. Deathbed Experiences
5. Direct Voice
6. Electronic Communication with the Dead
7. General
8. Materializations (Solid Ghosts)
9. Out-of-Body Experiences
10. Obsessions and Possessions
11. Philosophic Speculations Regarding Life After Death
12. Reincarnation
13. Spirit Photography
14. Light
15. Spirit Descriptions of After-Life Experiences

1. Angels

Besant, Annie, *Man and his Bodies*, Theosophical Publishing, 1983.

Burnam, Sophy, *A Book of Angels,* Ballantine Books, 1990.

Graham, Billy, *Angels,* Word Books, 1986.

Hall, Manly, *The Blessed Angels*, Philosophical Research Society, 1980.

Hodson, Geoffrey, *The Brotherhood of Angels and Men*, Theosophical Publishing, 1982.

Humann, Harvey, *The Many Faces of Angels*, DeVorss & Co., 1988.

Leadbeater, C. W., *The Devachanic Plane*, Theosophical Publishing Co., 1984

_____, *The Astral Plane,* Theosophical Publishing Co., 1968.

Moolenburgh, H. C., *A Handbook of Angels*, C. W. Daniel Co., 1988.

Newhouse, Flower A., *Rediscovering the Angels,* Christward Ministry, 1976.

Powell, Arthur E., *The Mental Body*, Theosophical Publishing, 1967.

Ronner, John, *Do You Have a Guardian Angel?* Mamre Press, 1991

Snell, Joy, *The Ministry of Angels*, Citadel Press, 1962.

Taylor, Terry L., *Messengers of Light,* H. J. Kramer, 1990.

2. Apparitions, Hallucinations, and Ghosts

Assorted Authors, *Ghosts and Things*, Berkley, 1962.

Bayless, Raymond, *Apparitions and Survival of Death*, University Books, 1973.

Fodor, Nandor, *Encyclopedia of Psychic Science*, University Books, 1966.

Fuller, Elizabeth, *My Search for the Ghost of Flight 401*, Berkley, 1978.

_____, *Poor Elizabeth's Almanac*, Berkley, 1980.

Fuller, John G., *The Airmen Who Would Not Die,* Transworld, 1979.

Green, C., and McCreery, C., *Apparitions*, Hamish Hamilton, 1975.

Holzer, Hans, *Yankee Ghosts,* Ace, 1966.

MacKenzie, A., *Apparitions and Ghosts: A Modern Study*, Barker, 1971.

Roberts, Nancy, *An Illustrated Guide to Ghosts*, McNally & Loftin, 1982.

Tyrell, G. N. M., *Apparitions*, Macmillan, 1962.

——————, "Six Theories about Apparitions," *Proceedings of the Society for Psychical Research*, Vol. 50, 1953–1956, pp. 153–239.

West, D. J., "A Mass Observation Questionnaire on Hallucinations," *Journal of the Society for Psychical Research*, Vol. 34, 1948, pp. 187–196.

West, L. J., ed., *Hallucinations*, Grune & Stratton, 1962.

3. Communications through Channels

Borgia, Anthony, *Life in the World Unseen*, Corgi Books, 1975.

Brandon, Wilfred, *Incarnation, a Plea from the Masters*, C. & R. Anthony, 1958.

——————, *Open the Door!* C. & R. Anthony, 1935.

——————, *We Knew These Men*, Alfred A. Knopf, 1942.

——————, *Love in the Afterlife*, C. & R. Anthony, 1956.

Burke, Jane Revere, *The One Way*, E. P. Dutton, 1922.

——————, *The Bundle of Life*, E. P. Dutton, 1934.

——————, *The Immutable Law*, E. P. Dutton, 1936.

Cooke, Ivan, ed., *The Return of Arthur Conan Doyle*, White Eagle, 1968.

——————, *Thy Kingdom Come*, Wright & Brown, 1969.

Cumming, G., *Swan on a Black Sea*, Routledge & Kegan Paul, 1965.

Darby and Joan, *Our Unseen Guest*, Borden, 1947.

Duguid, David, *Hafed, Prince of Persia*, W. Foulsham, 1935.

Ebon, Martin, ed., *True Experiences in Communicating with the Dead*, New American Library, 1968.

Edwards, Harry, *The Mediumship of Arnold Clare*, The Psychic Book Club, 1942.

——————, *The Mediumship of Jack Webber*, Healer Publishing, 1962.

Findlay, Arthur, *Looking Back*, Psychic Press, 1961.

——————, *On the Edge of the Etheric*, Psychic Press, 1945.

——————, *The Way of Life*, Psychic Press, 1962.

_____, *Where Two Worlds Meet*, Psychic Press, 1951.

Ford, Arthur, *The Life Beyond Death*, G. P. Putnam's Sons, 1971.

Greber, Johannes, *Communication with the Spirit World of God*, Johannes Greber Memorial Foundation, 1970.

Hapgood, Charles H., *Voices of Spirit through the Psychic Experience of Elwood Babbitt*, Delacorte, 1975.

Hayes, Patricia, and Smith, Marshall, *Extension of Life: Arthur Ford Speaks*, Dimensional Brotherhood, 1986.

Hilarion, *Nations*, Marcus Books, 1980.

_____, *The Nature of Reality*, Marcus Books, 1979.

_____, *Seasons of the Spirit*, Marcus Books, 1980.

Homewood, Harry, *Travis is Here*, Fawcett, 1978.

Kardec, Allan, *The Medium's Book*, Psychic Press, 1971.

_____, *The Spirits' Book*, Sao Paulo: Allan Kardec Editora Ltda.

Klimo, Jon, *Channeling*, Jeremy Tarcher, 1987.

Lees, Robert James, *Through the Mists*, Philip Wellby, 1906

Leichtman, Dr. Robert R., *From Heaven to Earth*, Ariel Press, 1978–1982. A Collection of 24 Books of Mediumistic interviews: *Edgar Cayce Returns, Shakespeare Returns, Cheiro Returns, Jung & Freud Return, Leadbeater Returns, Sir Oliver Lodge Returns, Thomas Jefferson Returns, Arthur Ford Returns, H. P. Blavatsky Returns, Nikola Tesla Returns, Eileen Garrett Returns, Churchill Returns, Yogananda Returns, Mark Twain Returns, Einstein Returns, Franklin Returns, Carnegie Returns, Wagner Returns, Burbank Returns, Lincoln Returns,* and *The Destiny of America.*

Litvag, Irving, *Singer in the Shadows*, Macmillan, 1972.

Lombroso, Cesare, *After Death—What?*, Small, Maynard, 1909.

Magus, *The Magian Gospel of Brother Yehshua*, Magian Press, 1979.

Mandel, Henry A., *Banners of Light*, Vantage Press, 1973.

Meek, George W., *As We See It From Here*, Metascience, 1980.

Montgomery, Ruth, *Threshold to Tomorrow,* G. P. Putnam's Sons, 1982.

Moore, Usborne, *The Voices,* Watts & Co., 1913.

Peebles, J. M., *Seers of the Ages*, Progressive Thinker, 1903.

Ramala Centre, *The Revelation of Ramala*, Neville Spearman, 1978.

Roberts, Jane, *The Unknown Reality*, Prentice Hall, 1977.

Roberts, Ursula, *Mary Barker Eddy: Her Communications from Beyond the Grave*, Max Parrish, 1964.

Smith, Suzy, *Life is Forever,* Dell, 1974.

_____, *The Mediumship of Mrs. Leonard,* University Books, 1964.

_____, *The Book of James*, G. P. Putnam's Sons, 1974.

Wetzl, Joseph, *The Bridge over the River*, Anthroposophic Press, 1974.

White, Ruth, and Swainson, Mary, *Gildas Communicates,* Neville Spearman, 1971.

White, Stewart Edward, *Across the Unknown.* Ariel Press, 1987.

_____, *The Betty Book*, Ariel Press, 1987.

_____, *The Gaelic Manuscripts*, Pantheon Press, 1977.

_____, *The Unobstructed Universe*, Ariel Press, 1988.

Wickland, Carl A., M.D., *Thirty Years among the Dead*, Newcastle, 1974.

4. Deathbed Experiences

Barrett, W. F., *Deathbed Visions*, Methuen, 1926.

Hunter, R. C., "On the Experience of Nearly Dying," *American Journal of Psychiatry*, July 1967, p. 124.

Kübler-Ross, Elisabeth, *Death: the Final Stage of Growth*, Prentice Hall, 1979.

_____, *On Death & Dying*, Macmillan, 1969.

_____, *Questions & Answers on Death & Dying*, Macmillan, 1974.

Matson, Archie, *Afterlife*, Harper & Row, 1975.

Moody, Raymond A., Jr., *Life After Life*, Bantam Books, 1976.

_____, *The Light Beyond*, Bantam Books, 1989.

Osis, Karlis, *Deathbed Observations by Physicians and Nurses*, Parapsychology Foundation, 1961.

_____, "Deathbed Observations by Physicians and Nurses: A Cross-Cultural Survey," *Journal of American Society for Psychical Research*, Vol. 71, 1977, pp. 237–259.

_____, and Haraldsson, Erlendur, *At the Hour of Death*, Avon, 1977.

Patison, E. Mansell, *The Experience of Dying,* Prentice Hall, 1977.

Ring, Kenneth, *Life at Death: A Scientific Investigation of the Near-Death Experience*, Coward, McCann & Geoghegan, 1980.

Rogo, D. Scott, *Nad, A Study of Some Unusual 'Other World' Experiences*, University Books, 1970.

5. Direct Voice

Flint, Leslie, *Voices in the Dark,* Macmillan, 1971.

Randall, Edward C., *The Dead Have Never Died,* George Allen & Unwin, 1918.

6. Electronic Communications with the Dead

Bander, Peter, *Carrying on Talking*, Colin Smythe, 1972.

Fuller, John G., *The Ghost of 29 Megacycles*, Signet, 1986.

Harsch, Maggy, and Locher, Theo, *Jenseitskontakte mit technischen Mittelgibtes!* Luxembourg, 1989.

Juergenson, Friedrich, "Voices of Phenomena," *Esoteric*, Oct.-Dec. 1975, Germany.

Raudive, Konstantin, *Breakthrough*, Colin Smythe, 1971.

Rogo, D. Scott, and Bayless, Raymond, *Phone Calls from the Dead*, Prentice Hall, 1979.

Senkowski, Ernst, *Instrumentelle Transkommunikation*, R. G. Fischer, Germany.

Sheargold, Richard K., *Hints on Receiving the Voice Phenomenon*, Van Duren Press, 1973.

Webster, Ken, *The Vertical Plane,* Grafton Books, London, 1989.

Welch, William Addams, *Talks with the Dead,* Pinnacle Books, 1975.

7. General

Barbanell, Maurice, *This Is Spiritualism,* Spiritualist Press, 1959.

Budge, E. A. Wallis, *The Egyptian Book of the Dead,* Dover, 1967.

Burr, Harold Saxton, *Blueprint for Immortality,* Neville Spearman, 1972.

Carrington, Hereward, and Meader, John, *Death, its Causes & Phenomena,* Rider, 1911.

Chapman, George, *Extraordinary Encounters,* Lang, 1973.

Crookall, Robert, *Imitations of Immortality,* James Clarke, 1965.

——————————, *The Supreme Adventure,* James Clarke, 1961.

——————————, *What Happens When You Die?* Colin Smythe, 1978.

Ducasse, C. J., *A Critical Examination of the Belief in a Life After Death,* Charles C. Thomas, 1961.

Evans-Wentz, W. Y., *The Tibetan Book of the Dead,* Oxford University Press, 1960.

Glasewski, Canon Andrew, *The Pattern of Telepathic Communications,* The Radionics Association, 1973.

Heindel, Max, *The Rosicrucian Mysteries,* The Rosicrucian Fellowship, 1943.

Hudson, Thomas Jay, *A Scientific Demonstration of the Future Life,* G. P. Putnam & Sons, 1896.

Hyslop, James, *Contact with the Other Worlds,* Century, 1919.

——————————, *Research and the Resurrection,* Small, Maynard, 1980.

Korein, Julius, ed., "Brain Death, Interrelated Medical & Social Issues," *New York Academy of Sciences,* Vol. 315, 1978.

Kübler-Ross, Elisabeth. *Death, the Final Stage of Growth.* Prentice Hall, 1975.

Myers, F. W. H., *Human Personality and Its Survival of Bodily Death,* University Books, 1961.

Noyes, Russell, "Dying & Mystical Consciousness," *Journal of Thanatology*, Vol. 1, Jan.-Feb. 1971.

Pearce-Higgins, Canon J. D., and Whitby, Rev. G. Stanley, eds, *Life, Death and Psychical Research*, Rider, 1973.

Powell, Arthur E., *The Astral Body*, Theosophical Publishing, 1978.

_____, *The Causal Body*, Theosophical Publishing, 1972.

_____, *The Mental Body*, Theosophical Publishing, 1967.

_____, *The Solar System*, Theosophical Publishing, 1971.

Roberts, Jane, *Seth Speaks: The Eternal Validity of the Soul*, Prentice Hall, 1972.

_____, *The Nature of Personal Reality*, Prentice Hall, 1974.

_____, *The Seth Material*, Prentice Hall, 1970.

Roll, W. G., "A New Look at the Survival Problem," in *New Directions in Parapsychology* (J. Beloff, ed.), Elek Science, 1974.

_____, "Survival Research: Problems & Possibilities," in *Psychic Exploration: A Challenge for Science* (E. D. Mitchell and J. White, eds.) G.P. Putnam's Sons, 1974.

Samuels, Mike, M. D., and Bennett, Hal, *Spirit Guides,* Random House, 1974.

Sandys, Cynthia, and Lehmann, Rosamund, *The Awakening Letters*, Neville Spearman, 1978.

Tiemeyer, T. N., *Jesus Christ, Super Psychic*, ESPress, 1976.

Tuella, *The Dynamics of Cosmic Telepathy,* Guardian Action Pub., 1983.

Vasilev, L. L., *Experiments in Mental Suggestion*, I.S.M.I. Pub., 1962.

White, John, and Krippner, Stanley, *Future Science*, Doubleday, 1977.

Whiteman, J. H. M., *The Mystical Life,* Faber & Faber, 1961.

8. Materializations (Solid Ghosts)

Bolton, Gambier, *Ghosts in Solid Form*, Psychic Book Club, 1957.

Crawford, W.J., *Reality of Psychic Phenomena*, Watkins, 1916.

_____, *Experiments in Psychical Science*, Watkins, 1919.

—————————, *Psychic Structures at the Goligher Circle*, Watkins, 1921.

Crookes, William, *Researches in the Phenomena of Spiritualism*, James Burns, 1874.

—————————, *Crookes and the Spirit World*. M. R. Barrington, ed. Souvenir Press, 1972.

Dingwall, E. J., *Some Human Oddities*, Hoore & Van Tha, 1847.

Edwards, Harry, *The Mediumship of Arnold Clare*, Rider, 1940.

—————————, *The Mediumship of Jack Webber*, Healer Publishing, 1962.

Fielding, Everard, *Sittings with Eusapia Palladino & Other Studies*, University Books, 1963.

Geley, Gustave, *Clairvoyance & Materialization*, Bern, 1927.

Hack, Gwendolyn Kelly, *Modern Psychic Mysteries*, Rider, 1929.

—————————, *Venetian Voices*, Rider, 1937.

Holms, A. Campbell, *The Facts of Psychic Science & Philosophy*, Kegan Paul, 1925.

Neilsenn, Einer, *Solid Proofs of Survival*, Spiritualist Press, 1950.

Price, Harry, *Rudi Schneider: A Scientific Examination of his Mediumship*, Methuen, 1930.

—————————, *Stella C: An Account of Some Original Experiments in Psychical Research*, Hurst & Blackett, 1925.

Rizzini, Jorge, *Otila e a Materlizacion de Uberaba*, Brazil: Editora Cultural Espirita.

9. Out-of-Body Experiences

Battersby, H. F. Prevost, *Man Outside Himself: The Methods of Astral Projection*, University Books, 1969.

Box, Oliver, *Astral Projection: A Record of Out-of-body Experiences*, University Books, 1962.

Crookall, Robert, *The Mechanisms of Astral Projection*, Darshana International, 1968.

—————————, *More Astral Projections*, Aquarian Press, 1964.

_____, *Casebook of Astral Projection*, University Books, 1972.

_____, *The Supreme Adventure*, James Clarke, 1961.

_____, *The Study & Practice of Astral Projection*, Aquarian Press, 1961,

Davis, Black, *Ekstacy: Out-of-the-Body Experiences*, Bobbs-Merill, 1975.

Green, Celia, *Out-of-the-Body Experiences*, Hamish Hamilton, 1968.

Monroe, Robert A., *Far Journeys,* Doubleday, 1985.

_____, *Journeys Out of the Body*, Anchor Press, 1973.

Ring, Kenneth, *Heading Toward Omega*, Morrow Publishing, 1985.

Smith, Suzy, *The Enigma of Out-of-Body Travel*, New American Library, 1965.

Tart, Charles, "Out-of-the-Body Experiences," in *Psychic Exploration: A Challenge for Science.* E. D. Mitchell and J. White, eds. G. P. Putnam's Sons, 1974.

10. Obsessions and Possessions

Wickland, Carl A., M.D., *Thirty Years Among the Dead*, Newcastle, 1974.

11. Philosophic Speculations Regarding Life After Death

Bailey, Alice A., *Death, the Great Adventure*, Lucis, 1985.

Beard, Paul, *Living On*, George Allen & Unwin, 1980.

Cannon, Alexander, M.D., *The Invisible Influence*, Aquarian Press, 1969.

Croissant, Kay, and Dees, Catherine, *Continuum: The Immortality Principle*, Continuum Foundation, 1982.

Fortune, Dion, *Through the Gates of Death*, Aquarian Press, 1968.

Fulton, Robert, et al, *Death & Dying*, Addison Wesley, 1978.

Grof, Stanislav; Cayce, Hugh Lynn; and Johnson, Raynor C., *The Dimensions of Dying and Rebirth*, A.R.E. Press, 1976.

Grof, Stanislav, and Halifax, Joan, *The Human Encounter with Death*, E. P. Dutton, 1975.

Hamilton, Margaret Lillian, *Is Survival a Fact?* Psychic Press, 1969.

Harlow, S. Ralph, *A Life After Death,* McFadden-Bartell, 1968.

Hick, John H., *Death & Eternal Life,* Harper & Row, 1976.

Hyslop, James H., *Life After Death,* E. P. Dutton, 1918.

Koestenbaum, Peter, *Is There an Answer to Death?* Prentice Hall, 1976.

Leichtman, Dr. Robert R., and Japikse, Carl, "The Role Death Plays in Life," in *The Life of Spirit,* Ariel Press, 1983.

Mitford, Jessica, *The American Way of Death,* Simon & Schuster, 1963.

Moody, Raymond A., Jr., *Life After Life,* Bantam, 1976.

Ring, Kenneth, *Life at Death,* Quill, 1980.

Rogo, D. Scott, *Life after Death: The Case for the Survival of Bodily Death,* Aquarian Press, 1986.

_____, *Man Does Survive,* Citadel Press, 1973.

Schneidman, Edwin S., ed. *Death: Current Perspectives,* Mayfield Publishing, 1976.

Weatherhead, Leslie D., *Life Begins at Death,* Abingdon Press, 1969.

White, John, *A Practical Guide to Death and Dying,* Theosophical Press, 1980.

12. Reincarnation

Cerminara, Gina, *Many Lives, Many Loves,* Wm. Sloane, 1963.

_____, *Many Mansions,* New American Library, 1950.

Challoner, H. K., *The Wheels of Rebirth,* Theosophical Publishing, 1969.

Ellis, Edith, *Incarnation: A Plea from the Masters,* C. & R. Anthony, 1936.

Endemann, Carl T., *Voyage Into the Past,* Alta Napa Press, 1981.

Head, Joseph, and Cranston, S. L., *Reincarnation: The Phoenix Fire Mystery,* Julian Press, 1977.

Kelsey, Denys, and Grant, Joan, *Many Lifetimes,* Pocket Books, 1968.

Leek, Sybil, *Reincarnation, the Second Chance,* Bantam, 1975.

Montgomery, Ruth, *Here and Hereafter,* Fawcett, 1968.

Russell, Lao, *The Continuity of Life—Why You Cannot Die!*, University of Science & Philosophy, 1972.

Shelley, Violet M., *Reincarnation Unnecessary*, A.R.E. Press, 1979.

Smith, Suzy, *Reincarnation for the Millions*, Dell, 1967.

Stearn Jess, *The Search for the Girl with the Blue Eyes*, Doubleday, 1968.

Stevenson, Ian, *Twenty Cases Suggestive of Reincarnation*, University Press of Virginia, 1974.

_____, *Xenoglossy: A Review and Report of a Case*, University Press of Virginia, 1974.

Steiger, Brad, *You Will Live Again*, Dell, 1978.

Wambach, Helen, *Reliving Past Lives*, Harper & Row, 1978.

Weiss, Brian, *Many Lives, Many Masters*, Simon & Schuster, 1988.

13. Spirit Photography

Barbanell, Maurice, *He Walks in Two Worlds*, Herbert Jenkins, 1964.

Holbe, Rainer, *Bilder aus dem Reich der Toten* (Pictures from the Realm of the Dead), Munich: Th. Knaur, 1987.

Holzer, Hans, *Psychic Photography*, McGraw-Hill, 1969.

14. Light

Leon, Dorothy, *Reality of the Light*, Anchor of Golden Light, 1984.

Ott, John N., *Health & Light*, Pocketbooks, 1974.

Russell, Walter, *Light*, University of Science & Philosophy, 1950.

Tibbs, Hardwin, *The Future of Light*, Watkins Pub., 1981.

15. Spirit Descriptions of Afterlife Experiences

Borgia, Anthony, *Life in the World Unseen*, Transworld.

Brandon, Wilfred, *Love in the Afterlife*, C. & R. Anthony, 1956.

_____, *Open the Door!* C. & R. Anthony, 1935.

_____, *We Knew These Men*, Alfred A. Knopf, 1942.

Burke, Jane R., *The Immutable Law*, E. P. Dutton, 1936.

Conacher, Douglas and Eira, *There is Life after Death*, Howard Baker, 1978.

Cooke, Ivan, *Thy Kingdom Come*, Wright & Brown.

_____, *The Return of Arthur Conan Doyle*, White Eagle, 1963.

Crookall, Robert, *The Supreme Adventure: Analysis of Psychic Communications*, James Clarke, 1961.

Darby and Joan, *Our Unseen Guest*, Borden, 1943.

Findlay, Arthur, *On the Edge of the Etheric*, Psychic Press, 1943.

_____, *Where Two Worlds Meet*, Psychic Press, 1951.

Hayes, Patricia, and Smith, Marshall, *Extension of Life: Arthur Ford Speaks*, Dimensional Brotherhood Publishing House, 1986.

Homewood, Harry, *Travis in Here,* Fawcett, 1978.

Leichtman, Dr. Robert R., *From Heaven to Earth*, Ariel Press, 1978–82.

Mandel, Henry A., *Banners of Light*, Vantage Press, 1973.

Randall, Robert C., *The Dead Have Never Died*, George Allen & Unwin, 1927.

Richelieu, Peter, *A Soul's Journey*, Turnstone Press, 1972.

Wetzl, Joseph, *The Bridge over the River*, Anthroposophic Press, 1974.

White, Stewart Edward, *Across the Unknown*, Ariel Press, 1987.

_____, *The Betty Book*, Ariel Press, 1987,

_____, *The Unobstructed Universe*, Ariel Press, 1988.

To order additional copies of this book,
please send full amount plus $4.00 for
postage and handling for the first book and
50¢ for each additional book.

Send orders to:

Galde Press, Inc.
PO Box 460
Lakeville, Minnesota 55044-0460

Credit card orders call 1–800–777–3454
Phone (612) 891–5991 • Fax (612) 891–6091
Visit our website at http://www.galdepress.com

Write for our free catalog.